FOREWORD
by Sandy G

Terry and Lesley: for all their friends, the inevitability of the words in the song 'love and marriage, love and marriage, they just go together like a horse and carriage … you can't have one, you can't have one, you can't have one without the other'.

Theirs is a wonderfully romantic story. Not just romantic but heroic as well. Terry was a handsome young airman during the Second World war, when to be in the Royal Air Force and a fighter pilot was to be a national hero. He was shot down twice and taken prisoner but survived, ending the war as a much decorated Squadron-Leader. Lesley, a beautiful young actress was just as courageous in her own way, continuing to work in the London theatre throughout the war, despite the Blitz. Only the brave deserve the fair, and if this were a film, they would have fallen in love and married there and then.

In fact, they still had not met, although they had both decided to leave the country for much the same reasons: Post-war Britain was too drab and restrictive to appeal to either of them. Having left the Air Force and become a ferry pilot, Terry was given the task of flying a small, single-engined Proctor 8000 miles to South Africa with the minimum of navigation aids and hardly a map. Lesley, who hoped to get a job with African Theatres, also flew to South Africa, in her case in an old DC3. They met in Johannesburg and after only three, one presumes extraordinarily exciting days of courtship, became engaged.

When their money ran out eight months later, they decided to return to England to get married. Terry at the time was flying the Proctor for an illicit diamond buyer who was in trouble with the law and in danger of having the plane impounded. Their interests coinciding, Terry agreed to fly the Proctor out of South Africa, the whole length of the continent, across the Mediterranean and Europe to England still without the benefit of radio, proper navigation equipment or emergency supplies of any kind. It was another amazing journey which, along with the outward leg, would have merited a book in itself.

After the wedding, Terry and Lesley returned to South Africa. Luckily for us Terry, who can turn his hand to anything, gave up flying and chose to be a photographer; first in the relatively mundane business of aerial photography and then much more excitingly as a Time-Life photo-journalist covering first Africa's hot spots and later Vietnam, the Middle East and just about everywhere else there was trouble. I was lucky enough to cover several stories in his company, notably the Congo which immediately after independence rapidly descended into anarchy. There were, however, lighter moments.

One day in 1961 Terry, the Time correspondent, Lee Griggs, and I went to talk to Conor Cruise O'Brien, then the UN special representative in Katanga (now Shaba), at his headquarters in Elisabethville (now Lubumbashi). His job was to being the secessionist republic and its president, Moise Tshombe, to heel. Understandably, O'Brien was not the most popular man in town and, as we were talking, a small Fouga Magister trainer, fitted with a baby machine-gun made a hostile pass or two over the UN compound. Militarily speaking, it was really a flea-bite, but to people who had seen little real combat like O'Brien, and indeed Lee Griggs and myself, unnerving. As the tiny jet hurtled downwards, Conor Cruise broke off his analysis of the situation and jumped into a conveniently placed fox-hole, closely followed by Lee Griggs and myself. As far as I remember, Lee Griggs landed on top of O'Brien who protested loudly. He protested even more loudly, however, when he saw Terry with a happy grin on his face and apparently oblivious of the Fouga's activities, photographing the UN man in the trench. To O'Brien's considerable annoyance, the photograph appeared as part of the publisher's note in the next edition of Time Magazine.

I also recall a much more serious occasion – at which I was not present – when Terry watched and photographed the slaughter of Malaysian troops by mutinous Congolese soldiers at Kindu. Apart from deservedly receiving a big play in Life Magazine, the brutal episode made a profound impression on Terry, who saw it as typifying the Congolese dilemma, combining as it did the fecklessness of UN rules of engagement, and the savagery spawned by the criminal incompetence of Belgian colonial rule.

Living Dangerously

With our very best wishes

Lesley & Terry

Lesley & Terence Spencer

ISBN 0-9542862-0-0

Published by
Percival Publications
166 High Street
Odiham
Hampshire
RG29 1JU

The right of Terence & Lesley Spencer to be identified as authors of this work has been asserted by them in accordance with the Copyright, Designs and Patents Act 1988.

All rights reserved. No part of this publication may be produced in any form or by any means – graphic, electronic or mechanical including photocopying, recording, taping or information storage and retrieval systems – without the prior permission, in writing, of the publisher.

Design & production co-ordinated by:
The Better Book Company Ltd
Havant
Hampshire
PO9 2XH

Printed in England

Cover photo by Terence Spencer

Like all great photographers Terry was eminently versatile and his record of a Beatles' tour of the UK, when they were just beginning their spectacular journey to the top, was later to make him a small fortune. As a shrewd operator he always retained the copyright of his photographs and his archive must be one of the most impressive, for its size and breadth of range, in contemporary photo-journalism.

This book is long overdue. All Terry's and Lesley's friends will be delighted that it has finally come to fruition. It will leave us all he richer in heart and spirit.

Sandy Gall

Acknowledgement

We are particularly grateful to Dr. Ted Johns for going over our original draft with a fine toothcomb, checking punctuation, style and vocabulary, making sure that our background remarks about our experiences were historically and geographically accurate, and then doing it all again once the final proofs were produced.

CHAPTER I

World War II

An incident occurred on the 19th of February 1946 that was to change my life.

I woke up one morning after a late night clubbing at the Coconut Grove in London, bleary eyed and with a hangover. I noticed beside the bed a packet of Players cigarettes on which was scribbled a telephone number in blazing lipstick. Girls were hard to come by at the end of World War II.

Pulling myself together, I walked across to the pub in Shepherds Market, had a beer and phoned the number from the quaint antique sedan telephone booth in the bar. Imagine my horror to be answered by a man who rather forcibly said, 'Is that Terry Spencer?' 'Yes,' I replied feebly. 'Good. Can you be at my office at 3.30 this afternoon?'

What it was all about I had not the faintest idea. The firm was the Percival Aircraft Company. I was greeted with the remark, 'Can you leave in two weeks?' 'Leave for where?' 'In the early hours of this morning you agreed to take a Proctor to South Africa.' 'My God! Did I?' I replied, only vaguely knowing where South Africa was. However, after six years of war this was my chance to get out of England and try my luck at the sort of travel stories I had so long planned.

The Percival's Sales Manager helped me get a passport, a flying licence and after some inoculations, I was on my way south to Marseilles. The Proctor was a small single-engined aeroplane. It had no radio, no dinghy or emergency supplies for the 8,000 mile flight. There were only maps as far as Cairo. But it was a job and it was peacetime.

In the tranquillity of that flight to Marseilles my mind wandered back to the war. I could not help it. Flying in civilian clothes felt odd to me.

I started the war in the Warwickshire Yeomanry: yes, horses. But I was reprimanded at my first camp for chromium-plating the metal

Living Dangerously

parts of the saddlery to save the tedious task of burnishing; I was transferred to the Royal Engineers but my heart belonged to the Royal Air Force. Engineers were then at a premium and transfers were well-nigh impossible. Being slightly short-sighted in my right eye, I discovered I could legally wear a monocle and knew this would displease my colonel, being his personal Field Engineer. When he was away on leave I wrote out a glowing recommendation for my transfer to the R.A.F. and signed it on his behalf rather illegally. When the colonel returned and saw my transfer documents coming in, he was happy to see me and my monocle go and did nothing to prevent it.

At my Elementary Flying Training School in Chester one of the pupils with only a few hours on Tiger Moths was landing in a field and taking villagers up for five shilling flips. What a great idea to help finance our bar bills! For me, revelling in the sensation of being alone in the open cockpit of a small Tiger Moth high up in the wintry skies and with the wind rushing by at 80 m.p.h. was just sheer bliss. I gazed down on the myriads of little people below, some of whose lives I was going to explore over the next 40 years.

Alas, I was posted to Cranwell to train on twin-engined Oxfords intended for Bomber Command, whereas I was set on flying fighters. My memories here were punctuated by spells of hectic parties and romantic evenings with the many W.A.A.Fs on the station. On one occasion with my great friend, Peter Bagshawe, we taxied out to a far corner of the airfield and took two of them up, determined to join the 'mile high club'. Little did the girls know that between us we only had a few hours on Oxfords. They soon found out and were so terrified that neither felt inclined for the adventures we had planned.

On another occasion in the air Pete tried to pee through the camera hatch. I gently pushed forward the stick and he received the lot in his face. Six years later Pete was to share our vast bed in the honeymoon suite of the Savoy hotel in London. Practising night flying at dusk, we took off over what appeared to be a mass of 'forget-me-not' flowers which turned out to be airmen and W.A.A.Fs in hot embraces. On one of these night flights we had an engine 'cut' but somehow managed to get the Oxford back on to the flare path without 'bending' it.

feel any emotions about the misery we had just wrought, not only to the soldiers but to their families and loved ones.

I was becoming very keen on a girl from nearby Horley (girls had to be transitory in those days as we moved often from one base to another). Jenny and I used to go to London, visit Shepherds in Shepherds Market or the Red Lion around the corner or to the Brevet Club and finish up in the Mirabelle before retiring to Hamilton House. This was a block of apartments on the corner of Park Lane and Piccadilly where you could hire a flat just for the night – even for a few hours.

The George and Dragon at Ightham in Kent became our squadron pub. It was run by 'Pissy' May and her daughter 'Doorknob' Dora (so called because she was alleged to have had an affair with a doorknob after a particularly hectic night). After hours May would lock the pub doors and one of the pilots would take over the bar as we drank through the night. In the mornings when May cashed up, she was invariably well in credit.

Peter Bagshawe was a good man to have around when things got tough in bars as often happened. He was a Sandhurst rugger and boxing blue and never lost his cool. In Chatham a gang of Canadian soldiers took exception to our behaviour – quite rightly – and decided we needed to be taught a lesson. Three of us left the bar first and as the Canadians came after us, Pete hit the first and the second, knocking both unconscious while the rest decided to 'call it a day' – much to my relief. We travelled up in the train the next morning with one of the soldiers who was smothered in bandages.

Our casualties were high on low level strafing. Not only were we flying a few feet above the trees but we were formating with a wingman, looking out for enemy aircraft and seeking targets. On one sortie I hit a high tension cable but only dented my air scoop. Morris Wilson was missing after an operation into Holland. His leader never saw him but thought he may have hit the sea. David Bell was another to hit the sea returning from his first operation in France but he lived to tell the tale. Keith Hazelwood was taking off on a short runway when he hit a house at 100 m.p.h and walked out of the debris without a scratch. Peter Arkle was killed when he and Tim

Living Dangerously

Phillips came in to land from both ends of the runway at the same time! Later, Tim failed to pull out after aerobatics and we watched him hurtling into the ground at 500 m.p.h. in the middle of the airfield at Detling. Tim was the 'whitest' of men and his cheery presence at parties was to be sadly missed by all, particularly the fairer sex. Even Flight Sergeant Manning had to bale out but only from a lorry when his brakes failed down a steep hill...

Generally one was not frightened during the war. I never thought I would be killed; anyway I have never been afraid of death but getting injured was another matter. Fear was more about the unknown, not necessarily danger, as when we started deep penetrations into occupied countries at night. We circled German aerodromes to keep their night fighters on the ground while our bombers flew overhead. Where possible, we operated in moonlight conditions flying only a few feet above the trees to avoid radar and 'flak'. Once I covered four countries in two hours. Being low and fast searchlights had difficulty following us but occasionally one did and being blinded 'on the deck' made life difficult.

One night I was sent to patrol a night fighter aerodrome at Dreux, south of Paris. Circling the 'drome' for 17 minutes, my Mustang was hit by intensive 'flak' and the radio shot out of its housing. Not knowing whether there was further damage to my plane, I set course for home, first attacking two barges, one of which blew up, presumably it was carrying explosives. I also shot up a locomotive whose firebox was clearly visible in the dark. Arriving over England now in dense cloud, I circled at 8,000 feet and hoped my I.F.F. (a radio recognition signal) was working. After what seemed an eternity a night Beaufighter flew up alongside and flashed his lights to follow him down to Manston where there was a long flarepath.

In November 1943 we were engaged on long, four-hour patrols out into the Atlantic escorting American convoys into Northern Ireland and Britain. The slightest hesitation from the single Alison engine started our adrenalin pumping. We soon found out the trouble when one dark and drizzly morning I put our engineering officer on the seat of the single seat fighter. I threw out the parachute and climbed in on top of him with only a cushion between us. We took off out into the Atlantic and after three hours sure enough the engine started missing. On returning to base, he ordered special plugs and we had no more trouble.

At last in December 1943 I achieved my ambition to get on to Spitfires, the most beautiful aircraft in the world and the most wonderful to fly. On my very first operation as No. 2 to the Commanding Officer, I crash landed at Ford as my undercart failed to lock down. Little damage to the Spit and none to me but not a propitious start. We did long hours on 'cockpit readiness' which involved being strapped in prepared to 'scramble' at a second's notice. On one such occasion my windscreen oiled up and I had to take off with the hood open only to have an engine cut at 10,000, feet fortunately right above the aerodrome.

165 Spit squadron flew many sorties after German aircraft but they were few and far between so we concentrated on low level strafing and shipping patrols in the Bay of Biscay and the English Channel. The evenings saw hectic parties. One such evening I walked through a plate glass door in the mess and was administered three stitches by the squadron doctor who had had as much to drink as all of us. That party ended at a quarter to six in the morning.

I was posted as 'A' flight commander to 41 Squadron, one of the great squadrons of this war and of World War 1. At the beginning it was difficult for me as most of the other pilots had considerably more operational experience. The clipped wing Spit XIIs were much faster than the older IXBs and much nicer to handle.

At Bolthead I met a most attractive girl from the operations room. I could share my problems with her as we strolled along the cliffs on beautiful moonlit nights. Our radios in the air were transmitted through loudspeakers all over the ops room and the language these girls heard when things got tough was enough to make any of them blush. I used to meet my girl most nights when she came off duty.

A dawn flight saw me leading six aircraft to St. Malo, flying across the channel a few feet off the water. We hit Sillon de Talbert and thought we were at Le Faucher island, but eventually finished up at Ushant. A very poor show which depressed me considerably,

Living Dangerously

especially as I was sent to 41 as an expert in low level navigation. To make matters worse a great pal of mine, David Bell, was shot down off St. Malo. He was on fire and failed to bale out.

A dilemma occurred when my No.2 was shot down off St. Peter Port in the Channel Islands. Wag was one of the few Americans in the R.A.F. Most had transferred to the American Air Force as their pay was almost double ours. Wag baled out and got into his dinghy. A Warwick amphibian dropped him a Lindholme craft and I saw a German patrol boat go out to pick him up. I could have shot up the boat but felt if I did he would be left to drown. The Huns picked him up but my Spit was hit several times by heavy flak and I had to leave him to become a prisoner of war.

It was June 1944. I had just said 'good night' to my ops room girl and tumbled into bed and was fast asleep when the C.O. woke me up to say the invasion of Europe was on. The rest of the night was spent in the ops room organising patrols and I took off myself at dawn to witness the most spectacular sight of my life. The Channel was littered with thousands of boats from warships to landing craft all heading towards the French coast in Normandy. Our job was to combat enemy aircraft, but we saw none that day. Returning from a later sortie my main petrol cock jammed and I was about to bale out at 500 feet off the sea when a feverish kick partially released it and produced enough petrol to get me back to Bolthead at 85 m.p.h. – just off the stall.

Later that month we received news that we were to go to West Malling to cope with the latest German secret weapon, the flying bomb. So very sadly I said 'goodbye' to my ops room girl at Downes Hotel but not without much heart rending. The 'doodlebugs', as the flying bombs were nicknamed, flew at 420 m.p.h. and at 4,000 feet. We would fly at 10,000 feet and dive in on them at 500 m.p.h. Shooting at these high speeds required new techniques. The Spit had to be very accurately trimmed to avoid any 'skidding' in the turns or our fire power was inaccurate. We learned not to attack from dead astern: when I once did, the flying bomb exploded 250 yards ahead of me and blew my Spit upside down: causing immense damage as I crashed through the debris. We were fascinated with these 'doodlebugs' and one such missile, flying relentlessly up the Thames, received all the ammunition of Flight Sergeant Chattin and myself. We slowed it down to 220 m.p.h. enabling me to fly alongside and take a close look. With my wingtip two feet from the bomb, it began to lift. This toppled its gyro and it crashed harmlessly into the water below. I became a bit of a hero that night in the British press as 'Tip it in Terry', the first man to topple a flying bomb with my wingtip although I never actually touched the bomb and anyway it was due to lousy shooting.

One of these doodlebugs dropped on to the R.A.F. Regiment's billets. I helped drag out the C.O. with his brains blown out. After this eight of us climbed aboard my two-seater Le Mans Singer, known as the 'Blue Peril', and headed for London. The Singer was beautifully maintained by my engine fitter who used it himself and ensured it was always full of 100 octane petrol. It was never taxed or insured throughout the war. Its canvas hood had long since rotted and we were all open to the elements.

Paris was recaptured on 23 August and soon afterwards we saw the ill-fated airborne invasion of Arnhem, when we escorted the massive armada of gliders and paratroopers. Our job was to attack German gun positions as they opened fire on the fleet. This was not dangerous as we attacked them from the rear; but we did not envy our poor Red Devils having to drop or land in that holocaust while we headed home to our girl friends and comfortable beds. About this time I took a Spit to see my ops room girl but was told she had just gone to Plymouth – 500 miles to be told that!

Ann Attree used to run the Lympne Flying Club before 1939. We had many fine parties at Ann's house when based at Lympne. She was a wonderful character, much loved by all the pilots. One night we crammed her into the Blue Peril with four other pilots to go drinking in Folkestone. At a bar someone put a condom in her long bread roll. Ann kept tugging at the roll until admitting defeat; she opened the roll and discovered what we had done. She never forgave us. Indeed, when my wife to be was going out to South Africa, Ann told her to look up 'one of the biggest bastards of all time'.

From Lympne I took a Spit IX up on an air test and was not happy with the engine when it cut on me at 400 feet as I was coming in to land with wheels and flaps fully down. We crashed into a wood running up the side of a hill when the wings were torn off and the engine broke away from the airframe. The fire crew were somewhat surprised to pass me walking up the road back to the 'drome' quite unscathed.

Arnhem was followed by large formations of fighters escorting American Flying Fortresses bombing heavily defended Ruhr industrial areas in Germany. Our Spits were usually top cover and we looked down on the dreadful turmoil below as the bombers flew through dense clouds of anti aircraft fire. Some blew up and disgorged their human contents with a few fortunates gliding earthwards on billowing white parachutes while others, as tiny dots in the sky, hurtled to their deaths.

About this time I was leading a squadron sweep into Germany when Tom Slack called up to say he could not get back on to his mains from his 90 gallon drop tank. Sometimes by yanking at the wires in the cockpit you could release the tank. I called up Tom, 'Pull your wire, pull your wire,' as Tom was about to force land in Germany to be taken prisoner. He called back, 'This is no time for jest!' ('Pulling your wire' was a schoolboy's phrase for playing with oneself). Some 30 years later Tom invited Lesley and me to a party in his London house saying, 'I have someone who has a bone to pick with you'. It was Wag, whom I had last seen in the 'drink' off St. Peter Port. He said he had never forgiven me for leaving him to be taken prisoner. However, years later we stayed with Wag and his wife, Brooke, in Baltimore and have become good friends since!

At this period of the war we were leading lives outside reality. On the one hand we were engaged in deadly aerial combat and on the other returning to a world that had seen little of the actual fighting other than the bombing – all in a matter of hours. This tended to set us apart from our fellow humans when neither could fully understand the other. I was to experience this again as a war photographer.

On a raid in the Liege area, we attacked two FW90s at Tirlemont in Belgium. I shot one down in flames and he blew up on hitting the ground. I was promptly bounced by the other who shattered my starboard elevator and wing. W/O Coleman got him but only after W/O Chattin was himself shot down. He baled out. I saw his Spit hit the deck. Fifty years later John Foreman, an aviation historian, told me the man I shot down was Hauptmann Emil Lang. Lang was the top scoring fighter ace of the Luftwaffe, having claimed 173 allied aircraft destroyed. His wingman, Leutenant Alfred Gross, shot down W/O Chattin then, in turn, was shot down by W/O Coleman. Gross was also a top scoring air ace, having shot down 29 allied aircraft, but he was so badly wounded he never returned to combat and died three years later. Foreman sent me a photo of Lang who looked a hell of a nice guy. It took me 50 years to realise this tragedy and the anguish of his mother, wife or girl friend. Up to that time the war had been totally impersonal to me. John Foreman also told me that Chattin was killed, possibly by Germans after he landed by parachute. On landing back from that trip we watched helplessly as one of our Sergeant pilots was burnt to death after he overturned on landing. Only a drink could eradicate that memory. Then we laughed and washed the event out of our minds.

The next morning I nicked the station commander's Tiger Moth for the weekend to visit my father in the Isle of Wight. On the Monday morning Dad drove me back to the field where a strong gale was blowing. I co-opted three villagers to hold the tail and wing down as I swung the prop. When I waved my arm, they were all to let go but the two on the wing held on. A sudden gust under the tail overturned the plane making it a total write-off! A short time after this event, a wild party took place in the sergeants' mess. In the early hours of the morning we strung a rope around the dancers on the floor and with a 'tug-of-war' on the rope, heaved on it, squeezing in the dancers until they could not move, to the laughter of those of us outside the rope. W/O Jimmy Ware hit a corporal and when another W/O came up to complain to me bitterly, I hit him - in my drunken state. We stole a 15 cwt truck and drove back to the officers' mess to continue the party until dawn. What a night! The next morning there was great 'stink' about the party. A few weeks later I had to fly up to Biggin Hill to get a reprimand from 11 Group A.O.C. This was for the Tiger Moth incident. Air Commodore Boucher was in 41 before 1939 and for an hour we talked about the squadron. After I had reached the headquarter gates on my way out, his ADC ran out to announce the AOC had forgotten to give me the reprimand. I returned rather sheepishly to see a smiling AOC. But those were the last few days of Boucher. When I went back yet again a few days later to get a reprimand for the dance floor incident, I was met by a very different AOC. After he had finished haranguing me for 'behaviour unbecoming an officer', he ended by saying he would never allow me to command a squadron. I could not have been happier: a flight commander in a great squadron was the best job in the R.A.F.

During the bitter winter of 1944 as we tried to keep up with the Allied advance across Europe, I left my beloved 41 to command 350 Belgian squadron flying the latest Spit XIVs but not before reminding Group Captain Johnny Johnson what the AOC had told me. Johnny was the top scoring fighter pilot of World War II and highly decorated. 'Fuck the AOC', said Johnny, 'we have a war on our hands.'

Low-level strafing in Germany was becoming a 'dicey' business. This was reflected in our casualties. We had to strafe locomotives and transport in the heavily defended Ruhr. This involved flying through the balloon barrage and 'flak' that at times was so intense it seemed impossible that any aircraft could survive it. Our Spitfires often resembled colanders after these trips. We soon developed a technique but it was a tantalising one. The Spit XIV had a tremendous rate of climb and we would climb at 8,000 feet a minute at only 90 mph. The German gunners could not calibrate their guns down to this low speed but it meant we were continually flying *into* the flak without getting hit.

Once based on the Continent, we were encouraged to visit our army colleagues in the front-line trenches. These men lived for days on end in frozen water and unbelievable cold; they were constantly shelled and seemed to take it all as routine. We watched the Germans shelling a nearby village when a shell fell within 30 yards of us. The four visiting pilots threw themselves flat on their faces to the laughter of the army boys. I have never been so frightened and in several wars to follow as a photographer, I was never to rid myself of this fear.

Food was desperately short for civilians in Belgium at this time, made the worse by the intense cold, but the R.A.F. club in Brussels was warm. I used to take a lovely girl called Denise there who relished a good meal followed by almost unobtainable coffee. I was to stay with Denise until the end of the war. A year or so after the war I gave Denise's telephone number to a friend of mine in South Africa but her reply to him was curt, 'Dites à Terry que la guerre est finie.' (Tell Terry the war is over.)

The weather conditions for our last Christmas in Holland were atrocious. We regularly had to climb up through some 10,000 feet of cloud when we formated with wing tips a mere three feet apart. The slip stream helped keep us in tight formation. On Christmas Day, leading the dawn patrol, we chased the Germans' latest jet fighter, the Me 262, but though we dived on him at 500 mph we could not catch him. That evening we had an excellent E.N.S.A. show with seven very beautiful girls whom we entertained until daylight.

On New Year's Day the Germans reckoned the British would have such hangovers that they launched their biggest aerial attack ever on our grounded fighters. We had taken off at first light and seen nothing until returning to find many of our Spits in flames on the air strip.

The 17th January 1945 was the coldest day imaginable: ghastly for men in the trenches and for our 'erks' living in tents and having to service our aircraft with frostbitten hands. On one such mission into the Ardennes where the Germans fought their last worthwhile offensive of the war, P.O. Smets had to bale out, Trip was badly wounded, baled out and landed in our local Mardega Club, Ken Matheson landed with a 'dead' motor, Fifi Verporten's jet tank was blown off and Tony Gaze had his wing wrinkled by an 88 shell. On landing we heard Jonah and Keith Lowe of 130 were missing, also Gibson of 41. Not a good day for us and it led to a heavy drinking session until 2 am in a local night club in Diest. One of the girls had a parlour trick. We would pile up her tip with masses of francs; she would come over, lift her skirt and accommodate the lot somewhere.

There was an old coal heater near the dance floor. We put a franc on it to get it hot and placed it one down from the top. In her usual fashion she came over, bowed, took the francs and had just got to the middle of the dance floor when she let out a scream, ran across the floor with francs pouring from her skirt. Later we heard Gibson had staggered back to our lines having lost his controls, then he baled out. Jonah lost a prop blade and crash landed with the Yanks shooting at him. Keith Lowe was in a Yank hospital.

Once in Germany we shot up everything that moved. Unlike in France, Belgium and Holland, where we had to be careful of civilians and even do dummy runs before attacking trains to let the civilians escape, at the same time alerting the German gunners, now we had a free hand. As the war was ending, we had plenty of Spitfires but pilots were scarce as no one wanted to get killed so close to the end of it all. Some used gags to avoid taking off by blowing radio fuses, until we told them they would have to take off without radio. That put an end to it.

All this came to an abrupt end for me on 26 February 1945 when I was shot down attacking ground targets near Munster in Germany. I had time to climb to 8,000 feet by which time the cockpit was full of smoke and uncomfortably hot. I called Roberto Muls, my No.2, that I was on fire and baling out. Unfortunately I then hit the tail plane and injured my hip. I felt no pain, only serene calm as I drifted gently down to earth beneath the silken canopy. The peace and quiet after the turmoil seemed like another world until I remembered I was falling into the hands of Germans who had little love for Allied fighter pilots. I landed in a field beside some French slave workers but was promptly surrounded by gun-toting German soldiers shouting and gesticulating at me. They took me to a military hospital where my hip was treated and then deposited me in a freezing prison cell. I spent the next two weeks in solitary confinement, lonely, cold, hungry and miserable before being taken to the air crew interrogation centre at Wetzlar. During the early hours of the morning on Frankfurt station I lost my guards. It was dark and miserably cold. I approached several German civilians announcing 'Ich bin Krieggefanger' (I'm a prisoner of war) but they thought I was joking.

Eventually, at the camp an arrogant major scowled, 'You arrived in our country uninvited and dressed in civilian clothes (we often flew in sweaters and I was not wearing a tunic). If you will not talk to me, I will hand you over to the Gestapo who <u>will</u> make you talk.' I felt very alone when realizing no one knew I was alive. The major stressed that point.

The war was coming to an end. The next night there was a heavy Allied bombing raid on Wetzlar and German civilians streamed into our camp thinking they would be safe. In the melée Jimmy Thiele, a New Zealander, and I slipped through the main gate just for the hell of it. Once outside the barbed wire, Jimmy turned round to me and said, 'Fuck going back inside.' We had not planned to escape and had no equipment beyond my silk scarf which was a map of Europe and Jimmy's tunic button, concealing a mini compass. We walked west all night and at dawn met a French slave worker who gave us a 98cc motor bicycle saying it was no use to him as he could not get petrol but there was a Hungarian unit down the road with plenty of petrol. The Hungarians wore khaki and so did we. We stole a couple of trays and queued up for food, the first proper food we had had in weeks - and were promptly sick! There were so many foreigners trudging eastwards that no one took heed of us. More vital was a stack of jerrycans. We removed one which would take us to the Rhine. Later that afternoon as we headed west we heard firing just ahead and dived for a culvert with our precious motor bike. An armoured vehicle rattled overhead, firing wildly. We rode on, one sitting balanced precariously on our jerrycan, passing several dead bodies beside the road. On entering an apparently deserted village, we were pounced upon by heavily armed Americans. Without identification we were arrested but managed to slip out of the back of the house, collect our motor bike and head for the Rhine once more. General Patton had just crossed at Remagen.

We hitched back to our wing, now in Holland, and on entering Johnny Johnson's caravan, he exclaimed, 'Terry! Where the bloody hell have you been these last five weeks?'

Throughout the war I had felt invincible. It could happen to others but never to me. On returning to my Belgian Squadron once more I now felt frankly scared and dreaded one of my flight commanders coming up in the mess and asking, 'Boss, will you lead the dawn patrol in the morning?' The war was ending as we trailed the victorious armies eastwards across Germany. At newly captured aerodromes I headed for their photographic sections and amassed a load of equipment to start my post-war life in photo journalism.

We crossed the Rhine on 16 April 1945 and were the first wing to operate east of the River Weser. My English adjutant, Jerry Gough, had been in British intelligence between the wars and as we flew in to Celle near New Hanover, knowing how I helped to pay my mess bill with photography, Jerry mentioned that we were near an infamous concentration camp called Belsen. He, of course, had no idea of the absolute horror awaiting us there. The next day I visited the camp with my camera shortly after it was liberated by the British army. The sickly smell of lime and death permeated the air from well outside the barbed wire. A terrible sight greeted me at the entrance to the camp where a skeletal frame of a woman had come to greet her liberators and slumped on to the wire gashing her neck in the process. She was dead. What I saw in Belsen was so horrific that I left the camp as though I had just experienced a most terrible nightmare.

The following day we were to be the first Spitfire squadron to patrol over Berlin. My pilot's log book entry simply says, 'Whacco'.

On the April 19th I was leading a section of four Belgian Spitfires, including Roberto Muls', attacking a tanker in the Bay of Wismar in the Baltic. It was late evening. I failed to see two German destroyers lurking in the long black shadows of the hills. We dived down at 440 mph, very fast in those days, to some 30 feet off the water. The sky lit up in what seemed a solid sheet of flame, so intensive was the 'flak'. The Spit was blown in two, the parachute blown out of the pack and I hurtled down towards the sea. 'What a bloody way to end it all,' I remember thinking quite clearly and without panic. In a split-second I hit the water and the canopy collapsed on top of me. Then I did panic. 'Jesus. I'm going to drown', I thought, while struggling to swim beneath the yards of silk. Then a foot touched the sand. I was in five feet of water! I cleared my parachute in time to see the front part of my Spit crash on land. The tail was in the water beside me.

I was now a prisoner of war for the second time. Having just seen Belsen I talked to Germans who knew all about concentration camps but I do not believe any of them knew of the horrors of what had taken place in those camps. I was liberated and rejoined my Wing a couple of weeks later. This time there was no comment from Johnny Johnson. My face and arms had been badly burnt but thanks to falling into the sea and a saline bath, I just looked an awful mess.

The thought of resuming a normal tranquil life was appalling. The war had germinated in me a desire for adventure. Perhaps I also felt I was living on borrowed time and had already become a fatalist. I did not realize it then but my R.A.F. experience was excellent training for photo journalism. It gave me quick reactions, taught me survival and the discipline to go one way towards trouble when the temptation was to do the opposite. Over the years to come I was prepared to take risks to get pictures but only if there was a strong chance of success. After all, Socrates said, 'The want of self-control in rushing into danger has been shown to be ignorance'. I agree and it is the reason I have lived so long.

For the final post-war months until my demob at Christmas, I was stationed in Germany. We lived the life of wealthy playboys. We had yachts, horses, little Fieseler Storch communication aeroplanes and Mercedes Benz cars. At nearby Travmünde we had a lavish country club and though we were banned from fraternising with German girls, they soon became Austrian! Together with Roy McGregor, we commandeered an 80-foot torpedo recovery boat. This had a large after deck where we danced the nights through with lovely E.N.S.A. girls from Lübeck to entertain the teoops. I was put in charge of wine stores in the area so we were never short of liquor. We kept our German crew of three alive by shooting rabbits on the aerodrome using looted shot guns.

Johnny Johnson attached Tony Gaze and myself to 616 Squadron flying our only jet fighters at that time. With jet experience I was put in charge of a phantom enemy aircraft flight. Our job was to fly most of the German aircraft doing consumption tests until Farnborough came out to collect them. This led to my sending German planes down to Berg Op Zoom in Holland to collect oysters for the mess, to Rheims for the champagne and to Copenhagen for wonderful cheeses and dairy produce. This job gave me access to vast stores of oil for our torpedo recovery boat on to which we fitted a radio so that our colleagues could drop us supplies by parachute when we were short of anything.

My demob came through at Christmas 1945. I felt there must be a market for travel stories after the British people had been cooped up on their small island for six years, virtually cut off from the outside world. Severe rationing had become a way of life. They were tired and dreary. Perhaps I could show them another life, so here I was on my way to the unknown.

Terence

Lesley

CHAPTER II

My flight to South Africa and Lesley's arrival

Arriving in Marseilles to refuel the Proctor before delivering it, as agreed to South Africa. I left the next morning for Corsica. The Mediterranean was looking sullen and pugnacious. I passed the scuttled French fleet in Toulon harbour and headed out to sea. Ninety miles from land I ran into the worst storm I have ever encountered. Battered about in what felt like being inside a gigantic washing machine, I retrieved a minimum of visibility by flying a few feet off the sea in a screaming headwind. After what seemed hours, my watch and declining fuel guage told me I should be making landfall soon. Still the minutes ticked by and no sign of land. I was beginning to wonder if I had somehow strayed through the narrow Straits of Bonafacio, between Corsica and Sardinia without seeing land. Suddenly, out of the murk loomed the 8,000 feet peaks of Corsica. I swung the Proctor northwards and landed at the quaint little town of Ajaccio.

After too many 'peroquets' (Corsican firewater) and goat's cheese, I left the next morning in the sunshine and saw the beauty of Corsica as I flew south-east over the rugged, green and snow-tipped mountains to Tunis in North Africa. My route took me along the North African coast to Cairo where I managed to scrounge 1/500,000 scale maps from an American Major for my onward flight up the Nile to Lake Victoria on the equator. At Entebbe in Uganda a South African Dakota pilot gave me maps to Johannesburg. Scouring the coast for Jo'burg, he told me to look 300 miles inland! I delayed my flights whenever possible to shoot pictures of the pyramids, temples, the native people and other scenes of the exciting countries I passed through.

Two weeks after leaving England I crossed the Limpopo river into the Union of South Africa. The progress of civilisation was transforming the tranquillity and peace of the thousands of miles of nature I had just flown over when my faithful little Gypsy Moth engine started running rough. However, two hours later the gold reef of the Witwatersrand stretched out for miles ahead of me: cyanide-yellow mounds of pre-Cambrian rocks, looking like the work of an army of oversized, madly manic moles. So this was Johannesburg. It was a welcome sight.

At Germiston airport a very English red-faced Colonel Robins took delivery of the plane and frostily asked, 'How are you getting back to England, old boy?'

'By the B.O.A.C. flying boat.' I replied nonchalantly.

'That costs £167.10s,' he answered menacingly.

'My contract states we are flown back after these delivery flights.'

'Really! Where's your contract?'

'In England our word is our contract.'

'Well, it isn't here.'

With only £15 in my pocket I had a problem.

Strolling round the busy streets of Johannesburg bounded by skyscrapers and gaily lit neon signs flashing every conceivable brilliance, I felt as though I had suddenly stepped into a new world outwardly untouched by the horrors of war and dreary blacked-out England. In a small restaurant I realised a seven years' ambition by ordering a large steak and three fried eggs. How matter of fact it all seemed.

The Proctor had been bought by a man I was subsequently to discover had spent periods in prison for crimes involved in I.D.B. (Illicit Diamond Buying).

Ben du Preez started his career as a clerk on the South African Railways and rose to be a multi-millionaire. He was lithe, slightly built, clean shaven and usually wore a brown trilby hat. You would not pick out Ben in a crowd. I became his personal pilot while making up my mind how best to get home. Ben was a delightful and generous character and paid me handsomely. He loved to talk about his encounters with the police on the Skeleton Coast of S.W. Africa (now Namibia) and how he usually outwitted them as he collected highly illegal uncut diamonds.

Ben was brave too. We had seven engine failures on the Proctor in the early days due to a fuel problem but he still continued to fly with me. I was glad there were none of these incidents over the Nubian desert or the Bangweulu Swamps.

My report to the Civil Aviation Council reads, 'On 1 November 1946 left Jo'burg at 1530 hrs for the three hours flight to Durban.

Living Dangerously

Eight miles from Durban weather clamped to zero feet while flying through the Valley of a Thousand Hills. No option but to climb up through 5,500 feet of cloud and head back for Ladysmith. Solid carpet of cloud as far as eye could see. Time 1815 last light. The sun dipping into cloud. Flew on N.W. course, climbing to keep above cloud which was billowing in places to 20,000 feet. At 1850 it was getting dark at our height. Mr. du Preez spotted a light below through a gap in the cloud. I immediately cut the engine and spiralled down from 8,600 feet. Light was from the firebox of a steam locomotive. We were in the mountains and realizing we were flying up the side of a steep hill, had no option but to throttle back and land with the help of one landing light. Hit ground hard, bounced and pulled up using full brake. Switched off.

Ben shook my hand and offered up a prayer for our miraculous escape. It was pitch dark, yet there was no apparent damage to our aircraft. We were relieved to see a Mr. & Mrs. McVie arrive on the scene and take us to their house for the night. We were somewhat shaken the next morning to see we had bounced over a sunken road to pull up in a field less than 50 yards long. A shock absorber rod had been damaged and McVie took this into his garage in Estcourt for welding. With a host of natives and a tractor, we managed to get the Proctor through a small river to a corn field only 400 yards long. At 4,700 feet the Proctor needed 500 yards to take off so I wanted to take off alone to lighten the aircraft but Ben insisted on coming along. We made it…but only just.

On another trip with Ben we flew a V.I.P. business man down to Port Elizabeth. This man had just lost his wife in a fire. Staying the night with him, I had just entered my bedroom in the dark when something fell on my neck. I hastily turned on the light to find a large deadly tarantula sprawling around the floor. One sure thing - it and I were not going to spend the night together. But, what to do? I opened the window and using a large watercolour of the recently deceased wife, I edged the spider towards the window and up the wall. I reached the sill and was about to throw it out when the spider ran up the painting. At that I just let the beast and painting sail to the ground below. I worried all night lest it rained. Thank God, it did not and I was able to rescue the painting before breakfast.

A few days after this incident, I met the girl who was to become my wife and still is 54 years later – Lesley Brook Learoyd.

Ann Attree had given Lesley my address in Jo'burg. Jackie Smith, my flat mate, knew the receptionist at the Carlton hotel. He phoned her to ask about a Mr. Leslie Brook, but the receptionist said, 'No. It is Miss Lesley Brook.' Jackie immediately asked her age.

'She is an actress and could be 17 or 70,' she joked, fearing competition.

Not being sure, I booked a table at the swish Roof Garden in case she was 17 and at the staid Langham in case she was 70. I was round at the Carlton at nine the next morning, phoned up to Lesley's room; she said she would be down in a minute. Women were in short supply in Jo'burg at that time. I waited anxiously at the lift. Imagine my surprise when quite the loveliest girl I have ever seen stepped out. She wore a silk floral dress displaying an elegant pair of legs. That was my first reaction. On closer study I saw she was wearing a simple gold necklace, had grey blue eyes and was about 5'4" tall. Her hair was fair and french-rolled at the back.

We had a blissful four days together before a close London friend of hers took her off on a ten day tour of South Africa. By then I knew the country so well I was able to guess most of the hotels they would be staying at and sent Lesley telegrams to most of them. Poor Jack hated it when they walked in and were told, 'a telegram for Miss Brook'. Lesley's most memorable telegram to me read, 'Returning to Jo'burg December 3. No accommodation, any suggestions? Much love Lesley.' I immediately kicked Jackie out of the flat without too much conscience as Jackie was poor and at £90 a month I was rich and paying our bottle store bill. Lesley moved in.

Our flat, 612 Denstone Court, was primitive in the extreme. It was just one divided room without even a fridge and a long walk to the toilet and bathroom. Costing £7 per month serviced, we could not reasonably complain, and being near mid-summer it was also hot. The next morning I asked Lesley if she would marry me and to my amazement she said, 'Yes.' I put my hand under the bed and drew out a bottle of warm South African champagne and two glasses: we drank to a long life together. However, I was in no doubt I had caught her on the rebound from a love affair she had had in England.

Living Dangerously

CHAPTER III

From the bright lights to paraffin lamps – Lesley recounts her arrival in South Africa

Now that the war was over and it was possible to travel abroad, I made the momentous decision to abandon my career in the London theatre and in films and go to South Africa. My mother was not happy when I broke the news to her but I made her a promise, 'I am going to find myself a rich diamond merchant and I ll fly back in my own aeroplane.' On the eve of my departure for South Africa I was staying with my parents on Romney Marsh and had driven over for a farewell drink with Ann Attree at the Lympne Flying Club where I repeated this prophesy.

A year later – yes – I did fly back in an aeroplane belonging to a rich diamond merchant. The pilot (alas not so rich) was my fiancé, Terry Spencer.

There must be few people less suited than myself to life in foreign lands, so why the decision, as soon as the war ended, to throw up everything – family, friends, a way of life and a career in the theatre which had been a burning ambition since childhood? I suppose I was disillusioned. I had always pictured us rejoicing and madly waving flags – something like those old newsreels at the end of World War I. There was not much of that – we seemed to spend most of our time complaining about fuel and food shortages. For myself, I had never been one for standing in a queue when a paste sandwich would do, so rationing did not really bother me. The butcher in Sainsburys had squeezed my hand with the change in it for four years but it had never occurred to me to ask for an extra chop.

Of course there was more to it than that. The love of my life, then, had left for the United States to marry the love of his life. At the time of his escape, finally, from my clutches, I was rehearsing for a new play by Frederick Lonsdale *But for the Grace of God*. I had acted in the West End before, playing juvenile leads in light comedies, but here was an opportunity to break away into something more serious and more demanding. The director was Peter Daubeny, who made a success in later years with his international theatre seasons – a gentle person, very different from our author who undoubtedly called the tune. One actress had already found the maestro incompatible and so had given up the part and left the company. Cynical and sophisticated though he was, one had the feeling that beneath the hard crust of worldliness Frederick Lonsdale was a romantic. Although he was a great deal older I felt he was attracted to me. One night he had asked me to dine with him in his own private suite on the sixth floor of London's Savoy Hotel. During the meal he started to talk about a Hollywood actor friend of his whose pretty daughter was to marry a young English air force officer badly burnt in the Battle of Britain. The coincidence was cruel. He was obviously referring to my ex-love. I think I changed colour as I looked down through the open french windows. It did not take long for the message to get through to Freddie that I was more interested in my own troubles than I was in him. From that moment relations between us deteriorated.

We were fortunate to have with us in the company the well loved veteran actor A.E. Matthews. Matty was the dearest and most charming gentle man you could wish to meet. We had worked together before in an unsophisticated little film called *Twilight Hour*. He wrote me the sweetest letter which I treasure among my possessions offering to help in sorting out my problems but my spirits were too low and I gave up the fight. Like my predecessor I reluctantly left the company.

And so instead of a West End run I went on tour with a rather undistinguished revival of *The Sport of Kings* starring Leslie Henson and his ex-wife Gladys.

The company was a happy one in spite of the new recruit. Leslie was a good old trouper to work with, the only slight flaw being his memory. Many a night I would hear him calling down from his dressing room, 'Gladdy, Gladdy' – I suspect he had temporarily overlooked the fact that although the best of friends the two were divorced and had each remarried, their respective spouses joining us, on and off during the tour. The week we played in Edinburgh Leslie went off on a day's outing by train, returning in time for the evening performance. He told us afterwards that on the way to the station he had seen someone whose face he knew well but could not place, so he greeted his old friend, warmly shaking him by the hand. Next morning there he was waiting at table and serving Leslie his breakfast!

After the performance one night at His Majestys Theatre in Aberdeen I confessed to the manager that I was giving up my stage career to go and live in South Africa. I repeated to him my intention to seek out a diamond millionaire. 'I'll bet you a bottle of whisky you will be back within the year,' he said. In the circumstances I am not sure who wins but perhaps one day I can sort it out with Jim Donald.

My friends in the theatre were naturally horrified when they heard of my decision. We were all so dedicated that to go anywhere except on tour or on location with a film unit was literally the end of the world. 'What ever will you do?', they gasped. It was a good question.

I had gone straight from the R.A.D.A. to Croydon Repertory where I earned the princely sum of two pounds a week and paid 25 shillings for a week's bed and breakfast. Highlights, however, were going to London where I escaped the bus conductor by sitting on the top deck and looking out of the window, and of course the shop talk when we all went to a café after the evening performance - even though we were rehearsing a new play for the following week.

In the early days of my career I landed a job understudying Vivien Leigh in *A Midsummer Night's Dream* at the Open Air Theatre in Regent s Park. During rehearsals I fell asleep in a chair and woke to find Oberon towering over me! I beat a hasty retreat. Phyllis Neilson Terry was a formidable character. I was to work with her again in *The Millionairess* in Bristol. She was full of sympathy when my hotel room was ransacked and all my precious belongings stolen, including clothes costing not only money but irreplaceable coupons.

For reasons unknown to me Vivien Leigh never spoke to me once during the six weeks run of the Dream. She was very beautiful and graceful and we all envied the fabulous clothes she wore. At this time I was having a pleasant relaxed liaison with a boy called Lindsey. On the last night of the season he and I were walking away from the park after the curtain had fallen when he stopped in his tracks and said, 'I've forgotten my shoes. I'll have to go back.' I didn't wait. I knew he hadn't forgotten his shoes. It was suddenly clear to me that he cherished a hopeless passion for Vivien. As I walked on I thought how sad, that is the end of a relationship and I am going to be miserable. I only wasted one moment of regret. I looked up at the sky through the trees: it was a beautiful clear starry night – 'No. I'm not,' I said and started to run. Oh, how I wish all the broken romances in life could end so easily.

Of course I often miss the life I left behind. I played the juvenile lead in over 20 films and worked with many well known actors. Yet, when I look back, it is the simpler things that I treasure most, the E.N.S.A. tour of *George and Margaret,* for example. Janet, the stage manager, and I shared digs. If it was a double bed we put a bolster down the middle. In Southport she and I walked round for five hours because we would not pay more than 27/6d for full board. Janet was earning £5 per week and my salary was £7 a week. Between us we had devised a plan for other towns, where digs were more plentiful and we were able to bargain. I would attract the landlady's attention while Janet had a quick look to see if the sheets were clean. If this was satisfactory she would whip out her family photographs, including one of her small son. These helped to counteract our gallery of boy friends which followed the others on to the mantelpiece. On one occasion the bed linen did not pass the inspection. 'Mrs. Lowther-Wilson,' said Janet on her return. 'I think you have forgotten to change the sheets.' 'Well Miss,' replied Mrs. Lowther-Wilson, 'It was an officer and only the one night.'

Janet was always ready to tell a story against herself – so here goes. Our landlady was talking about me in a very complimentary way to a friend. When she saw that Janet was standing nearby she added, 'And the other one has got nice teeth'.

There were serious moments too, such as the time when a land mine fell in Bridlington not far away and Janet remembers coming towards me, hand outstretched for a final 'good-bye'. It is hard to believe but we did get used to the air raids. When I first heard the sirens at my parent's home in Kent, I ran in and sat on the stairs but did not find either of them there! I had to go back to London because of my work and was living in a fifth floor flat in Baker Street which meant we had to go down to the ground floor if the raids were bad. I only remember going into a shelter twice. Once was under Baker Street station and the other was when my mother and I were driving down to Kent. All hell was being let loose above us so we wisely stopped and enquired where we should go. The people we met down in that shelter were so nice and friendly and asked us back for hot drinks after the raid had passed over. So Sidcup is imprinted on my memory. I was in a play at the Q Theatre when in mid September 1940 the greatest raid on London seemed to set the whole city alight. Standing outside in the street I could only imagine the horror of that night as I stared at the ghastly but dramatic scene in front of me.

I was in Croydon Rep when I learned that I had landed a film contract with Warner Brothers First National. They gave me a retaining fee together with a fair sum for every day I worked in the studio, sometimes with Hugh Williams, sometimes with Claude Hulbert and also with Emlyn Williams – none of whom, sadly, is still with us.

For the first time in my life I was able to wallow in the luxury of buying expensive clothes and other things of which I had only dreamed before. So no more cheating on the buses and I could now afford several pairs of stockings instead of one and a half and having to wash one at a time. 'No stint in the home,' I proclaimed to a great friend from student days who arrived to spend the weekend. Peggy looked in the cupboard and there was one egg and one tin of baked beans for the two of us!

My brother Barry and I moved in to a charming mews flat with its own garage off London's Gloucester Road and we were there when war broke out. I was then doing a season at Stratford on Avon playing Olivia in *Twelfth Night* and other leading parts. Our flat was the scene of many hectic parties during one of which some reveller brought back the top of a Belisha Beacon from the street and Barry painted a fish on it to use as a table lamp. Famous names to be – among them Peter Ustinov, Geoffrey Keen, Maurice Denham and, of course, Michael Denison and Dulcie Gray – were among the many who came and drank with us. We were not adept at providing meals. Whatever happened to those tins of baked beans and sausages? We did not want to spend money on eating in restaurants but occasionally branched out for a light meal in a nearby café. There one day I was approached by a very good looking young man. We may even have shared a Welsh Rarebit before Barry intervened and spoilt the fun. Several years later when I was filming at the studio with Stewart Granger he asked if I remembered how he picked me up in a snack bar near our flat!

When I was not trotting round the provinces I was as likely as not to be playing a character which Irene Handel and I christened 'Auntie Smug' in a series of films made by Butchers at Riverside Studios. They were romantic comedies in which as leading lady I was usually involved in a spot of 'mercy marrying', as Irene called it – only being rescued in the last reel by the hero to whom my heart truly belonged. As movies they were about as different as one could imagine from those of today.

A cold, foggy autumn followed the summer of 1946 and when the day of departure arrived my mother stood, a desolate and bewildered figure, as I waved her 'goodbye'. My other brother, Roderick who won a V.C. during the war, was dubious but encouraging, and gave me his welcome moral support as far as Croydon airport. After that I was on my own and as the Dakota took off for Belgium I had an immediate sense of freedom and adventure. I had not been away from Britain for eight years. Air travel held far more glamour in those days and though we were an ill assorted lot, the individual attention we received was marvellous.

So I continued my journey to Johannesburg from Brussels in October 1946. The first night of our journey to the Southern Hemisphere found us in North Africa. Could any doctor prescribe a better tonic than to exchange damp, foggy England for the warm climate, the sounds and smells of the Middle East? There would be relapses still, and loneliness, but when we landed at Castel Benito, the cure for my bruised heart had already begun. Even the meal provided could not destroy the spell. Arabs, unused as yet to foreign palates, had cheerfully mixed tea and coffee together as a beverage and this, along with greasy fried eggs, proved too much for some of us.

Our route south took us through Kano in Nigeria where lively, chattering Africans displayed their colourful leather goods, beads and wood and ivory carvings. On to Léopoldville in the Congo (now Zaire) where we stayed at an inviting little guest house comprising of rondavels, the white man's copy of an African dwelling. From the windows we watched African women walking by with their graceful swinging gait balancing their bundles precariously on their heads. Our next stop was Elizabethville where the roads were still unmade – quite unrecognisable as the modern city of today. The Lido had a swimming pool in picturesque surroundings. We sat down to dinner on the terrace with eight different nationalities in harmony around the table.

We landed at Germiston airport near Johannesburg at the beginning of an African summer. Sad to relate, there was no red carpet laid out for the actress who had thrown up a promising career in England, but only the bus from the Carlton hotel. African Consolidated Theatres, who had suggested I might work for them, were conspicuously absent. The realisation that there was little or no professional theatre in South Africa soon dawned on me.

Well, then, if my hopes of earning a living were fading, social life was the next thing to be investigated. As soon as I had settled in at the Carlton Hotel I put a call through to a friend, Jack van Os, whom I had first met at Ivor Novello's house where Bobby Howes had taken me to meet representatives of African Consolidated Theatres. Bobby and I had become friends when I played opposite him in *Halfway to Heaven* at London's Princes Theatre, now renamed the Shaftesbury. He was a darling to work with and made everyone in the company feel relaxed and happy.

I had scarcely time to put down the phone when Jack was round to collect me, such is the hospitality of the South Africans. He said my phone call gave him the surprise of his life. He had not believed when we talked in London that I would pull up my roots and arrive in the Golden City. Through Jack I was to meet many colourful personalities in Jo'burg where gin and brandy flowed like water and where swimming pools and tennis courts were the order of the day. The conversation of this somewhat decadent society was basic to say the least with most of these people now dead – long before their time.

Within two days of my arrival my fate was sealed. Without having a notion of what it might lead to, I followed up my introduction from Ann Attree who knew Terry Spencer when he was stationed at R.A.F. Lympne. I was to see a lot of Terry over the next few days when out of the blue came an invitation to accompany Jack to the Cape by car. However Terry was not going to give anyone else a chance and on every possible occasion when we entered a hotel, I would be handed a telegram or a letter from him.

The day after my return from the Cape with Jack, I became engaged to Terry and for the next seven months we led a gloriously happy and carefree existence.

Then one night Ben du Preez asked us to meet him in a Greek café in Fox Street.

It was like a scene from a Humphrey Bogart film as we sat around a white plastic covered table in an ill-lit room. The great news was that Ben wanted Terry to take the Proctor to England, leaving within a week. We were to get married and meet him in Rome. Surreptitiously, Ben took from his pocket a crumpled piece of tissue paper, slowly opening it to reveal nine beautiful polished diamonds weighing upwards of 1.7 carats. 'Select one of these, Lesley. It is my wedding present to you. We will choose the setting at Katz & Lourie (the Aspreys of South Africa) in the morning. For you, Terry, my present is my XK120 Jaguar'. It was hardly surprising, but we never received either!

The reason for this sudden departure may have been suspect but it was a Godsend for us. My savings had just about run out and Terry could not afford the return flight.

Lesley (profile)

Thistledown

Lesley with Robertson Hare

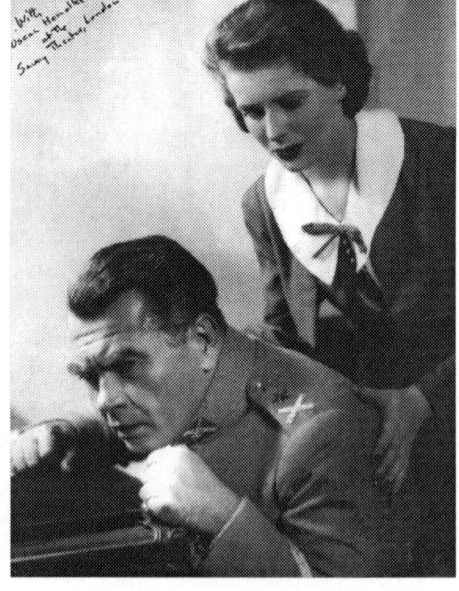

Lesley with Oscar Homolka

Lesley in 'Side Street Angel'

*In Ben du Preez's suite at the Hotel Bernini in Rome.
His immaculately dressed 'secretary'.*

CHAPTER IV

Lesley recounts our flight back to England

We had a feverish week ahead getting packed and ready for home, with the added prospect of flying thousands of miles before returning to Johannesburg. We still did not have a radio and only the minimum of navigational instruments.

It was a cold, bleak morning on 16 July 1947 when Ben collected us from our flat and drove us to Germiston airport. We weighed our paraphernalia consisting largely of brandy, nylon stockings, rolls of material and other luxuries so rare in England, before we took off at 9 a.m.

We flew over 'The Valley', where my Uncle Cyril had settled since the Boer War and dropped a small gift on a makeshift parachute down to his little thatched rondavel home bordered by a mass of petunias. The couple waved their thanks and good wishes. The airport Manager in Bulawayo, Southern Rhodesia (now Zimbabwe) asked our destination. 'Kent,' I replied. 'What! In that small machine?' It transpired he came from Dymchurch, a few miles from my family home.

I had been on flights round South Africa in the Proctor with Terry but I was still not all that happy in a small aircraft. However, by now I learned to maintain a straight and level course on the compass gyro directional indicator (G.D.I.) once in flight.

It was on the next stage of our journey that a small crisis arose between Terry and myself. He hit me! I have never been good at heights so could not look over the side. Terry said I was the only 'pilot' he knew who flew entirely on instruments. For some reason I was unaware that apart from a sideways movement I must also move the stick backwards and forwards. There I was 1,500 feet up with my eyes glued to the G.D.I. At one moment in time our faithful Proctor, laden to the hilt, was climbing at a dangerous angle and about to stall. My hands, as Terry explained afterwards to his tearful fiancée, were frozen on the controls and hitting me was the only way to make me release my grip so he could take over and prevent disaster. I forgave him – he has never hit me since!

At that moment Terry had been checking the next stage of our flight. He never seemed to bother about pre-flight planning until we were airborne. I must have been gullible but was continually assured everything would be all right. The habit has now been transferred to our expeditions by road!

My first view of the Victoria Falls was dramatic. We saw the spray 40 miles away, looking like a vast jet of steam projected 300 feet into the air with its myriads of rainbow colours sparkling in the blue sky. Green and pretty trees surrounded the Falls. Flying low around this awe inspiring masterpiece of nature, digesting its beauty, we saw the Zambezi River plunge into the deep abyss below.

We left Livingston near the Falls at dawn the next morning and flew over dense jungle until reaching the desolate Bangweulu Swamp, riddled with malaria-carrying mosquitos and the dreaded tsetse fly. The swamp stretches for 100 miles and is certainly not the place for the engine to falter. We sometimes flew at treetop height to see the crocodiles and other wild animals and soon ran into two terrifyingly fierce tropical storms when the rain hit the windscreen like a tattoo of machine-gun fire. We laboured up to 9,000 feet through the storm to cross the rugged peaks of the Ukonongo mountains and had trouble finding Kasama in Northern Rhodesia (now Zambia) in the blinding rain. Terry had to land with his head hanging out of the side window. He got out looking like a drowned rat and found the officials surprised to see such a small aircraft drop out of this storm.

Terry had fitted something called a drift guage which helped him navigate these vast stretches of country often without a single landmark, sometimes for three long hours, when a small dirt airstrip would appear ahead carved out of the bush. The Proctor gave us a few frights with its sluggish take-offs at high altitudes from short airstrips. Terry still could not judge the speed of the wind so our E.T.A. (Expected Time of Arrival) was often erratic. At best, our maps were only 1/500,000 scale and showed few contours of mountains. Many parts of this vast black continent were virtually unmapped.

When we flew low over natives in their remote, primitive villages, people would scatter in all directions, arms and legs whirring like windmills, as they had never before seen such a large bird just above their heads!

I felt very nostalgic about Lake Victoria. It looked so beautiful, still and peaceful from the air with the gentle green sloping down to the dark blue water, the neat and tidy kraals and the Africans who were visible in their numerous little fishing dugout canoes. We seem to travel back in time. We crossed the equator and after nearly four hours had our first view of the White Nile.

Juba was tucked away in dense jungle and not easy to find without radio. In those days it consisted of a small jungle airstrip with a single-level tin roof hotel and a few huts belonging to a handful of whites. Tall, distinguished Dinka men strolled around stark naked. It was unbearably hot and sultry. You felt if you blew too hard a portion of the atmosphere would collapse in a sheet of water.

Later that evening, sitting outside our thatched hut listening to the nearby tom-toms, my mind was carried away by the many stories I had read as a child about darkest Africa. At that moment over the airwaves of our small transistor radio drifted a familiar voice, 'Late dance music will be played for you tonight by Jack Jackson from Grosvenor House, London.'

Like the many way-out places we dropped in on, the locals were glad to see new faces and invariably offered us generous hospitality. Juba was no exception, especially as the manager had happened to see me act in a play in Scotland – a little embarrassing, as Terry and I were not yet married. That night there was a birthday party at which the best champagne flowed. At 2 a.m Saki Michaelides, a big game hunter, took Terry out and they found a lone elephant. He handed Terry a powerful rifle which he fired, the recoil almost blowing him backwards out of the Jeep, fortunately missing the magnificent creature.

There was a slight setback here when, with no radio, we were refused permission to proceed without an aerial escort. The country to the north was the Sud, considered one of the most dangerous jungles and swamps in Africa. The authorities were tired of sending out search parties for missing aircraft.

We knew it would be difficult because of our slow cruising speed. Two days later a twin-engined Consol came in and we persuaded the pilot to 'say' he would cruise at our speed of 140 m.p.h. en route to Khartoum, so we were allowed to leave. We had loaded a hand of bananas on to our already overladen aircraft, making for a precarious take off. Our wheels would not come unstuck as we raced down the short dirt airstrip. A few yards from the end, by which time our hearts were beating overtime, we collected the top of a small tree and staggered into the hot atmosphere. The Consol outpaced us and we lost him in the first bank of clouds.

The jungle was changing into sparse bush, then sand. We saw the glow of the lights from Khartoum ahead. Even at our cruising altitude of 8,000 feet, the heat was almost intolerable with our perspex hood intensifying the sun's rays and penetrating our bodies. Combined with the continual bumping of the little plane, one needed a strong stomach to survive. Khartoum is where the Blue Nile from Abyssinia meets the White Nile and continues its long journey to the Mediterranean. Northwards from Khartoum our view was just sand, sand, sand for hundreds of miles without a living soul to be seen, not even a camel. Huge volumes of sand had been blown up into mountains of grotesque, unfriendly shapes allowing no possibility for a landing. Our ears tuned in to the even beat of our single engine. After Khartoum the Nile takes a 250 mile loop to the north east but Terry had decided to fly the 400 miles direct across the desolate Valley of the Kings and pick up the Nile again at Merowe. There was a brief fuel stop at Wadi Halfa where Terry had to hold a towel over the controls which were too hot to handle.

At our next stop, Luxor, we were refuelled by hand pump from 40-gallon drums by a flock of Arab boys in turbans and dirty white jellabas. It was striking how the jet black skins of the natives on the equator gradually became lighter the further north we progressed until they became white in Europe. We were now in the land of the Pharaohs and the green cotton fields along the river ended abruptly in sand as far as the eye could see. Terry flew low to show me the Pyramids before landing at Cairo but Luxor and its age-old buildings were something I will never forget. In Cairo we took a break from the rather arduous flying for a night at the famous Shepherds Hotel where the large fan in our room was most welcome. The following morning we went shopping for fruit in the market and took off around lunchtime, reaching the desert almost right away. Terry decided to follow the North African coast westward. Our navigation was easy with the relentless shimmering sand of the Sahara on our left and the welcome blue of the Mediterranean on our right.

The horror and waste of war came to me as we flew over some of the famous North African battlefields of el Alamein and 'Marble Arch'. All along there were crashed and burnt-out aircraft and any amount of tanks and lorries lying where they had ceased to be serviceable or where their crews had lost their lives.

We found el Adem just before six o'clock with the R.A.F. in residence, so there were white N.C.Os in place of Africans and German prisoners of war to wait on us. In the mess that night we had a good old time 'thrash' as we used to call it and it is no good pretending that either of us felt our best next morning.

Tunis looked so clean and white from the air but was full of strange sights and smells on the ground. We hitched a lift with Shell to the Majestic Hotel which was a badly run monstrosity. Worse, there was a water shortage and everything stank to high Heaven. It was 100 miles on to Palermo in Sicily. Here the Italians refused us permission to continue through Italy as they said our aircraft documents were incorrect. During bitter arguments, worsened by the language difficulty and their anti-British feeling, I was followed around by strange, sinister women in black whenever I made the slightest move. After four precious hours, a tight-lipped official allowed us to take off providing we returned to Tunis.

Nothing daunted, Terry set course south as if for Tunis flying a few feet off the water to avoid radar. Fifteen miles out he altered course to the northwest for a three hours sea crossing. Although our one and only engine had behaved superbly to date, with no radio our flight over the sea was not the safest form of travel. However, my betrothed informed me there was not a thing to worry about. I was to keep my eyes skinned for any kind of craft and if, by any chance we were to have an engine cut, we would land happily on the sea and get picked up. I was blissfully unaware then that with a fixed undercarriage and large spats, we would have nosed over on striking the water. Well, there was gullible Gertie cheerfully spotting the odd fisherman and there was Terry at the controls grimly listening to the engine and imagining how rough it sounded. He was also a little worried as he had no proper maps of this area. We climbed to 3,000 feet and were over water for three long hours. Some 250 miles out in the Tyrrhenian sea we saw jagged flashes of lightning ahead and then ominous, forbidding black clouds bubbling up 8,000 feet. It forced us down to within a few feet of swirling white crests. It was getting dark and Terry could not risk getting caught up above cloud. We tightened our seat belts to maintain contact with our Bucking Bronco seats while peering vainly through the rain for a sign of the rugged mountains of Corsica. The minutes ticked by and no sign of land. Terry made a point of being very careful with his navigation here, so careful, in fact, that we missed the landmark we were making for simply because we flew right over it! We rounded the southern tip of Corsica and followed the coastal lights north to Ajaccio, nestled snugly in the mountains. Terry knew the airstrip but there was no flarepath. This was another worry as we had insufficient petrol to get us to Marseilles. He beat up the town for some ten minutes and eventually saw two cars driving out. They positioned their headlights to enable us to make a safe landing.

What a pleasure now was our warm reception from the French islanders. We drank Pernod with them at the little airport bar and when supper came they produced out of nothing (rations were very short and there was much poverty after the war) a meal such as I have seldom tasted better, even to this day. Naturally it was enhanced by the fact that it was so unexpected. We were provided with simple accommodation for which we were not allowed to pay. Fortunately, we had tins of coffee: these being a luxury, they were accepted with unconcealed delight.

The last stage to England was uneventful. Nevertheless, our emotions were overwhelming as we saw the white cliffs of Dover looming up in the haze ahead and then my own home below. The wheels of our faithful little Proctor came to rest at Lympne airport in Kent – ten days, 72 flying hours and 9,720 miles after leaving Jo'burg.

Very soon my parents arrived to greet us. I sometimes wonder how my mother stood up to the strain, knowing little of our whereabouts since leaving South Africa. By a strange coincidence another Terence Spencer was killed at Victoria Falls during our flight home.

A few days later we took the Proctor back to Percivals for a major service. Entering the circuit, the engine cut dead for the first time but fortunately it was a simple glide landing on to the large grass airfield. It was Terry's fault, he had to admit he had not done a service since leaving Tunis and there was water in the carburettor.

On our flight back to England, we stop off in Juba in the Sudan.

40   *Living Dangerously*

CHAPTER V

Adventures in Europe

I would like to be able to claim a triumphant return to stage and screen after Terry and I were duly married.

The spell was broken however though I did make a couple of mediocre films, playing supporting roles and I also appeared in a stage production at the Kew Theatre, now sadly no longer in existence.

We took the Proctor to Switzerland for our honeymoon. There were few private aeroplanes at the end of the war so people took us for young millionaires. Little did they know we were so broke we could not afford taxis into town but hitched a lift on petrol bowsers or airfield transport. After a week of our honeymoon, Terry was summoned to Rome to meet Ben du Preez. I was bundled on to a train from Geneva while Terry flew the Proctor to Rome returning ten days later.

We were living at the time in a pleasant small flat in Devonshire Street in London which I had occupied before I went to South Africa. I'll never forget the suppers Terry prepared for me when I came home after the evening performance. He still maintains I married him because he could cook and he married me for my money; but I soon ceased to be a wage earner and he to be a chef!

It was beginning to dawn on us that Ben du Preez's business was not going well and that was the reason Terry's salary was not forthcoming. He had been generous to us and working for Ben certainly had its exciting moments – like choosing a large diamond for my wedding present though I am still waiting for it!

The need for security finally catches up and makes dullards of us all! Terry, through a friend, found a job selling toy steam engines to Harrods and other shops. The pay was a pittance and although we enjoyed life in our comfortable flat, we were more than somewhat restricted socially and often walked miles to a favourite pub to save the money for our beers.

Without money but with an aeroplane we flew all over England, landing illegally on disused R.A.F. aerodromes as with our South

African registered plane, we could get away with murder. We then decided to complete our broken honeymoon and took off this time for France, only to be summoned by Ben once again to fly to Rome. To impress his business associates, he wanted me in the role of a private secretary though I could not even use a typewriter! Terry was to act as his private pilot.

We sampled the luxuries of the Bernini Hotel until suddenly one day Ben told us he was in serious trouble and could not pay the bill. He then took Terry off on a secret mission leaving me as security.

Terry will pick up our story.

It was late after Ben had given a lavish party to his business associates when he sidled over to me and said, 'Terry, we've got to fly to Paris tonight and meet a contact of mine urgently.'

'Ben, without radio we cannot possibly take off until two o'clock in the morning when we can make Marseilles in France at daybreak.'

Once airborne, we followed the coastal lights northwards over Genoa on the five hour flight to Marseilles. After an hour in the air Ben produced a large packet which at first I thought was something to eat until Ben explained it was South African money which he would have to change with a contact in Paris. 'For God's sake Ben, that s illegal,' I said. There were severe restrictions on currency moving across borders and as Captain of even this small aircraft I would be held responsible if caught. Our luck held, as Paris Customs at Toussus le Noble airport were on strike! Ben checked in to the chic Georges V Hotel and after a shower we went down to the bar. A small plump character, dressed in black and wearing a black homburg hat drifted in. He looked like a con man straight out of a central casting film agency.

'There's your contact, Ben.' It was…

Ben handed over the large package only to learn the next morning that the notes were counterfeit. 'That is bad news,' Ben remarked without due concern. He had already talked the man in to some other deal producing enough cash to meet our immediate commitments. Two days later we were back in Rome.

Ben returned to South Africa after completing his seemingly successful business and we flew back to England remaining there for almost a year without pay.

We should have known that nothing was straightforward with Ben. We could not make any contact with him in South Africa and were now getting desperately worried. Our money was running out and Lesley was three months pregnant so we decided to return to South Africa. Lesley sold up her apartment to pay the deposit for our aviation petrol. Fortunately I knew Douglas Bader, the legless air ace, who then ran Shell Aviation. Bader agreed to give us a petrol carnet for £100 on the promise that the balance would be paid when we reached South Africa.

I persuaded Woody Woodward of the Black Star Picture Agency in London to get me assignments for our long return flight. Naturally, he wanted to see a portfolio of my work. 'Unfortunately, it is on its way to South Africa'. I lied. Nevertheless Woody got me my first ever assigned journalistic job. It was for the *Aeroplane* magazine. The Proctor was to be the first private plane to land in Spain after the war and the editor wanted the story and pictures.

CHAPTER VI

Our return to South Africa

It was almost twelve months to the day when we received the green light for our return to South Africa. I suppose we were both pleased to climb out of our little rut though I had always secretly hoped that Terry would find a way of earning a living so we could remain in England. It was not to be. In July 1948 we set off once more in the same small aeroplane. We had £180 in our pockets and no back-up this time.

Terry had decided before we left that we should return via the West Coast of Africa despite the rainy season south of the Sahara and the longer route.

An early port of call after we left Paris was Biarritz (hardly the society Biarritz from the youthful days of our parents). We had a pleasant if simple meal in the flying club where the barman found us a room in a nearby farmhouse. Here the walls were covered with religious pictures and icons and the bedside table looked like a tiny altar with its cross and other small objects of worship. We could not help feeling a little out of place; however in spite of our weariness we talked long into the night about our very uncertain future, the flight ahead and the prospect of Terry finding himself unemployed. On the other hand we reminisced about the happy times we had spent in England and the Continent during the last year – the love and romance we had shared together since we met that evening in Johannesburg and the added happiness our forthcoming child would bring.

On our way to Seville Terry suffered a severe 'Spanish tummy' and was taken short in mid air. He had to resort to opening a sardine tin, being the only available *receptacle!* Not a romantic sight.

Will I ever forget the reception committee awaiting us in Seville? This, after being royally entertained in Madrid by the Duke of Almadova del Rio, cousin of King Alfonso and President of the Aero Club of Spain. Lined up on the tarmac in Seville in a row of chairs as we taxied in, were the Mayor and Mayoress, a Colonel in full uniform who was in charge of the air force base and other dignitaries. A large bouquet of flowers was handed to me as I stepped out in my crumpled white T-shirt and shorts. Due to a small misunderstanding in communications, it was Lord Brabazon, President of the Royal Aero Club of Great Britain and Lady Brabazon who were expected – not Mr. & Mrs. Terry Spencer. However, such is the warmth of Spanish hospitality that the whole programme was carried through as arranged. Fortunately, I could at least replace the shorts with my 'going-away' wedding outfit, but this had to serve from dawn to dusk. Before we left home Terry had impressed on me the absolute necessity to travel light, so imagine my surprise when unpacking I discovered he had brought with him eight pairs of shoes!

Our entertainment included a visit to the XI century Arab castle of the Alcazar where despite the lighting, we were able to see something of the pastel ceilings, carved mosaic walls and gorgeous tapestries. I wonder if General Franco used the suite containing all the Louis XV furniture, elaborately draped four-poster bed and crystal mirrors. Wallpaper, however attractive, will never quite replace for me that pale blue moire silk!

We were fortunate to be there at the time of the festival of Santa Anna in Triona, a suburb of Seville just across the river – but then there is always a Saints' Day somewhere in Spain.

After wining and dining in a nearby park with the mayor and his charming family and friends, we joined in the festivities until the early hours. Next morning with affectionate farewells and hopes voiced on both sides for continued friendly relations between our two countries, we waggled our wings and flew off.

Tangiers was next – a strange cosmopolitan town abounding in such obvious racketeers, where titles grew not on trees but on branches. We had an introduction to Baron Flick Sommery-Gade who invited us to dinner along with a Prince and a Count among others. Flick lived in the Kasbah with an Arab girl. Although Tania had become a Christian, this was not accepted and life was no bed of roses for the pair, particularly at the time of Ramadan. There were many unpleasant demonstrations of disapproval.

We were very late back to our little hotel and as a result Terry had to develop film far into the night and spent most of the next day writing his *Aeroplane* article on our balcony.

The sea looked inviting so needing a break, we decided to go for a swim. Much refreshed, we repaired to a milk bar for a cool drink and ice cream. While sitting there Terry became on good terms with the French proprietor. Remembering we needed to change some dollars we discussed terms with him which seemed fair. He sent his assistant away with our precious money while we sat biting our nails for what seemed hours. What could have possessed us to take such a risk in Tangiers of all places? However the messenger did finally re-appear and our fears were laid to rest.

We were entertained the second night on board a luxury yacht owned by the Prince we had met the day before. Nevertheless it was no hardship to come down to earth - or more literally to take to the skies next day and head west along the North African coast over Casablanca to Cape Juby at the extreme north west corner of Africa. This was a Spanish military 'Beau Geste' type of fort surrounded by the Sahara with an airstrip graded out of the sand. A woman arriving was a rare treat for the soldiers. The military commander at Cape Juby gave us emergency rations, a Verey pistol and water, as the chances of rescue on the next leg were remote. These, of course, should have been part of our equipment in the first place.

The long flight over nothing but sand was boring and tiring. We were both exhausted. I sat in the back to keep cool while Terry occasionally dozed off at the controls. I suddenly spotted a large fly on his back and whacked it hard with a magazine. He woke with a start wondering if the plane had blown up.

We reached Port Etienne at last in French Mauretania and cir-cled several times vainly trying to find the airstrip in a howling sand storm with winds gusting up to 60 m.p.h. at right angles to the strip. The only alternative was to land on the beach. Terry knew that the hardest sand would be close to the water's edge. We secured our gear to the rear seats, tightened our harness and left the rest to God. With His help we made it but when a Jeep came to tow us in, the aircraft sank into the soft sand and had to be dug out by the local wild-looking Africans.

There were no facilities, so a handful of French officers invited us to their house, shared by these 'grass-widowers'. They gave us a good meal, beer and plenty of wine, ending up in quite a party. We felt here, as in many remote corners of the African continent, that people were genuinely glad to see new faces, especially if one one of the faces was a woman's. We wondered at the cheerfulness of these men living with frequent sandstorms, biting winds and no entertainment other than strolls into the desert. They ate no fresh food other than fish and depended on restricted water supplies coming by tanker from France. Some of them painted or carved in their spare time.

We took off in another sandstorm and it was a blessed relief to find some vegetation around St. Louis before the long and tedious flight to Dakar – where we wasted no time. Our next stop was Bathurst in the Gambia. Here it was the rainy season and everything was fresh and lush. Our reception was equally cheering – especially from the radio chief who had seen me in a repertory production in Coventry.

We were delayed in Bathurst by bad weather and made the most of it by going for a swim and also buying mangoes, nuts and other luxuries in the open markets. We were shown the native gaol where a former British Civil Servant was just starting a two year sentence in a little thatched hut for embezzlement. This cost him his savings and lifelong pension. Worse was the scandal and derision of the local Africans.

The 3rd of August 1948 is a date long remembered by us for the worst flying conditions of the whole trip, with one possible exception. (The following Sunday we flew almost literally into the Cameroon Mountains.) Without a 'met' report, we took off and almost immediately ran into a line-squall. There was no option but to continue climbing until we reached 8,000 feet where we felt safe from any mountains not marked on our small scale map. We were on instruments solidly for an hour and a half. It was a very lonely and eerie feeling up there. Without radio there is no way of contacting the ground and sharing your problems! I was doing a bit of darning in the back but somehow I could not concentrate. We both sat there waiting until at last there was a break in the cloud and we descended to 50 feet flying in and out of whisps of cloud looking for a landmark. With difficulty we found Conakry aerodrome but when Terry circled we lost it again until a miracle found us taxiing straight into the luxury of a hangar out of the pouring rain!

One of our more civilised night stops was Roberts Field in Liberia, then the only black republic in Africa. It was a joy to land for once on a long concrete runway and glimpse American women smartly dressed and made up. It was almost too much of a temptation! However, we could not stay long because the landing fees were beyond our dwindling finances. So we had to push on. The sun shone through for the first time in West Africa and allowed us to sit back and relax. Offshore, frail-looking dug-out canoes were leisurely riding the surf as they fished. Rounding Cape Palmas at the extreme southwest tip of Africa we celebrated with a thermos of hot coffee, delicious ham sandwiches and fruit served by the air hostess.

It was already dark when we reached Abidjan on the French Ivory Coast. Terry and I repaired to our separate loos. They were equally disgusting – of the stand-up variety – so we decided to leave at once for Accra on the Gold Coast (now Ghana). The flying control officer thought we were quite mad to fly that distance at night without radio. 'If you want to go, it's up to you', he said. 'Furthermore, I cannot contact Accra to advise them of your arrival as it is too late. Takoradi is about half way. If you have any trouble, circle and they will light the flarepath for you.'

This was my first experience of night flying and I did not enjoy it. However, I settled down, my eyes glued as usual to the gyro indicator. Suddenly, I looked out and could see nothing ahead except a red glow over the port wing and a green glow to my right. As I woke Terry from his reverie, he exclaimed. 'My God! We are in 10/10 cloud.' He took over and steered due south for Takoradi where we decided to land. We saw the lights of the town but endless searching failed to produce a flare path.

Without too much petrol, we followed the intermittent lights of little native fires all along the coast till at last we spotted Accra's welcome flashing beacon. We were so relieved to find the longest runway in Africa – in our eagerness to get there we started our descent the wrong way – fortunately a red Verey light soared into the air and Terry flew round to land into the wind. What a relief! Terry was particularly exhausted and retired to bed as soon as we had wined and dined in the airport hotel. I took myself along to the bathroom, hardly ensuite, to find it inhabited by a huge flying cockroach. My cries for help were ignored by my beloved who slept soundly on.

The weather was bad all through Nigeria. We flew low over some unpleasant-looking swamps and forests. We had been warned that the natives were hostile to casual visitors. Having reached this far, we had no desire to end up in their cooking pots. From Port Harcourt we skimmed across the waves, our eyes glued to the windscreen for signs of the Cameroon Mountains which we were told rise up sharply out of the sea. When we saw the dim outline, Terry turned hard to port and made for the open sea before edging back. Suddenly, I yelled, 'Look out!' The mountains seemed only a few feet ahead of us. It was a moment I will never forget.

South of the Cameroons the weather improved and with some relief, we landed at Libreville in French Equatorial Africa. Fabric had been ripped off the port wing in a severe hail storm. Terry carried out emergency repairs with Elastoplast from our medical kit.

The next day we left the Atlantic behind and had a last look at the ocean which had been our constant companion for many thousands of miles. We then headed inland for Léopoldville (Kinshasa) and booked in to the same Sabena Guest House which I remembered from my earlier flight to South Africa. Our petrol carnet ran out in Léo and put us in a fix. How were we going to get back to Jo burg? We decided on dinner in the best restaurant and here our luck changed. The Shell representative arrived to tell us the petrol account had been paid by du Preez, so he was presumably out of jail and our money was secure in our own bank. We celebrated the news with a bottle of wine that we could now afford and then decided to stay over and see something of the Belgian Congo, as it was then. Little did we think that in 1960 Terry was to be back on and off over a period of three years covering the Congo revolution for LIFE magazine. The following afternoon we took the boat across the Congo river into Brazzaville but we found it poor and primitive by comparison and were not sorry to return to Lépoldville.

During the war Terry commanded a Belgian Squadron and it was a pleasant surprise when one of his erstwhile pilots walked into the bar one evening. Like many others from 350 Squadron, he was a pilot for Sabena.

From the navigational point of view, the next hop was surprisingly the most challenging. In 500 miles of bush and jungle there was only one landmark, Kikwit, which boasted a few thatched rondavels and tin roofed trading stores. Our drift gauge helped us find it after an hour and a half and then Luluabourg.

After what we had been through we were blessed with good weather for the next 1400 miles to what was then Salisbury in Southern Rhodesia (now Zimbabwe). Here Terry had a battle with flying control who insisted he flew to Johannesburg via Bulawayo, adding several hundred miles to the flight, but as we had the range to fly direct, he refused. Finally he agreed to sign a 'blood-chit' absolving them of any responsibility and we were on our way via Naboomspruit in the Northern Transvaal in South Africa. As on our flight north, my aunt and uncle came out of their rondavels as we executed a 'beat-up' and dropped the daily papers.

Du preez was at Germiston airport to meet us.

All dressed up in Paris

Lesley & Terry on the Proctor

Terry & Ben in Johannesburg

Living Dangerously

CHAPTER VII

Lesley describes our early life in South Africa

Once life had settled down after the excitement of arrival and reunion with our various friends, a grim reaction was to set in. I knew then as I knew for the next 14 years that South Africa was not the country for me. I do not mean for one minute that I was unhappy. This was not the case. I had Terry, we built our home and we brought up our family, but I never settled. Every Sunday paper my mother sent was scoured for English country cottages. When we left South Africa for good, our furniture hardly filled a van.

Well, Happy Person, here was the beginning of your 14 year sentence. Neither Terry nor I can quite explain how we came to settle on a 21 acre smallholding at Honeydew, 15 miles north of Johannesburg, when we had set out to find a house and small garden in the suburbs. For 13 years we were involved in building or extending. We started with one small hut and ended up with ten thatched buildings, including the house, another cottage, a tennis court and swimming pool. When we bought the property which was on the side of a hill with a fine view over the Magaliesburg Mountains, it was already fenced and the previous owner had planted fir trees along the main drive. Eventually, there were 400 peach trees but we always seemed to be away when they were at their fruitful best.

At the time contracts were exchanged the owner had 150 day-old ducks on order and asked if we would like to have them. There was a windmill drawing an abundant supply of crystal clear water and a dam so we agreed to take them over. In order to care for our livestock we had to stay on the property.

Though the South African spring was on its way, the nights were still very cold and so we had all the baby ducks with us in the concrete block hut measuring 8' x 12' and boasting little more than an outside water tap. 'Five minutes, please. Your call, Miss Brook. Curtain going up.' Oh, where were those bouquets of lilies and roses?

Regrettably inexperienced, I had provided the ducks with drinking water in their boxes, not realizing that they would spill it and then succumb to the wet and cold. By the time we launched them on the dam, their number was sadly reduced.

Building was now starting in earnest and we had little time to devote to farming, although we had acquired a cow providing both ourselves and the ducks with milk. One important factor had not been made clear: when should these super milk-fed ducks be ready for market? By the time we got around to it, they were far too old and tough, so the only thing to do was to pressure cook them for hours and serve them up for dinner parties.

Our living conditions were improved when a neighbour offered us the use of his double rondavel cottage situated just over the dirt road and looking across bare veld. We had given up our Jo'burg flat now that we were property owners and this offer was a stroke of luck – much appreciated. There was no bathroom so occasionally we would take a run over to the Muldersdrift Hotel in our buggy truck, bought for £50, or we would visit one of our friends not too far away.

It was to the Muldersdrift Hotel I took myself a couple of weeks before our daughter, Cara, was born and it was just as if I had moved into the Ritz. Not so the Frangwen Maternity Home: I would not wish my worst enemy into the hands of those Afrikaans nurses. At the height of my distress I was hanging on to the metal head board looking desperately for help, only to find the room was empty.

With my ordeal at the Frangwen mercifully over, Cara and I, together with a nursing sister (those were the days) were brought home to Southern Valley, named after my uncle's little property, the Valley, in the Northern Transvaal.

I think it has something to say for our sense of values and way of life that the cocktail bar was beautifully finished and ready to welcome us, whereas the floor of the bedroom the nurse was to share with our valuable offspring was just bare cement and about one inch deep in water.

*Johannesburg, South Africa Sept 1948.
Ablutions outside our first 'house' on the farm. Peter Bagshawe by tap.*

*South Africa, Nov 1949. Margerine boxes as tables in our early days at
Southern Valley when we had no proper furniture.*

South Africa Feb 1947. Our first transport.

Terence, Pete & Pipa Cub.

Living Dangerously

CHAPTER VIII

Building the farm and aerial photography

As Lesley said, Ben met us on our arrival and drove us in to our simple little flat in Fox Street that had been well looked after in our absence. Ben told me to come in to his office in the morning where I collected a cheque for £2,300. So life was looking good until the bank phoned to say the cheque had bounced, 'Account closed'. What a bastard. Lesley and I were literally down to our last penny when Peter Bagshawe came to our rescue with £15 – about all he possessed. Peter had just arrived in Johannesburg after an adventurous flight from England in a little Auster. On one occasion his unlicensed 'co-pilot' took off and left Pete stranded. He eventually caught up by road and found to his relief that the aircraft was undamaged.

Ten days later our lawyer phoned to say he had the money from Ben. We immediately put this down on Southern Valley, a 21 acre plot 15 miles to the north of Johannesburg. Soon after, Pete and I started digging the foundations to incorporate the shack in the main house. We cast the cement blocks ourselves and, having persuaded an Indian in Sophiatown to give us building material on credit, we bought doors and windows.

We worked 14 hours a day until we managed to get two bricklayers from the Pretoria Central Prison on greatly subsidised government grants. It turned out that one had been on death row for high treason. He was Patrick O'Malony, very Afrikaans despite his name. He had vowed, after endless stews in jail, 'If my wife gives me stew on my first night of freedom, I'll murder her'. Lesley did. It was all she could cook on a Primus stove. However, laced with plenty of red wine, she survived. The other man was hanged a year later for murder. On several occasions we left Lesley on the farm with these two men but they invariably behaved impeccably, though I have to say I always slept with my Colt automatic beside the bed – just in case.

I have never been adept with a revolver, but one day Willie, our farm 'boy', came running to the rondavels shouting, 'Baas, Baas. a rinkaals!' (a venomous snake which spits at you). Lesley gave me the gun and I raced down the track after Willie to see the beast sitting up waiting to attack.

In true cowboy fashion, I fired as I ran and the brute dropped. Willie went over to find I had shot it clean through the head. My reputation soared throughout the valley, even though it had been an absolute fluke. We then agreed, I must never fire a gun again!

We housed our two men in a bell tent on the site. They lived on 'mealie pop' (a thick sort of porridge, usually associated with the natives) which they cooked themselves, washed down with gallon jars of wine.

Sometimes they joined us for more stews. They would work fiendishly for four or five days then go on outrageous 'blinds' with 'dagga' (marijuana) for the next two. However, the walls were soon completed.

One night late, Lesley, Pete and I returned from the Muldersdrift Inn to find all hell letting loose in the bell tent as the two builders fought each other. Pete waded in, floored both of them with two punches and the next morning they were gone. We still owed them £20 – a lot of money for us then.

The R.A.F. ball in Johannesburg was something we did not want to miss but we had no money for tickets. Nevertheless, we were determined to go. Lesley wore her converted wedding dress and I donned my dinner jacket and off we set in the buggy truck for the 15 mile drive into town. We walked in through the kitchen and were wandering around the ballroom, looking very lost, when the President, Group Captain Haysom, invited us over to the top table. In the *Rand Daily Mail* the next morning was a photograph of Lesley and me and in the social column, 'And other important guests were Mr. Terry Spencer and his charming wife, a former London actress, who wore a striking white gown encrusted with jewels'.

Sadly, Pete left us to seek his fortune elsewhere. With the help of Willie I erected gum poles interlaced with wattle sticks for the roof, then two Africans thatched it. A friend, Eddie Thiele, did the plumbing and connected the water supply to our windmill pump and borehole. We had to rely on paraffin lamps and a paraffin fridge which only worked well in the winters. Even then, we had to turn it upside down regularly for it to work at all.

Yet again, the boring subject of money cropped up. I had to get work. I answered an advertisement in the *Johannesburg Star* for a photographer but when the Art Director asked me if I knew about Speed Graphic cameras, I had to answer, 'I've never used one, I only use 35mm'. Then another advertisement for a 'C.P.A.' This sounded rather naval so I applied and got the job only to find it stood for Chief Pump Attendant. However, I remained with Brinkworth Garage for a year, working weekends to get two days off during the week to continue work on the farm.

Our life style improved from eating off a plank across wooden margarine boxes to a table; from paraffin lamps to a small 12 volt electric generator; until the great day when electricity arrived. We soon had a cow, pigs, chickens and a donkey – all suitably christened by Lesley after well-known personalities in the world of entertainment.

Pete rejoined us. It was his turn to be broke but he had the bright idea of taking aerial photographs of the many wealthy houses around Jo'burg. We borrowed £260 from our local doctor, bought an old Piper Cub aeroplane, graded an airstrip 500 yards long on the farm and built a rickety hangar of gum poles.

SkyFotos was now ready to start work. Pete flew, and using a 35mm Contax and 135mm lens I had 'confiscated' from a German officer, I undertook the aerial photography. We photographed the houses and gardens from 50 to 150 feet above the ground, not worrying about air regulations as no one bothered us. On one occasion we caught in a photograph an African servant walking off with a bottle of scotch after a lunchtime party. Such was the detail of our pictures.

Sometimes we had a problem starting the Piper Cub after wet weather, when we had to remove both magnetos and warm them up in our old coal oven. When replaced she inevitably started on the first or second swing. It was a year before we had a professional service on the plane but we had already discovered that Elastoplast repaired torn fabric very well.

I processed the film in a makeshift darkroom on the farm and made 10" x 12" enlargements. We hired Gilbert Mokali, a coloured man, to do the framing. These were then taken by Pete who canvassed the smart areas selling the framed prints for three guineas each. He was good-looking and had enormous charisma. He was known to sit on the beds of wealthy socialites selling them big enlargements and masses of postcards and Christmas cards. It caught on like a 'bush fire' and we never looked back. Eventually we bought proper aerial cameras and worked for the mining companies and industry, ending up with a proper studio and laboratory in Jo'burg.

The large sow off the farm was the cause of some hair-raising experiences. When she produced a litter we failed to remove the piglets from her mum and consequently she became mighty fierce. On at least two occasions she escaped from her pen and chased Pete and me around the farm, showing little respect for the broom handles we wielded. When we finally took her to market she became most belligerent along Eloff Street in the middle of Johannesburg. The pig leapt out of the back of the buggy truck and ran amok amongst the traffic. Two burly Afrikaans policemen, probably both farmers, tackled her and put her back in the truck, restraining her for the last few miles to the market.

Around this period I became official speedway photographer at the Grand Central tracks giving me invaluable experience with high speed flash photography at night. It also brought us in a nice income, selling prints of the riders to fans.

In the spring of 1952 our newly installed telephone rang. 'Terry, can you help me out of a jam?' It was the diminutive Ernie Shirley, top reporter on the *Johannesburg Star* and also a part time 'stringer' for *Time* and LIFE magazines, 'There's been a dreadful catastrophe in a shanty town'. This was Albertynsville which had been struck by a severe tornado followed by torrential rain. Twenty blacks lay dead in the slime, 400 were injured and 4000 were made homeless. This was the first of many tragedies I was to witness as a photo journalist over the next 35 years. Somehow, this one was more poignant than anything I had seen during the war. I was deeply moved while watching people as they searched the debris for their pathetic belongings, wondering where they would find another shelter. They knew the white racist government would give them little help. It was my first story for LIFE magazine.

Duncan's arrest

Albertynsville Disaster in South Africa, Dec 1952

Coelacanth. Grahamstown, Jan 1954.

CHAPTER IX

Terry's venture into journalism

In the early hours of New Year's Day, 1953, someone drove me home from a very hectic party and put me to bed. Lesley was in England. I had not been asleep for more than an hour when I was shaken into consciousness by the irate scottish accent of Alex Campbell, recently made the first Time and LIFE correspondent for southern Africa.

'I have been trying to get hold of you all night. Where have you been?'

My bleary eyes told the story. Alex had driven the 15 miles out to the farm at 4 a.m., so was in no mood to hear me refuse to get out of bed.

'A large fish named a coelacanth has been brought in to Grahamstown in the Cape Province.'

'For God's sake, Alex, you're joking! Who cares?'

'Listen boy, it is the greatest natural history find this century. It is a 300 million year old clue to evolution and that's no joke. Now, in case you don't know it, today is Tuesday. You have to ship the picture packet to New York aboard the PanAm flight leaving at 10 a.m. on Thursday morning. It is 700 miles to Grahamstown where you must shoot the pictures, interview the Professor and get back to Johannesburg in time to write the text. So GET CRACKING.'

Mind does take over when it has to because somehow, after Alex and I had drunk large beakers of black coffee, I set off in our old Chevvy on roads that were not great in those days and, other than the odd meals and petrol stops, drove non-stop to Grahamstown, arriving at 7.30 p.m. that evening.

The next morning Professor J.L.B. Smith rolled out the grotesque monster which I photographed in black and white and in colour. I was a little worried about the colour as I had had limited experience with it. The fish was in full sunlight. I bracketed my exposures hoping that one would hit it correctly.

What with a delayed hangover and the foul smell of the fish, I was not feeling too well.

During and after lunch I interviewed the Professor who was like an excited little boy with a new toy.

'Since it became known that the long considered extinct coelacanth was in fact alive somewhere in the Indian Ocean,' he told me, 'I offered a reward of £100 for a specimen in reasonable condition. Then I heard a fisherman, named Ahmed Hussein, in the Comores Islands, had landed one nearly intact. I pulled prime minister Malan out of bed and persuaded him to give me an aeroplane to collect it. Here it is, a living relic from prehistoric times. It is the closest surviving relative to the ancient creatures linking water and land animals. Man, himself, is considered a direct descendent of the coelacanth.'

I left that evening and drove back to Jo'burg through the night taking the unprocessed film straight to Jan Smuts airport where I wrote the text. It was aboard the PanAm flight and made two pages in LIFE.

I was amazingly lucky with my first few assignments. LIFE in those days assigned some ten stories for every one used in the magazine. My first two stories in the first two weeks both made it. Fortunately, New York had no idea of my lack of experience but felt that, at last, they had a photographer they could use in southern Africa.

That year, 1953, was to be a tough year for me. I had taken over the sales operation of SkyFotos knowing little about the job. I was doing an immense amount of building on the farm, knowing little about that as well, and was trying to make the grade as a professional photo journalist, knowing little about that either.

Working for LIFE soon involved violence, something I had to get accustomed to while working in Africa. With Alex, I was in the Western Native Township near Jo'burg covering the forceable eviction of the blacks. There was an African on the roof of a broken down shanty and as I lifted my camera, he screamed abuse at me and let fly an iron bar. Before beating a hasty retreat I was able to take what is still one of my best photographs illustrating the lot of a news photographer. (See cover).

In April there was a crucial election in South Africa, won by the Afrikaaners. The Nationalists saw this as an endorsement of their 'apartheid' policy that had swept them into power in 1948 with a mandate to pursue segregation to the limit. The word 'apartheid' (separateness) entered the English dictionary and set in motion a chain of events that led to South Africa's isolation from the rest of the world. Politics had never played an important part in my life but it was impossible not to feel revolted at the lack of human dignity displayed against the blacks. The Group Areas Act denied the blacks freedom of movement and the Homelands policy made them aliens in the land of their birth.

Certainly, one realized the predicament of the white man when one saw what was happening to whites in other parts of Africa after a black government took control, usually resulting in a one party state.

Working as a freelance, I soon discovered that to make money one had to get a story pre-assigned and so I soon gave up doing stories on speculation.

I covered the case of a woman who gave birth to quintuplets in a remote village in Mozambique. When the story broke, I had no time to contact a possible buyer, so hopped in to the old Chevvy, piled in my ever-growing load of camera equipment and drove the 400 miles to the village. I arrived in time to shoot pictures of the mother and her proud set of quintuplets, only to have four of them die in the night. I then had to cover the pathetic funeral the next day. The story did sell but did not retrieve anything like the considerable expense involved. Great distances in Africa coupled with the problem of communications killed freelancing for all but a few.

In July Ernie Shirley and I drove leisurely south along the monotonously straight roads on the 700 mile route to the Cape Province. It was to be my first effort at a photographic essay for LIFE. Not for 400 years had two rival South African tribes been united in a royal wedding. The couple had never previously laid eyes on each other but the Paramount Chief of the Gaikas had already paid his lobola of £1000 in lieu of the customary 100 cows on behalf of his son.

This was accepted by the Paramount Chief of the Pondos. Recognising that South Africa had changed since their tribes had first united, they planned a ceremony combining ancient tribal customs with the solemnity of a Christian wedding.

Five thousand Gaikas and Pondos rallied to the Great Place, the royal kraal of Chief Sandile, father of the groom. They brewed oil drums full of strong kaffir beer which they drank throughout the night before the wedding, feasting, dancing and merrymaking.

The opportunity was too much for a local tobacco company to miss. In the cool of a koppie under the blazing African sun, a Christian altar had been erected for the ceremony by the Bishop of Grahamstown. Emblazoned across the top of the altar was a large banner, 'COMMANDO ROUND THE TOWN', with a large advertisement for their cigarettes. Encouraged by the advanced publicity, 3000 uninvited camera-toting white tourists invaded the scene.

The whole spectacle became a shambles. The bridegroom appeared in his leopard skin, his lips painted white. The bride was smothered in a blanket to hide her face. With the help of her escorts she fought her way through the mob where, by tradition, she swept aside her wrappings and sought approval from the bridegroom and the Gaika elders, few of whom were even able to get a glimpse of her. Then she tried to drive her spear into the gatepost of the royal kraal but, with no room to manoeuvre, she missed as she cried, 'This is my kraal'. Even so, the elders shouted 'Enter!'

The couple changed into western clothes for the Christian ceremony. The beautiful location in the trees on the hill saw tourists poking their cameras over the altar, some of whom climbed on to the back of it, spilling the communion wine across the stark white drape. The vivid streak of crimson looked as if some fearful sacrifice had been made to the Great White God.

Ernie and I soon decided to forget the colour and the unique African ceremony and concentrate on the shambles. My final frame showed the bridal couple leaving for their honeymoon. While jostling and scrambling in the crowd, my camera was momentarily knocked out of my hand. The bridegroom, seeing my predicament, stopped and with his bride, looked straight into the rescued camera.

'Damn it!' I said angrily, 'I missed the candid shot.'

Returning to Johannesburg, we were inundated with cable picture queries from New York. One read, 'WHAT IS NAME OF MAN ON BRIDE'S RIGHT?' How could we ever find out and who cared anyway? So we cabled back, MAN ON BRIDE'S RIGHT IS BRIDEGROOM'S SISTER'. We heard no more.

Imagine our delight when a cable arrived the following week,' HOLD YOUR HORSES STOP GAIKA PONDO WEDDING IS SIX PAGE SUMMER LEAD WITH TWO FULL PAGE PICTURES AND TEN OTHERS STOP CONGRATULATIONS GREAT JOB CATURANI.' George Caturani was on the LIFE news desk. Eagerly we awaited arrival of the magazine to find the full page closing picture I had been late in getting, was now captioned, 'As they pose for their official wedding picture'. You can't win!

South Africa - Kewla Dec 1959. Lemmy Special plays his pennywhistle in a Johannesburg street with two other members of his gorup.

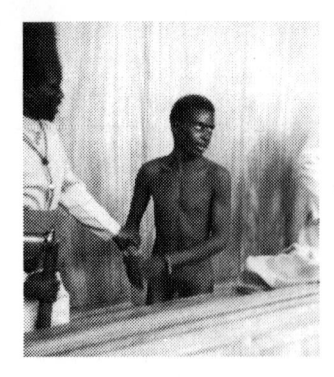

Mau-Mau Civil War in Kenya, May 1954. A convicted murderer goes berserk in the Supreme court in Nairobi. He strips naked in the box. I was arrested for taking these pictures but Alex Campbell took the film roll off me before the police got me.

Centre: Tom Mboya's big rally in Nairobi, Kenya, March 1960.

Below: Reporters in Nyasaland during riots, August 1953 l-r: Adrian Porter (AP), Terry Spencer & Ross Mark (Daily Express)

CHAPTER X

Trouble flares up all over southern Africa

I was assigned to cover a party meeting with the future prime minister, Johannes Strijdom, It was about as near to one of the old Nazi campaigns as anyone would ever want to see. Photographers were attacked by burly Nationalist supporters. You let off a flash and then ran like hell, dissolving into the crowd for protection.

There was a serious revolt against white domination further north in Nyasaland, so Alex Campbell and I caught a South African Airways DC6 to Salisbury where we transferred to an old DC3 taking us into the beautiful country of Nyasaland (now Malawi). We landed at Blantyre and checked into Ryall's Hotel, the rendezvous of the rest of the press corps. A quick wash and shirt change and we met in the bar to get 'filled in' on the situation by colleagues.

Hiring a self-drive car we set off at dawn the next morning to cross the Shire River to Chikwawe where most of the trouble seemed to be centred. Rounding a sharp bend in the dirt road on the descent to the river, we pulled up abruptly where a tree had been felled, serving as a roadblock. Being the only whites around this desolate area and fearing an ambush, Alex and I jumped out of the car and ran for shelter in the nearby trees. We could not turn the car and, if it was an ambush, the road would already be closed behind us. Our hearts were pounding while listening intently for sounds of rebel tribesmen who were known to be on the rampage in the area.

Suddenly, we both looked up. Yes. Unmistakably there was the distant sound of an engine. It was getting nearer. A lorry rounded the sharp bend and ground to a halt in a cloud of dust as the driver spotted the roadblock and our deserted car. Soldiers leapt out, automatic weapons at the ready and took cover in the trees around us. Keeping our heads low, we shouted at them. The soldiers told us to show ourselves.

'Aren't you Spencer?' inquired the officer in charge.

'Yes,' I answered, surprised.

'Weren't you at Cheltenham College?' I nodded. We had indeed been at school together.

'This is great. Why not join our patrol?' he invited.

We were soon through the roadblock and on the rickety pontoon ferrying vehicles across the river. Many more road blocks were encountered and each one had to be taken seriously. At one of these we were stoned by a mob who hastily melted into thick undergrowth when they saw the soldiers.

Our army patrol was joined by armed police. When raiding a nearby village, we were met by a large crowd of hostile Africans led by a man who was shouting and gesticulating. The crowd started shooting at us with bows and arrows. The police superintendent dropped on one knee, took careful aim with his .303 Lee Enfield rifle and hit the leader straight through the heart. His legs just gave way as he crumpled like a punctured bag of maize.

The effect of that one shot was electric. For a moment there was dead silence; then everyone started screaming. It was a terrifying, blood-curdling sound. In seconds the crowd had vanished as though a conjurer had waved his magic wand. We cautiously entered the village but it was deserted. Pots were gurgling over wood fires and chickens were scampering about in circles, cackling wildly. Soldiers amused themselves by trying to kill these chickens with the abandoned bows and arrows but without much luck. I still have the bow and arrows I picked up in that village.

It was getting dark and not a good time to be on these lonely roads so the police superintendent ordered the patrol to move a few miles down the road to an open clearing. The vehicles were parked in a circle with their headlamps pointing outwards. Tents were erected inside the circle and sentries were posted. Supper was cooked over a large camp fire. A few us of huddled in a corner and knocked off a bottle of scotch I had brought. My old school mate told me, 'I'm glad the police shot that man. It would be more than my life is worth to shoot one of these bloody wogs. The military enquiries would never end and I would be the scapegoat for the top brass if anything went wrong.'

A few days later I was in a tea plantation in the Cholo district with Arthur Mapleson of the London *Daily Express* when we ran into another minor battle in which the police were being attacked with bows and arrows. We heard the young officer in charge reporting the incident over his Landrover radio back to his headquarters.

After the 'battle' Arthur and I felt we needed a drink and retired to the Cholo Club where the press had been made honoury members. I left Arthur with a large gin and tonic and phoned the senior police officer at command headquarters, 'I understand there has been trouble in the Cholo district. Could you please give me some information?'

'Who are you?' he asked briskly and rudely.

'Terry Spencer of LIFE Magazine.'

'No, we have no information of any trouble in the Cholo district.'

'Had there been any trouble,' I persisted, 'would you have heard about it?'

'Don't be so bloody facetious. Of course we would.'

'Damn right you would, you bloody liar!' I shouted back at him over the dilapidated instrument, 'we have just come from there and heard your Inspector reporting the incident to you over his radio.'

We were waiting for just such an incident. We expect 'bumsteers' from the police, as they often have to keep information quiet, but direct lies cannot be tolerated. We were constantly being fed lies by the Nyasaland police so we used this event to complain to the Governor, Sir Geoffrey Colby, and had no further trouble in that respect.

Kenya was now the land of Mau Mau, taking its strange and terrible hold over that most beautiful and exciting of African countries. On our arrival the flowering jacaranda trees were a blaze of purple, but oaths and rituals were an integral part of the life of the Kikuyu tribe, steeped in pagan superstition and ideology. Originally, the secret oaths were designed to unite and discipline members of the tribe. As Mau Mau momentum gained strength and success, so the design of the oaths was directed at acts of violence and terror against the 30,000 strong white population. They made men perform acts, often sexual and with animals, so degrading that any other atrocity (they were ordered to commit) would seem mild in comparison. They were made to fornicate with dead bodies and to drink the Kaberichia cocktail, a mixture of menstrual blood and semen.

In any event, these oaths achieved a solidarity among the Kikuyu either by desire or by fear necessitating immense British forces and money to counteract. In fact, during the seven year Mau Mau campaign, only 95 whites were killed, but on the African and Asian side the situation was desperate, with 13,000 deaths, some by garrotting. Several victims had their penises removed while still alive. These were eaten by fellow tribesmen.

Alex and I travelled long distances around Kenya by car to cover the trouble spots. We were alone, unarmed and could easily be ambushed or shot at from the thick forests and undergrowth suffocating many of the roads. Trains were ambushed until they started carrying armed guards.

A night on a lonely farmstead in the White Highlands brought home to us the fear which the whites were living through every 24 hours of the day. There was always one member of the family awake and on guard with a considerable armoury close at hand. He would sit up through the night listening, listening. On a dark and lonely night the imagination can run riot when one hears strange noises. The telephone line would be cut before an attack. This would sound a light 'tinkle' on the telephone. One would rush in panic to the phone to be engulfed in relief by the calm voice of the operator, 'Can I help you?' Another time it was only the wind or a tree touching the wires. But next time….? Even with weapons the chances of surviving an attack were small. Worse, you knew that death would not come quickly. This was not the practice of Mau Mau. 'We are all going slowly round the bend, said our host. 'How long can we go on like this?' All he needed now was an atrocity to strike one of his friends and he would move out, leaving his life's savings behind. Others took to drink or became irrational.

Mau Mau had won another round.

We went on trips to the Aberdare Mountains with two British Special Branch police officers, Ian Henderson and Bernard Ruck.

Both were subsequently decorated for bravery. Ian was one of the few whites in Kenya who spoke fluent Kikuyu. Most of the farmers spoke a bastard Swahili. Thus, Ian was able to converse and interrogate with immense success. These two men used to go up into the mountains at night, unarmed, to confer with Mau Mau leaders.

At this time my brother, John, was a Senior Superintendent of police at Nyeri in the heart of Mau Mau country. When his younger brother working for LIFE Magazine turned up in his area that May morning in 1954, John was a worried man. He planned to take early retirement and did not want his chances spoilt, but he did invite me to stay with him. However, Alex and I decided to stay at the White Rhino Hotel in company with other members of the press corps. It was essential in covering this sort of story to swop clues and exchange snippets of the story with colleagues so that pieces of the 'jigsaw' would fall into place. Someone always seemed to have the right contact. Then there was the cheque book. It is said that every man has his price. It is very difficult to keep a story from a determined press corps.

Our Special Branch contacts in Kenya were excellent. It was imperative to protect these sources for the 'off the record' information we were getting. Coupled with our own investigations, we knew that a mass Mau Mau surrender was imminent. But where and when...?

I was having dinner one night with John and his wife, Melba. He had warned her to say nothing in my presence. However, certain casual remarks made during dinner, together with what I already knew, told me that the surrender was expected in the early hours of the morning.

I bade 'good night', returned to the hotel, roused Alex out of bed and parked our car in a clump of trees within sight of the police station. Sure enough, at 1.30 a.m. police Landrovers swept out of the station. Alex accelerated to catch up with the convoy. It was pouring with rain and no one noticed us. At the rendevous they were far from happy with our presence and questioned us relentlessly as to how we got there. We hung around, cold and miserable until dawn but nothing happened.

Alex and I headed back for Nyeri and decided that he would stay in the car to watch the roads for any additional police movement while I checked with the Provincial Commissioner's office. Walking past his open window I realised that the P.C. was on the scrambler telephone to the Governor in Nairobi. He was describing in detail what had just gone wrong. Much of what he was saying we knew already from our Special Branch contacts but that was entirely 'off the record' and could not be used. Now, I was hearing it from the P.C. himself. Admittedly, I should not have been listening, neither should his security have been so lax. I was concentrating on what the P.C. was saying and checking it against what we already knew when I heard a shout, 'Stop Sir! Stop! The Press!' It was Dick Gribble, Commissioner of the Special Branch. He was standing in the open window below which I cowered. In a second I ducked around the corner of the building and raced over to Alex, 'Start the engine.' I shouted as I ran. He opened the door and I piled in as he let out the clutch and accelerated south for Nairobi.

'Be bloody sure to tell me what you heard and not what you know,' said Alex.

'Most vital is that the P.C. mentioned the names of Generals China and Kareba who had been released from the death cell to supervise the surrender and had not returned.' I told him breathlessly.

Through these two convicted Mau Mau murderers, Ruck and Henderson had arranged a delicate truce. For the first time in a year the familiar sound of gunfire was absent from the forests. 'Last night,' I recounted to Alex, 'hundreds of Mau Mau headed towards the village of Gethvini to surrender. Inadvertently, however, they crossed the prohibited but unmarked boundary of the Kikuyu reserve in the dark and a company of the Kings African Rifles opened fire on them. They dispersed into the forests with their wounded but left behind 25 of their dead.'

The surrender had been shot to smithereens and with it an early end to Mau Mau.

We had a unique scoop for a weekly magazine.

Our bid to reach Nairobi was short-lived. The police had radioed ahead and a Landrover blocked the road. We were escorted back to Nyeri and met by an irate Gribble. 'How much did you hear?'

'Everything.' I replied.

'What are you going to do about it?'

'It's a big story and we can't just sit on it. We've expended a lot of sweat and blood tracking it down.'

It would have been too embarrassing to detain us on some pretext or the other so they did the clever thing by releasing our exclusive story to the rest of the foreign press corps. At a drinks party some time afterwards Dick Gribble congratulated us and turning to Alex queried, 'Weren't you the reporter who called General Erskine 'the cocktail party General'?'

'Let's put it this way,' said Alex, 'I filed it but it was never printed.' This told us conclusively what we suspected – that the police were reading our cables. Press cables, like any other, are supposed to be confidential.

This type of story is always difficult for photographers. You travel hundreds of miles through tricky and often dangerous countryside for little pay-off. It illustrates the paramount difference between journalism and photo journalism, in that the photographer has to be there before the event. To do this he has to have far better contacts, get involved with much greater 'in depth' reporting and be continuously on the move. Some correspondents, on the other hand, can roll up at the local bar after the event and get 'filled-in' by his colleagues, add his own embellishments and write his story – without ever having seen a thing.

I had shot some pictures under difficult circumstances for *Time* magazine up in the Aberdare mountains and was not happy when Alex handed me a cable, 'SPENCERS PIX UTTERLY UNUSABLE - HARTSHORN'. Barker T. Hartshorn was the *Time* picture editor. Next day Alex handed me another, 'SPENCERS UTTERLY UNUSABLES USED - HARTSHORN'.

The supreme court in Nairobi seemed an odd place for a picture story so it was only from personal interest that I accompanied Alex into a press seat. Photography is strictly prohibited in court but, as always, I had a small Nikon concealed under my jacket. They were trying a Kikuyu who was alleged to have murdered a small white girl in particularly brutal circumstances. Suddenly, he leapt out of the dock, threw his manacled wrists in the air while the blanket covering his body fell to the ground. He scrambled around the court room stark naked, crashing his handcuffs on the benches and screaming in a wild, beserk manner. Forgetting the dignity of the court I jumped across the top of the benches to photograph this bizarre scene. So preoccupied was I with the prisoner that I barely felt a powerful police hand on my ankle wrenching me off the bench as I crashed to the floor. I managed to get the film out of the camera and pass it to Alex who came to my rescue. While waiting to be seen by a senior police officer I loaded another film into the camera. After receiving a severe reprimand for my disgraceful behaviour, my film (unused) was confiscated and I was released.

Returning to Johannesburg I learned the great news that Lesley had produced a son in London.

The dour, bespectacled little Scotsman, Alex Campbell, left the Johannesburg bureau to be replaced by a young, ebullient and amusing American, Ed Hughes. After a riotous New Year's Eve party our first job together was to fly the 800 miles south to Cape Town to cover an unusual gathering – Boere sports. The meeting was held on a large shimmering white sandy beach. In traditional Afrikaans style steak, mutton and boereworst (a spiced sausage), were sizzling on expertly-made wooden fires and metal grills. Boeremusik was being played on squeezeboxes and concertinas. Many of the sports dated back to the old voortrekker days when the Boers were on the march northwards seeking new places to settle. There was pillow fighting on horseback, tug-of-wars where the rope went round men's necks instead of their waists. There was 'thumbtrek' in which men intertwined thumbs and tried to force their opponents to roll on their faces plus other curious events.

It was a lovely sunny day and a gentle breeze off the sea kept us cool. Ed was forming a quite different picture of the Afrikaaner than the one he had read about. Around mid afternoon there was a call for silence and the Master of Ceremonies stood on the platform and announced in English, no doubt for our benefit, 'The two men at the foot of the stage are from *Time*, that dastard American magazine printing all those lies about our beautiful country and folk'.

My stomach rolled as I waited for the reaction from the hostile Afrikaaners surrounding us. To my horror Ed jumped up on to the platform, grabbed the microphone and turned to the large crowd, 'Yes, I work for *Time* and my colleague works for LIFE. Who says we print lies about South Africa? That's not true. I have only been in your country for ten days and I have had a most enjoyable time but never before in my journalistic career have I known a man stand up and try to incite a crowd against two defenceless people'. Ed received a rousing applause and we survived the rest of the afternoon.

In 1955 the increasing heat of African nationalism was being felt in the black ghettoes of Johannesburg. At 4.30 one February morning I was awakened by the telephone bell. It was Ed. 'Get off your arse and down to Sophiatown fast. All hell is breaking loose in the township'.

Ed had been tipped off by Ernie Shirley who in turn had been called by one of his many black contacts in Sophiatown. Police sources became increasingly difficult in South Africa though we still had a few. We relied more on lawyers connected with the underground movements and blacks in the townships.

Arriving outside the shanty town as dawn was breaking, I had little difficulty spotting Ed in his sleek white open Chevrolet. Heavily armed police were everywhere. I parked my car well away from the trouble spots, grabbed my camera bag and equipment and hopped in beside Ed. 'If you go into that bloody Kaffir township, you're going to get hurt.' We were not sure if the cop warning meant getting hurt by the police or by the African inmates.

Ed and I regally toured the township, photographing confrontations of Africans and police as we tried to avoid being hit by missiles on the one hand and obscene abuse from the police on the other.

At dawn hundreds of white police with automatic Sten guns and rifles led black police armed with clubs and spears into the sleeping warren of Sophiatown. This was no ordinary raid, it was the South African government's method of enforcing 'apartheid'. 'No black may own property in a white area,' declared Prime Minister Verwoerd, so 60,000 blacks were being evicted from their homes.

All day a tall gaunt Anglican priest wandered among his parishioners giving them encouragement, 'Do not fear. The day is coming when these madmen will regret this fiendish, evil act.' The Africans called him Makhaliphile (Dauntless One). The whites called him a dangerous agitator. He was Father Trevor Huddleston, the nearest live and walking image of Christ I have witnessed. He had a powerful personality and yet he was gentle and serene.

There was no religious sentimentality about him. He was one of the few white men who could talk to a black man without patronising him.

That night the bulldozers moved in to Sophiatown. There was nothing left for the Africans.

Soon after this event Huddleston, who had openly and bravely opposed 'apartheid', left South Africa, virtually expelled by his own church. When the Archbishop of Canterbury visited South Africa and spoke out against 'Too rapid de-segregation', Huddleston openly criticised his views and the false impressions they created. All this did not prevent him becoming a Bishop in England.

One of my favourite pictures in South Africa was taken in Huddleston's little tin shanty church in Sophiatown. It shows a small black boy praying in front of his Christ. What struck me was that this statue of Christ was, like the boy, pitch black.

Ernie and I made it part of our jobs to communicate regularly with the people of the African townships although it was illegal for us whites to be there. It was essential to be their guests, to drink their brandy. In that way we could talk to them as equals – something unknown between whites and blacks in South Africa where only a master-to-slave relationship existed. I like to think we later returned their brandy.

The South African police informer network in the African townships was devastatingly efficient – because it paid well. Our presence in a shack would soon become known to them despite the precautions we had taken. We used to enter through the guarded gates into the gloomy, dimly lit townships, crouched in the back seats of one of their ramshackle cars. As soon as a police raid was on we would be warned and slip out the back way climbing over rusty barbed-wire fences and creep stealthily in the footsteps of our host to another safe hideout.

Ernie probably had the best contacts, both black and white. Later these contacts enabled us to meet up regularly with the great black Pimpernel, Nelson Mandela, then on the run for two years. The police were searching the country for him but missed him when Mandela returned to his office guarded by a policeman. He was dressed as a cleaner with his bucket and broom. He saluted the policeman, 'Morning Baas', went upstairs, collected his papers hidden under floor boards, stuffed them in his bucket and walked out of the building.

Ernie was the most organised reporter and fastest writer I ever met. He carefully prearranged his lines of communication, vital in areas where copy was being transmitted on a Morse code key. Where necessary, the palms of various hands were well greased to ensure speedy and priority transmission.

After a story Ernie would dash to his car, to a table somewhere or to his room; take out his battered typewriter and 'bang' out his piece straight on to a cable form. I never saw him read over anything he had written. His piece would then be handed to a locally hired piccanin who would rush it to the cable office. Sometimes, Ernie would hand it to me to telephone over the local 'party line' to the nearest 'stringer' for onward transmission by cable or telex. While this was going on he would be 'bashing' out his second cable to another paper, he strung for, the *New York Times* etc. All the stories were written for the particular editor and were quite different in character though seldom in content. I gained valuable experience from him early on in my journalistic career.

In September 1955 Ernie, Lesley and I drove 400 miles down to Natal to shoot a story on a beautiful nun who rode a white horse into the Valley of a Thousand Hills administering to the sick and dying T.B. cases. This was a story suggested to LIFE by Ed Hughes.

When the three of us turned up at the mission station set high on a hill overlooking dramatic undulating countryside, we took the Mother Superior by surprise. She was horrified at us doing a story on one of her nuns.

'I know LIFE,' she said in her broad Irish brogue and there was a glint in her eye. 'They are likely to run the picture opposite a big Maidenform bra advert'.

'Oh No! Mother,' I answered, 'LIFE has just done a series on the religions of the world and they will treat this story with the deference it is due.'

'What religions did you do?' she enquired.

'Catholicism,' I immediately answered; then paused to think of others. 'Christianity, Judaism, Buddhism'. I was fast running out of candidates and trying frantically to think of the one the magazine had run on the Middle East when I victoriously spluttered, 'Oh - and Ramadamism! The Mother Superior doubled up laughing, tears running down her ample cheeks as she turned to me, 'You're in the wrong job, my son. You ought to be in the church.'

However, she introduced us to the riding nun. Riding was a euphemism. She barely knew how to mount the animal. Ernie was going to have to do most of the riding if we were going to get a story at all. Not by any stretch of our imaginations could we describe the girl as 'beautiful'. If that was not enough, she told us that there had not been a T.B. death in the hills for months. Anyway, the surrounding country was beautiful and we followed her around for three days, at least getting some good pictures.

We were accepted into the community and came to love the nuns. It was my first close relations with these people and I was surprised to discover how normal and broad-minded they were. When the Mother Superior first showed us to our rooms, she advised, 'For goodness sake lock up everything. These little black 'skellums' (urchins) will steal your last button'.

Life at the mission station was Spartan and simple. We rose before dawn to photograph our girl at mass. After breakfast one of us would have to work the pump outside the toilet for the other. We had not had an alcoholic drink for three days when I gave the Mother Superior money for our stay. With almost indecent haste she said, 'Well now, I must be off to the town.' Ernie interjected, 'Mother, I need some toothpaste. Can I come with you?'

'Make it Gilbeys!' I called out to Ernie as they walked across to the car. Mother looked back and laughed. She knew I was refering to Gilbeys gin.

A night I shall always remember was 12 August 1957. Against a clear crystal sky high above South Africa we spotted the weird flashing dots as the Russian Sputnik sped around the world. We saw man's first flight into space. Alas, the dots were too faint to register on my film.

Because of the great distances and bad communications in Africa, we seldom had time to cable New York for permission to go on 'fast-breaking' news stories. We simply hopped on to the next plane and asked Fiona Ilic in our Johannesburg office to advise New York and give them a contact address. The New York office had a large map of the world in the foreign news room but we decided it was not nearly large enough. We once had a cable in Salisbury, 'CAN YOU URGENTLY HOP A TAXI TO NAIROBI TONIGHT? Actually, it is 2,000 miles on dusty, tortuous dirt roads.

In March 1959 Curt Prendergast, who had taken over the Time Life bureau from Ed Hughes, phoned me, 'Get to Jan Smuts (airport) fastest. Trouble has broken out all over Nyasaland again.'

Business, personal engagements and dinner dates all went by the board. In seconds I had gathered together film and equipment while Lesley threw clothes into a bag. Then we had a hectic 80 m.p.h. drive to Jan Smuts after Fiona Ilic had tipped off the airline that we were running late but had to catch the flight. You could do that sort of thing in those days.

Many times I arrived at Jan Smuts to hear the boarding instructions being announced for passengers. A quick word at the counter and they would hold the plane as I checked in the gear, dashed through customs and immigration and slumped hot and breathless into my seat. An ice-cold gin and tonic shortly after take off settled me for the trip. In the meanwhile, Fiona would be trying to get through to Eric Robins in Salisbury to brief him to join us and, at the same time, get us all on to the first plane out of Salisbury for Blantyre in Nyasaland. Somehow, we always managed it.

The hostility between the Central African Federation and Rhodesia had exploded once again into violence. African nationalism was gaining momentum as steadily as a veld fire. Nearly three million blacks were determined not to be dominated by a mere 8,000 whites. Trouble flared from the misty mountains to the clear blue-grey waters of Lake Nyasa. Europeans were being stoned in the capital, Blantyre. At Karonga a mob wrecked the airfield and stormed the jail, releasing 13 prisoners.

The scene which greeted us on our arrival in Blantyre was much the same as before. We watched the African riot police with their evil-looking black helmets and military webbing, going into action against stone-throwing mobs.

They carried steel shields to protect themselves against these jagged missiles. Alas, I had already learned that riots had to be covered with a wide angle lens, recording the expressions and emotions of men in action – and we carried no shields. I have often initially been near paralysed with fear but once in the 'thick of it', fear is forgotten. I know that whatever I have seen is recorded on film, though I often do not remember taking the photograph.

After a riot I saw a man, obviously a Special Branch policeman, unobtrusively trying to take my photograph. He noticed I had seen him, smiled and asked, What exposure should I give? Leave that to the experts. I quipped, giving him a passport photograph. We carried these in quantity for a mass of visas we needed while working the African continent. He wanted it for my police dossier. His name was Bob Mushett and he became a good contact, although his closeness to the foreign press corps, especially in Ryall's bar, made us suspicious and careful.

Most, if not all white police departments in black Africa attached such importance to press investigations that they detailed at least one officer solely to monitor the activities of the press. Nyasaland was a country where press contacts were better than police contacts. We could 'hobnob' with 'terrorists' as the police called them, 'freedom fighters' as they called themselves. While no respectable journalist would impart confidential information on terrorist activities, he could inadvertently let slip the odd clue in the bar which, coupled with the information the police already knew, could greatly help Bob Mushett. That was why he liked to join us in the bar. All over the world I was to notice Special Branch men hanging around press bars - listening... You developed a 'nose' for them.

Late one evening Curt Prendergast, George Clay of N.B.C. and I were drinking in a corner of the bar when Bob came over and whispered, we're going to arrest Banda tonight. We intend to cordon off the whole area so get in quick. The gnome-like Hastings Banda was the great African nationalist, 'extremist of the extremists', he once called himself.

We parked our car in the dense undergrowth surrounding Banda's house. It was 10 p.m. His bodyguards were drinking and making a lot of noise so they had not heard our car engine as we drove in without lights. We had four long hours to wait and hoped they would not discover us. We would have been taken as Special Branch men and dealt with accordingly. One of us kept watch. If a single twig cracked we would all sit rigidly upright and listen. It could be a rifle bolt. We heard several people patrolling around but they did not find us. As 2 a.m. approached we glanced at each other and felt the tension; then we heard the distant rumble of truck engines. Suddenly the shooting started and bright flares lit up the whole area. It was actually tear gas canisters and star shells being fired by the police as they surrounded the house. That was the last we saw of any action as a dense cloud of thick, choking tear gas engulfed the area. We even lost sight of each other. Tears were running down my cheeks, my skin tingled and felt as though it was on fire. By the time the three of us joined up again and made our way stealthily over to the house, all we found were three black policemen on guard. Banda had been arrested with most of his henchmen and taken away.

During a night like that I did not take a single picture though Curt and George wrote good stories. This is another twist on the paramount difference between journalism and photo journalism.

Jomo Kenyatta in jail in Kenya's NFD province, April 1961

*Sophiatown Sept 1955.
His Black Christ*

*Father Trevor Huddleston, visiting
one of his flock, May 1960*

Sophiatown move - 1956. Blacks were moved out to make way for an all-white area near Johannesburg.

Nun on horseback at dusk, Zululand, 1956.

Living Dangerously

CHAPTER XI

Lesley returns to Johannesburg

Terry agreed to my trips overseas about every two years. These visits were important to me as I had never been able to break away from my way of life in England and wanted to see my parents, other relations and friends. There was a problem on my return as I always had difficulty in settling down again on the farm. On one occasion when I arrived home after a longer than usual spell away, Terry took me into the ill-lit kitchen to introduce me to the new 'staff'. I confess I was sickened by the poor bundles of rags who eyed me suspiciously as they sat on the stone floor picking their noses.

At least things seemed to be going smoothly on the business side if not on the home front. I have never been one for living on my own in the country and although we did have African servants in their own quarters, I was still nervous and used to dread the dark evenings which descend so quickly in the southern hemisphere. I would then have to wrestle with the wretched paraffin lamps.

Once, after ten days away in Natal, Terry arrived home in the early evening and I offered him a glass of sherry. 'What's this?' he asked as I passed him a tumblerful. 'Well, that's how I drink it!' I said. Soon after that we let the farm.

During the last, rather prolonged visit to England, something happened 'out of the blue' that was to alter the course of our lives. Terry started working for LIFE Magazine. This was the beginning of 20 years association with LIFE until it closed in 1972, only to resurface many years later. So from now on I was to compete not only with aerial photography but with LIFE magazine as well.

We were still running SkyFotos. I was on my own at Southern Valley trying to keep things going. When people rang up about their aerial photographs, I tried to blame the weather but continuously cloudless blue skies defeated me, so I escaped down to Durban.

In the early days before I was tied up with the children I was asked by one Cecil Williams to play the lead in a play called *Deep are the Roots*. By coincidence I had seen the London production but it was only now I was in South Africa that the message became clear – it was a very liberal play connected with apartheid. Cecil became a good friend and was a brave man indeed. He was with Nelson Mandela in the car in Natal when they were ambushed and arrested. Cecil was kept for some time under house arrest in his top floor flat in Johannesburg. He eventually escaped to England. He once told me something I will never forget about an incident he had once observed involving a black man with a shirt and tie and wearing a hat standing at a bus stop. Two young Afrikaaners came along, took exception to the man's appearance and beat him up. Could it have been this incident that started Cecil on his courageous stand against apartheid?

We had a series of African cooks and nannies, some good and some bad. Our favourite was Natalia. We found her in her native province and she spoke not one word of English. I am ashamed to say we never tried to speak their language while they struggled valiantly with ours. Mary came to us towards the end of our stay in South Africa. She was cook and part time nanny to Raina (our second daughter) and was the most beautiful and dearest to us. She was coloured (in other words of mixed blood, not pure African) with huge wide-apart eyes, a lovely smile and sense of humour. Her morals, I am afraid, left much to be desired!

Our Willie, who was with us from the start as farm hand, found a friend of his to come and cook for us. One morning I woke early and it seemed unusually light. I drew back the curtains and knew the reason why. The farm was lit from end to end, or so it seemed, by veld fires. The alarm was quickly raised and we all set to with sacks or whatever we could lay hands on to beat out the flames spreading perilously near our house and the other thatched buildings. One person, however, was not taking any part in the drama. Pausing for a moment I happened to catch sight of our new cook and was amazed to find him calmly chopping wood to light the kitchen range.

Pioneering was never on the agenda when I planned my life and career. However we came close to it in those early days on the farm at Honeydew. Our cooking was done on an old kitchen range which somehow heated the water and we had a stone sink which we had picked up for £4 in the Indian market. We had no telephone (that was still to come) and our nearest neighbour was a quarter of a mile away. Gas lighting, which replaced the dreaded paraffin lamps, was a lifesaver for me, even more so than electricity which followed later.

A splendid half-Persian cat called Micky joined us. Micky was fastidious and if his minced meat was even slightly off as a result of the inadequate refrigeration, he would not touch it. One Sunday some friends arrived for drinks and it soon became obvious they expected to stay for lunch. On Terry's suggestion, I took out Micky's rejected mince and after cooking it with plenty of onions, garlic and tomatoes, we served it up with spaghetti for lunch. From that day onwards our friends, who learnt the secret, still talk of that excellent Micky bolognaise.

I used to console myself with the thought of these simple coloured people who perhaps did not work so hard or make so much money as the next man but at least they can tell St. Peter at the gates how they talked and laughed and danced and enjoyed what freedom they could under their summer skies.

Some strange experiences came our way connected with witchcraft. Having been recommended by my uncle in Naboomspruit, a certain Gilbert arrived from the Northern Transvaal to cook for us. He was especially welcome since cooking was not my favourite occupation then or now. He started well and then his work deteriorated and he became difficult and morose. Unknown to us he visited a witch doctor and came back with an incision in his chest. In this instance the treatment was not a success and in due course Gilbert went into hospital where he died some months later of cancer of the liver.

On another occasion we took on a fine looking man called Simon and the same sort of thing happened. He started well and then became more and more difficult. When I spoke to him and tried to get at the trouble his head went down to his chest and he would not look at me. I decided to consult Watch who had succeeded Willy as 'boss boy' or chief farm hand. Watch had been in the army in North Africa and spoke quite good English. When I told him my story, he hesitated, whether it was because he thought as a European or whether he too was sceptical, I shall never know. This then is the explanation he gave me. Someone who disliked Simon (perhaps jealous) must have placed a spell on one of the objects in the kitchen. Although Watch looked rather furtively around, he saw nothing visible to the naked eye; so he then thought the only solution would be to find a witch doctor to exorcize the poor victim. One of our English neighbours had the same experience, he told me, with a much valued servant and he actually went to those lengths. Simon, alas, ended up in court on some petty theft charge after he left us. I really do not believe he was wholly responsible.

This now is a shameful tale to tell. A married couple once worked for us. They did not appear to be very happy and neither were they satisfactory from our point of view. At the same time friends were staying with us and one of them missed a sum of money from his rondavel bedroom. Small pieces of jewellery, of no great value, also disappeared. The couple had given in their notice and it was decided I should go through their baggage before they left. They offered no resistance. We did not find anything. I do not think I will forget to my dying day the pathetic collection making up their entire personal belongings. It later transpired that a lunch guest that day was subject to fits of kleptomania…

Emma, out first wash girl, showed me how to bake bread, wrapping it in blankets to keep it warm for the yeast to rise. She spoke the most beautiful biblical English.

Because we had no telephone in the early days and our nearest neighbour was a quarter of a mile away, I was never happy to be left on my own in the evenings. This was sometimes unavoidable, and when Terry and Pete were invited to an R.A.F. reunion party, I agreed as cheerfully as I could that they should go. When it started to get dark and it was time to light those dreaded paraffin lamps, I began to regret my generosity. Then again, as it came near to 11 o'clock when they promised to be home, I felt a little halo round my head. However, 11 o'clock passed, then midnight and when they finally rolled in at 1.30 a.m., they were in no state to be welcomed or forgiven. Only one thing saved the day. Our local store at Honeydew was inadequate so I had given them a list of things to buy in Jo'burg before going to the party. This included mincemeat for us and some cheap dog meat for our Ridgeback. Sensibly, because of the heat, they gave the parcel to the porter to put in the fridge and surprisingly remembered (on pain of death no doubt) to collect it after their drunken party ended. When we opened it next morning, what did we find? A large leg of lamb and a couple of pounds of best steak! I would like to have seen the expression on the face of the person who undid our parcel...

Sadly, this idyllic way of life was not to last. We were at a dance one night at the Muldersdrift Hotel when Pete met an Afrikaans policeman's ex-wife, Cornelia, known to her friends as Babe. I sometimes wonder if the contrast of the rather pseudo social characters we sometimes mixed with at parties drove Pete into Cornelia's arms, attractive though she was. They were unsuited in many ways and parted company after a few years of marriage.

Early in 1951 we needed to expand the business so after they were married Babe came in on the sales side of SkyFotos. The three of them went off into the country to canvas and photograph the larger farms. On the business side things went well but tension grew between Terry and Cornelia and the time came for the parting of the ways. We drew up a settlement and paid Pete out for his share. Not long after the break he started a crop spraying business which was successful if dangerous because of the extreme low flying. Terry took over our flying himself and trained a young man called David Shirley to do the aerial photography. It was easier than finding someone suitable with a commercial pilot's licence.

The time came to uproot ourselves from the comparative comfort of Hebron Haven in Natal where we had spent the last months and move to a new area of Natal, rich in another type of farming – forestry. Greytown is suitably named and is imprinted on my memory for the mist that sat on the hills around us and never ever seemed to lift. Marvellous for the trees but not for my morale.

We found accommodation with an English Colonel and his lady but they were hardly a cheerful couple. We had with us our nurse girl for Cara, Natalia, and they provided her with a room of sorts but their own house girl slept on the kitchen floor at night. She may have derived some consolation from the warmth of the stove.

The ongoing problem of finding rooms for ourselves and Natalia, let alone a place for our Ridgeback, Limmy, led us very reluctantly to accept Ernie Shirley's offer to look after the dog for us. It was very hard to part with him as he had joined us in the early happy days of Southern Valley and we loved him dearly.

Terry was away a lot at this time covering the Mau Mau uprising in Kenya. When Ernie phoned to tell me that Limmy had run away. I was devastated. A kind person told me not to worry as a Ridgeback would always return to his home – but where was his home? Some time later, I took the children to stay with friends and then drove on up to the Northern Transvaal. I had 'LOST/REWARD' notices printed and placed them wherever possible en route to Naboomspruit, Pietersburg and Louis Trichardt. I covered about 600 miles looking for our beloved animal – but in vain.

Not long after Terry's return from Kenya we completed our canvassing for aerial photography in Natal and for a time lived in a small flat in Johannesburg. Meanwhile our problems on the farm were being solved. Already under way was the building of a two bedroom cottage only 100 yards or so from our own house. When it was finished, we let it to a couple we knew who had two Boxer dogs. I was happy to have them close when there was trouble.

One night up at Watch's house the 'boys' had been drinking, illegal for Africans but we were not to enforce a law we did not believe in, They were gambling as well. A fight started. Mary came in from her room to tell me to call the police. I could hear repeated thuds as one African was beaten almost to death. He survived when no white man would have done. The police came later and took him to hospital.

Living Dangerously

CHAPTER XII

Terry visits Kariba for wild animal rescue and trouble in South Africa

In April 1958 Kariba, the biggest man-made lake in the world was created in the narrow gorge separating Northern and Southern Rhodesia or Zambia and Zimbabwe as they are known today. Some 50,000 Batonga tribesmen lived on the banks of the Zambesi river and had to be forcibly evicted from their homes to make way for the lake. But, for the teeming masses of wild animals who also lived in the valley, considered to be one of the richest game sanctuaries in the world, the problem was equally serious.

As the waters rose to form the lake, small islands were formed, only to be submerged beneath the relentlessly ever-rising water. Thousands of animals and reptiles were trapped on these islands, destined to drown except for the few who could swim to safety.

There were only eight black and three white game rangers in the area. Funds were raised, boats equipped with outboard engines were bought and these stalwart men planned to rescue as many of the animals as possible. For a parallel, we must return to biblical antiquity and the time when 'The waters prevailed exceedingly upon the earth', and Noah took the animals into his ark. We have no clear details as to how Noah captured his animals; nor did Rupert Fothergill, the leader of the rangers. They had lived with wild animals most of their lives and understood them. They knew the techniques used by men trapping wild animals for zoos but the latter were dealing mostly with young animals in reasonably ideal conditions. Nevertheless, they were determined to find a way. This was when I joined them.

Fortunately for the rangers, the lions were the first to sense danger. They swam to the 'mainland'. The elephants needed a little prodding and driving; then with a lot of hooting and flapping of large ears they entered the water and also made it to dry land.

The immediate concern was for the main species of delicate and nervous antelope who feared men more than the water and often died of fright when caught. Most of the rescued animals, no matter how exhausted, believed at the instant of capture that it was their last moment on earth and fought accordingly.

Highly strung animals like bush buck and impala were given tranquillizer shots to help them through their ordeal. Warthogs are dangerous animals. One 'swish' from their powerful necks and their horns can sever a man's leg. Wild pigs worked themselves into a frenzy but once securely tied up, relaxed and often slept peacefully.

Baboons and monkeys have a nasty bite and can only be caught under water. After being ducked they were gripped behind the neck, their jaws tied before being unceremoniously dumped into sacks. It was not easy. I tried to rescue a bedraggled, sad little bush baby stranded on a branch, within inches of being submerged. His great big eyes looked pleadingly up at me. He was weak but not too weak to give me a painful bite.

Vervet monkeys proved a problem as they could swim under water for up to a couple of minutes. Many of these animals were emaciated and mad with hunger. They gripped the upper branches of mopani trees, climbing ever higher to escape from the rising water that eventually engulfed them, with the merciful relief of drowning. Others were reduced to eating the bark of the trees. There were the heart-rending bush babies and other less exotic-looking animals like the antbears and the porcupines which had to be rescued, and even the ever changing coloured chameleons, trying so hard to make friends with us.

Rupert's first task was to reconnoitre the flooding valley and gauge the extent of the task ahead of him. So for three days we travelled up the Zambezi in one of the boats. The equatorial sun beat down mercilessly on us and I was impatient since I was getting no photographs. I voiced this casually to the very British, ex-Indian army District Commissioner at the end of our journey who remarked, 'Dear boy. Three days! Don't let that bother you. Here we work by the calendar, not by the clock.'

That remark stuck with me all over Africa and Asia in the coming years.

We set up camp on an island now measuring only 150 x 400 meters and teeming with terrified, half-stunned animals. Worse, it was plagued with every form of venomous snake, including deadly green and black mambas. A bite from these fanged reptiles gave one only minutes to live. A ranger from the Salisbury snake park visited us and was bitten on his finger by a mamba he was trying to catch. Without hesitation he blew off the tip with his shotgun. He had no illusions. He shot antibiotics into his gory stump, bandaged it up and suffered no further effects.

We were bothered by the tsetse fly, and the mosquitos were unbearable in the steaming, swampy Gwembe valley. When dusk fell soon after six o'clock each evening, we had to get into our camp beds beneath mosquito nets. Even then, evil swarms bit us and kept us awake with their incessant buzzing. In the mornings we invariably turned our kitbags inside out and on several occasions, venomous snakes and scorpions slithered away. During all the years the rangers operated on the flooded islands of Kariba where the snake population was many times the normal, only three men were bitten and on each occasion they were trying to catch the reptiles. I soon discovered that snakes were even more afraid of me than I was of them – if that was possible.

Soon the rangers developed techniques for catching, transporting and releasing any type of animal. The practice was to allow a doomed island to reduce in size to not more than 200 x 400 metres. To the cries of 'Ahaa, ahoyie, ooooola, whaaaaai, whaaaai,' the animals were driven to one end. A strong net rope was stretched across the narrower end of the island and the animals were driven in to it. Rangers enmeshed them, trying to avoid kicking hooves, ferocious tusks and savage teeth. Four men then each jumped on a creature and tried to subdue it. They fastened ropes around its jaws and legs and carried it to the boat for release in a safe area away from native hunters. Releasing could also be hazardous for when frightened they sometimes turned on their rescuers.

The rangers discovered too that it was simpler and safer to catch animals in the water where they were in a strange element. They also saw that all animals and reptiles, even tortoises can swim if they have to. The Zambezi contained crocodiles, just to add to the problems of the many hours spent in the water. Far worse was the ever- present danger of meeting an exhausted mamba or other deadly snake heading for you, thinking you were a floating log and a heaven- sent resting place.

It was arduous and hot work. The water was too warm to refresh our burned bodies. When thirsty we simply ducked our heads beneath the surface and took a deep gulp. It was rather like drinking one's own bath water. We diluted our evening brandies with this lukewarm liquid and commented on the taste which varied according to the undergrowth beneath us.

While final arrangements were made to capture the rhinoceros, Ranger Lofty Stokes and I used to sit in a boat in the cool of the evening catching tiger fish and bream. I loved the peace of those African evenings out on the lake, listening to the various noises of the animals and the weird music from nearby native kraals drifting across the mopani trees. With it came the smell of wood burning fires. A little later the myriads of insects started humming as the sun sank down behind the Zambezi in a blaze of ever-changing splashes of crimson and gold.

At 5.30 one morning we set out behind Rupert in search of a large rhino. It must be remembered that these animals knew they were trapped. They were on the defensive and therefore dangerous. Nevertheless, Rupert stalked the bull to within 15 yards. Mad with rage, it charged and hit Rupert. I was too busy shooting the incident with a motor-driven camera sequence to realize just how close I was to the snorting, panting brute. I felt a thud when hit by its armour-plated hulk and found myself under Lofty. Above the screams I heard Rupert shout, 'Get the bastard off me - quick...' African scouts closed in and the rhino escaped. Somehow it did not put a foot on Rupert nor did he experience its full two ton weight, otherwise he would certainly have been killed.

We were picking ourselves up when someone shouted, 'Look out!' The rhino was charging again. We scattered. I climbed a small spindly tree and for a moment the rhino's horn was only inches from my foot. I was terrified he would lean against the tree and it would collapse. Instead, he saw an African scout up another tree and charged him before being driven off. Rupert was later discovered to have two broken ribs, Lofty was only bruised and I had a small gash in my thigh, a little too near to where it mattered.

When the Batonga tribesmen were forcibly moved out of the Zambezi valley to new villages, they took with them their witch doctor who was responsible to Nyaminyami, the mythical monster and guardian serpent of the river whose whiskers are the rainbows of the Victoria Falls. Daily, John Siajanka, the witch doctor, pined away. There was nothing white doctors or their fellow witch doctors could do for him. He was dying. The District Commissioner decided to return him to his nearly submerged island.

We heard that Siajanka had returned a weak and sick man. Two days later Ranger Barry Ball and I visited him and found him fully recovered and very much alive. The water was already lapping at the entrance to his mud and grass hut. He was sitting straddled across the door on a small hand-carved stool with a snuff box filled with African 'moetie (medicine) strung around his neck.

We knew that the following morning the water would enter his house. Although he had a dug-out canoe, his island was now a long way from the mainland and we decided to see if he wanted rescuing. He was hostile and did not want us to land.

The white man will never succeed in stopping the waters of the Great River. Nyaminyami will destroy the sticks (referring to the vast concrete dam) that he has built.' He would not let me photograph him until I showed him the snake tattooed on my arm at which he smiled and we were friends.

Barry and I returned the following morning. The house was half submerged. The witch doctor was sitting under a mopani tree on high ground, crying, 'Nyaminyami is dead! My work is finished.' Still he would not accompany us. Finally, we returned on the third day and saw that the dugout canoe had disappeared. There was no sign of John, only his two stools bobbing about in the eddying waters. I have and cherish these two stools today.

Rupert Fothergill summed up the lessons I learned from my four weeks with this marvellous group: 'Man is the most dangerous of all animals.'

Since I was returning to Salisbury, Rupert gave me a 12 foot python to deliver to the snake park. I practised endlessly to ensure I could handle it and then put it back in its sack in my tent. I secretly planned to produce the monster in the crowded press bar in Meikles Hotel the next night. I returned to my camp bed with a chuckle and fell blissfully asleep. The next morning there was a hole in the sack and my joke had escaped!

After a short spell at home I flew south to Cape Town for British prime minister Harold Macmillan's visit and his speech that was to echo throughout the world. In a wood-panelled parliamentary dining room filled mostly with stern-faced Afrikaners, Macmillan rose to his feet,

'The wind of change is blowing through this Continent, whether we like it or not, the national conscience is a political fact and we must come to terms with it.'

Later, banging the table for emphasis, he told his white audience, 'We reject the idea of any inherent superiority of one race over another. I know South Africa, but I hope you won't mind me saying that some aspects of your policies make it impossible for us to support you without being forced to abandon our own deep convictions about the political destinies of free men.' Prime Minister Dr. Verwoerd did not applaud.

Not long afterwards I went with Grey Villet, the LIFE photographer whose job on the *Star* I had applied for, to the Rand Show Ground as Dr. Verwoerd was to appear at the Easter show. We waited almost to the end and then went over to Ellis Park to cover a Rugby match. We returned to Lee Griggs flat for a drink. Lee was to be replaced by Jim Bell as the new Time Life bureau Chief when the telephone rang. It was Jim Bell. 'Verwoerd has been shot!'

'Impossible,' said Lee, 'Grey and Terry were with him to the bitter end.'

'Not to Verwoerd's goddamned bitter end they weren't,' said our irate bureau chief. 'Now I suppose you know it is Saturday. Get cracking.'

LIFE 'closed' on a Saturday night but New York was eight hours behind us. Lee hotfooted it into the office to help Jim. They cabled the news desk that full files on the assassination would follow in an hour or so. I telephoned my many contacts, seeking anyone who might have a picture. Yes, a commercial photographer had been there taking official photographs of the presentation and had one picture of the drama. I knew J.J. Wesselo well. He told me, 'I saw a guy leap out of his member's seat and put a gun to Verwoerd's temple. I hardly heard the shot but he collapsed.'

'Listen!' I said, 'I'll give you £500 (quite a sum then) and will be right over.'

This was one of the few radio pictures LIFE ran in those days. They did not like the loss of picture quality.

Incidentally, Verwoerd did not die. By some miracle the .22 bullet missed his brain and it was his personal bodyguard, Major Carl Richter, who fainted! It was Richter's prostrate body being carried out that fostered the assassination rumour.

That episode long haunted me and was the reason why I was always the last photographer to leave an event.

Meanwhile the canvassing struggle was going on throughout the country to get the white population to vote for and against South Africa becoming a republic away from Great Britain. The Nationalist supporters came to opposition meetings to beat up United Party supporters and prevent speakers being heard. Attacks were made on English-speaking pressmen, especially if they discovered they worked for the four-letter magazines, - *Time* and LIFE. Verwoerd won his republic but only just – by a 52% majority.

In March 1960 South Africa reached the day of reckoning. Nothing would ever be quite the same again. At Sharpeville. 68 hapless blacks were killed and 200 wounded, some seriously.

It all started in Durban when 500 police tried to quell the rioting after nine policemen were murdered in Cato Manor, a nearby black township. Entering Cato Manor alone was a hazardous business at such times, not just because of the blacks but the police did not want our presence, particularly foreign correspondents. It was important to go in with a colleague who could be a vital witness. Without him God help you as far as the police were concerned.

The seeds of discontent had spread up country to Johannesburg.

Fifty years ago a law had been passed on all non-whites – negroes, coloureds (those of mixed blood), Asians and Chinese – making them carry pass books in which were entered their personal details: where they lived; the taxes they paid; their employer's name and crimes committed. A man could not move from one job to another without the signature of his last boss. He could not travel outside his area without permission. To the non-white the pass book became his passport of oppression. When the ubiquitous police wanted to get tough, they waged war on pass book offenders. If caught without a book the person could be thrown into a waiting police van surrounded by wire mesh to be caged in like a wild animal. Japanese residents were later declared 'white' – because of their economic standing.

The time seemed ripe. The Pan African Congress urged Africans to descend on police stations without pass books and invite arrest. More than 20,000 angry Africans surrounded the four foot high barbed wire fence of Sharpeville police station. Around 130 police reinforcements and four Saracen armoured cars arrived and were stoned by the mob. The police commander, G.D. Pienaar, ordered his men to load and like a chain reaction they began firing their revolvers, rifles and automatic Sten guns. Pienaar was quoted as saying afterwards, 'If they do these things they must learn their lesson the hard way.'

Many people wondered whether this was not police retribution for the death of their colleagues at Cato Manor.

Ian Berry of the Magnum picture agency was in the middle of the throng during the firing. His pictures of the dead and dying probably did more to portray to the world the horror of that moment than all the words written about Sharpeville. He was lucky to get out with his film and his life.

A few days later a work boycott was ordered by the African National Congress (A.N.C.). Gangs of thugs policed the townships to prevent people going to work, many drank the fiery skokiaan, workers were dragged off trains, kicked and beaten. One man had both his hands slashed off with a panga. This was black fighting black in black territory so, wisely, the police kept out. By nightfall the streets were strewn with dead and wounded.

Whites could not enter black townships without a pass. At times like this, the last thing the police wanted were pressmen, particularly foreign pressmen, reporting how they dealt with the blacks.

Our contacts told us that there was going to be a mass burning of pass books at Emdeni. This would involve a six-mile drive through trouble-torn Soweto, a militant black township. Peter Bagshawe volunteered to drive my old Chevrolet. We rendezvous-ed with our contact at dawn and he drove us past the police post into the township with Pete and I crouched down in the back. The blacks suspected us of being Special Branch police and were hostile until our contact explained we were journalists. They were still afraid of my cameras, knowing the pictures could be used in evidence against them.

After several such hold-ups we arrived within a mile of Emdeni. On an open stretch of land a mob of about 100 men walked menacingly down the dirt road towards us. Our contact leant out of the back window and shouted, 'Journalists going to cover the pass book burning at Emdeni. Let us pass!' They took no notice. Shouting, screaming and waving clubs, they surrounded our car. I yelled to lock all car doors. A powerful arm struck Pete in the face and equally powerful arms tried to drag me through the open car window. Men scrambled over the bonnet and banged on the roof. The noise was deafening. Others tried to overturn the car but with the weight of men on top, found it impossible. Inside it became pitch black as the mob pressed tightly round the car and the windscreen.

Suddenly, as though a spring blind had been released, a strong ray of sunshine cut in through the windscreen as peopled tumbled off the car. Our friend screamed, 'Get going!' Pete let the clutch in with a bang and the powerful car leapt forward, scattering bodies in all directions. What made them suddenly flee, we will never know. They told us later at Emdeni that this mob had just murdered a fellow African and their blood was up.

At Emdeni a crowd of several thousand had gathered and were shouting and screaming around a large pile of pass books. A small bearded character wearing a sackcloth skirt and wielding a heavy baton was doing a wild, fanatical dance urging people to throw their books on to the pile. Thanks to our contact they let me photograph the scene as kerosene set the bonfire alight to the accompaniment of wild cheers.

Stringent precautions were taken for the mass funeral of the Sharpeville victims. The police prevented even local black newsmen attending. Aerial photography being my business, we had no problem. While they had thought of most things, they did not bring anti-aircraft guns to the funeral.

The authorities would soon find out who was in our aircraft, so we had to get the film out of the country quick. At Jan Smuts airport we had a contact to handle sensitive packets. For a £5 bribe he could bypass normal customs clearance and get the packet aboard the Pan Am New York flight with the correct documentation. In extreme cases, one of us would hand-carry the packet to Rhodesia where Eric Robins, our Rhodesian 'stringer', would tranship it to New York via London.

There was rioting all over the country. Verwoerd declared a state of emergency, introducing press censorship and arrest without warrant among many other stringent restrictions. This was aimed to prevent people like us covering the disturbances.

I flew down to Durban to meet a contact who gave me a detailed list of those detained and those about to be arrested. He told me that Joe Mathews, now leader of the banned A.N.C., and Moses Mabhida had escaped high into the mountains of Basutoland and we should make contact with them in Maseru.

In trepidation I carried this list to Johannesburg knowing that if caught I would be in serious trouble. Every figure at the airport seemed to me to be a dreaded Special Branch man.

We suggested to New York that we do a major in-depth essay on the escapees and the underground movement generally. We did not telex this information through the Johannesburg post office as we knew all press cables were being read by the police. Furthermore, the Afrikaans telex clerk would object to the message and delay sending it, so we telephoned it direct to New York from an unknown number. George Caturani on the foreign news desk gave us the immediate go ahead.

Jim Bell who had replaced Curt Prendergast in the bureau, decided that since Eric Robins was not known locally, he should work on the story with me. This was good news. Eric was a close friend. An ex-Fleet Street *Daily Mirror* man, he was a top professional, exuded enthusiasm and enjoyed adventure.

The major arrests took place at dawn on Friday March 25, 1960. Two who were previously tipped off and went into hiding were Ronald Segal, a white Cape Town magazine editor, and a black lawyer Oliver Tambo, today President of the A.N.C. based in London. They agreed to let Eric and me accompany them on their escape out of the country. We made it clear that we would not help them but would go as observers only. Certainly, we would be circumspect in taking pictures in order not to draw attention to them, especially if things got tough.

We cruised westwards out of Johannesburg at 80 m.p.h. in Segal's Vauxhall for 130 miles on good tar macadam roads through flat, uninteresting bush country. Ten miles short of Zeerust, a sleepy Western Transvaal town, we had to ask the way to Lobatsi in Bechuanaland. A black man and white men in a car would rouse suspicion in a Platteland town at a time like this. Just the spot to be on watch for escapees.

The graded dirt road to the border was dusty and corrugated. Segal had to slow down for an ox wagon and, on accelerating again, heard an ominous 'knock' from the engine which started to lose power. We anxiously struggled on. We knew that normally the South Africans did not 'man' their border post at Pioneer Gate but it seemed inconceivable that such an obvious escape route would not be guarded that Sunday morning, just two days after the mass arrests. However it was not. Perhaps the route we had taken was too obvious. Our car was stopped by the Bechuanaland police who merely took details of the driver and his car. Tambo and Segal were eventually granted political asylum.

Finally, Eric and I wanted to visit the secret hideout of the A.N.C. so we checked in to the Lancers hotel in Maseru in Basutoland – now Lesotho. Within an hour a waiter told us someone wanted to see us. We were taken to a ramshackle corrugated iron shack where we met Joe Mathews himself. With him was Bob Tsolo, chairman of the militant Pan African Congress and the man who had led the people into the Sharpeville massacre.

We chartered a small single-engine plane and with Joe and Bob we flew to the latter's house near Sekakes, 10,000 feet up in the Basutoland mountains. We passed over beautiful, wild rugged country with Bob directing the pilot who landed us on the side of a gentle slope leading up to the house.

They had chosen the ideal retreat for their new headquarters. It was impossible to approach without prior warning. After Eric's interview and my pictures, we returned to Maseru to find a well-known liberal journalist waiting to charter our plane and fly the two to Bechuanaland and safety. I believe this is wrong. Journalists should not use their press privileges to help underground movements. We are there as observers and have to remain as impartial as is humanly possible.

Our film was 'dynamite' and certainly too hot for anyone to handle at Jan Smuts airport. Eric decided to fly it to Rhodesia himself.

In contrast, an urgent cable from New York sent me North to join Kermit Roosevelt on a safari to retrace the footsteps of his famous grandfather, President Theodore, in 1909. This safari should have been a peaceful, pleasant trip for me but it was not. LIFE magazine had paid the bulk of the costs but the Roosevelts felt I had been pushing them too hard and spoilt much of their fun. This was exemplified by a passage in Kermit's *A Sentimental Journey,* 'We returned to camp to meet LIFE photographer Terence Spencer who turned out to be a most pleasant, lively, affable Englishman – except when manipulating his cameras when he became, like most members of his profession, a ruthless, demanding monomaniacal tyrant or if he thinks tyranny won't work, a wheedler. When he was taking pictures nothing else mattered.'

The 'big five' animals in Africa are the lion, elephant, buffalo, leopard and rhinoceros. The professional rangers agree that the buffalo, particularly a wounded one, is the most dangerous. They are cunning and revengeful. The elephant is shortsighted and seldom attacks unless provoked. The fleet-footed leopard is shy and prefers operating at night. The rhino is short-sighted and makes mock charges which are frightening but a loud shout and a clap and he will abort his attack. Lastly, the lion. He is the king of the jungle and knows it.

After my weeks with the game rangers at Kariba, it was difficult to accept the tales around the camp fires at night. They were designed to inculcate fear, danger and excitement into ultra-rich clients on these luxury safaris. One appreciated that the white hunters had a job to do and a living to promote.

I had only one fright on this safari. From dawn we had been trailing a herd of buffalo. Around ten o'clock we were closing in on them down wind. We were crawling stealthily along on our bellies and I was having trouble keeping my four cameras from clanking against each other. I could feel the tension of the Roosevelts. Suddenly, the herd took fright and bolted. Simultaneously, something grabbed my ankle. My heart hit my Adam's apple! It was one of our waiters in his green velvet uniform offering me a dry martini out of a thermos flask.

The news on my small radio was interrupted with the announcement that revolution was sweeping throughout the Congo. On my return to Nairobi I cabled New York asking if they wanted me to go back. To my surprise and relief they answered, 'LARRY BURROWS ON WAY FROM LONDON WANT YOU RETURN SOUTH AFRICA FOR TROUBLE THERE BEST CATURANI.'

The atmosphere in Johannesburg was still tense. I had hardly been at home in 1960 and Lesley was not happy. She was alone on our farm 15 miles from Johannesburg with two small children. Thank God, the troubles so far had not spread out of the townships.

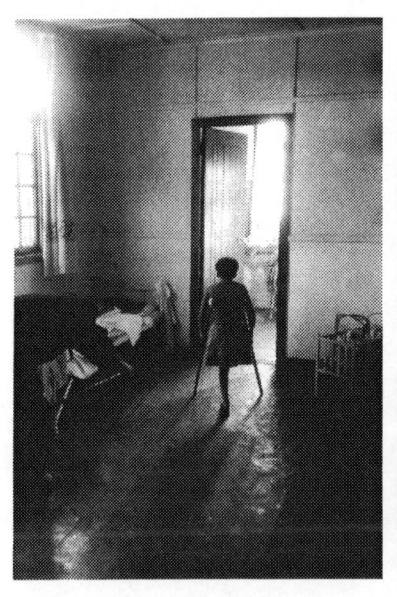

*South Africa - Busiwe, Nov 1953.
Little girl who had her leg bitten off
by a crocodile awaits her artificial leg*

*Oliver Tambo escapes from arrest
across the border into Botswana,
April 1960*

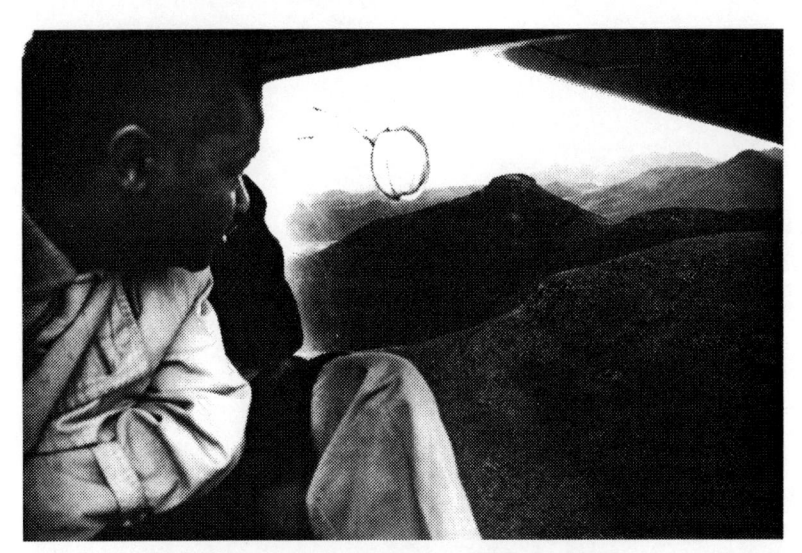

Flying over Basutoland with Joe Mathews

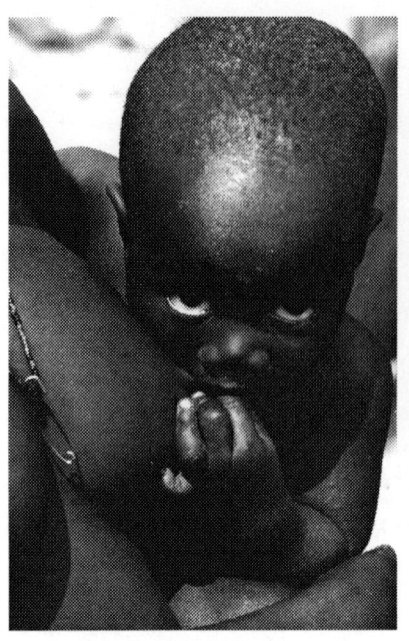

Okavango Swamps, October 1963. A local baby suckles her mother, keeping clear of the dangerous safety pin.

A small bushman, July 1956, in the Kalahari desert of South west Africa (now Namibia). He is drinking from an ostrich egg.

South Africa, Sharpeville, April 1960

Burning the detested pass books.

South Africa - Sharpeville, April 1960. Phographing the funeral was banned so we covered it from our own aeroplane.

Rioters in Orlando Native Township, Johannesburg, stop and surround our car. They nearly overturned us, Pete Bagshawe and self.

Living Dangerously 105

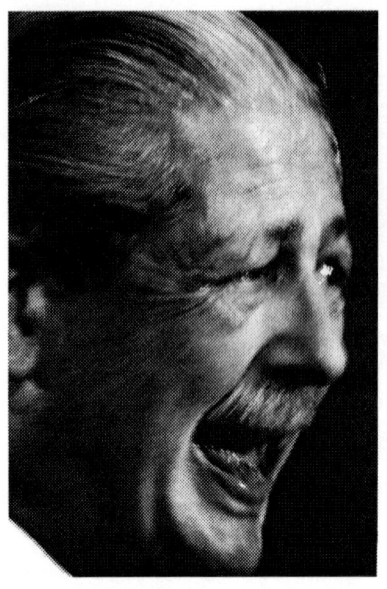

Harold Macmillan at a Conservative rally meeting – almost in tears. Jan 1963.

The Kabaka of Uganda, Oct 1955 on returning to Kampala after his banishment to England.

Cape Town, May 1961 – two of the local girls.

CHAPTER XIII

Terry in the Congo Revolution

'The foulest, the dirtiest, the bloodiest and the most revolting assignment any member of the foreign press corps ever had to cover'. Donald Wise of the London *Daily Express* summed up what we all felt about the Congo.

Lee Griggs, phoned from the Johannesburg office, 'I have bad news for you, we have to leave right away for the Congo.' It certainly was bad news. After Independence and the departure of the Belgians, the power struggle between the various black factions had turned in to a bloody revolution. I did not know how to break the news to Lesley.

As we crossed the mighty Congo river from Brazzaville to Léopoldville in July 1960 we saw columns of smoke rising from many parts of the city. There was no sign of any whites but there were 20 or 30 Congolese soldiers awaiting us on the jetty. After ten minutes of noisy vernacular between our captain and a corporal, we came alongside. Although I travelled light on this sort of job, I still had 60 kilos of equipment, film and clothes and this had to be lugged in the oppressive heat up into the centre of the city as there was no transport.

I had been to Léopoldville several times previously and knew my way to the Memling Hotel. The place was in chaos. Cars were burning, shops were barricaded with iron bars, others burnt out. Gangs of youths roamed the otherwise deserted streets lootting anything they could see.

The foreign press corps, numbering about 100 at that time, was confined more or less to the 'white' area around the Boulevard Albert. Wandering around the 'black' parts was hazardous. We gathered in the bar of the Memling to exchange information with colleagues. It was here that I met the bespectacled Larry Burrows and also Bob Morse of LIFE. Larry had been beaten up a few days before and some of his cameras had been smashed. He welcomed his replacement with a broad smile. Bob was to stay on with me.

There was a total break-down of law and order. Power-crazed, heavily armed soldiers and unruly drunken gangs were holding up civilians and robbing them, others were stopping cars, beating up the occupants and stealing their vehicles. The 25,000 strong Force Publique mutinied against their white officers and disregarded their new black leaders. A nation of fourteen million people was reverting to near tribal savagery.

The Belgians were on the run. The airport at Njili was closed and anyway it was impossible to get there without being murdered. So they flocked in their thousands down to the 'beach' in an effort to board the irregular ferry to Brazzaville. Alternatively, they paid large sums of almost worthless money to be taken across in any craft that floated, often at considerable risk with the rapids so near.

White Léopoldville became a ghost city. Mobs gathered outside our hotels, shouting and screaming as rifle shots rang out. Congolese military police chased journalists out of their rooms at bayonet point and assembled them in the lobby until someone secured their release.

Prime Minister Patrice Lumumba tried to restore some order and went to the infamous Léo II barracks. I accompanied him. We were promptly chased out by dishevelled troops swinging their belts like whips and shouting in French, 'Kill Lumumba and all whites.' I left as fast as he did. Lumumba went into hiding.

Four of us photographers would join forces and patrol together from dawn to dusk in our commandeered cars left behind by the deserting Belgians. We swapped information with colleagues in other cars and tipped each other off when trouble started. We patrolled with the car windows lowered, not because of the heat but to avoid shattering glass from a flying rock or from a loaded rifle jammed into the car with a shaky finger on the trigger. We soon learned the signs of impending riots: small groups of men talking excitedly on street corners; rising columns of smoke; rifle shots and the sound of screaming.

Screaming, which I was to hear so much of in the next year, still rings terror in my ears. There is no sound so blood-curdling as the high pitched yelling from a mob of drunken, frightened men and women on the rampage. Worse was having to head for this din when every instinct in your body was urging you to go the other way — which was what most other people were doing.

A camera is not a healthy weapon in these situations. At various times in the Congo, in common with most photographers who were there any length of time, I had been dragged out of our car, had cameras ripped off my neck, the shirt ripped off my back and, worst of all, been attacked by vicious, screaming women trying to claw my face. Somehow, one feels on even terms with men but with wild women... In these circumstances I ducked into the mob and vanished. I amazed myself at the speed and agility I could run whilst carrying heavy equipment. Often a powerful kick on a hostile shin or in the balls gave one a good start. I soon learned to look after myself and cease using gentlemanly tactics. I also carried a tear-gas pen which was effective indoors.

Daily we faced fierce, often drunken savage-looking Congolese troops careering through the streets of Léopoldville in vehicles mounted with machine guns. They would pull ahead and make you stop. Glistening jet black faces, some wearing sun glasses, others with goggles slung loosely round their necks and contrasting white cigarettes drooping from the corners of their mouths, would slouch over towards us. Their hefty, well camouflaged steel helmets added to the fearsome sight. We smiled, trying to avoid showing fear. I would produce my LIFE press card telling them that we were American correspondents. This seemed to have a more salutary effect than the mention of other nationalities. We gave them cigarettes and beer and they let us go.

Horrendous rumours filtered in to Léopoldville of Catholic nuns and white women being raped upcountry. When we could get there, the large passenger hall at Njili became jam-packed with Belgian families uncharacteristically laying out their blankets, setting up small cooking stoves and surrounding themselves with their bright metal or fibre suitcases bulging to capacity. Children cried and others played. Some taps spouted brownish water but not so the toilets where conditions soon became diabolical. Many of these families pleaded with us to take their cars, use them and then try to get them across to Brazzaville. We became a little choosey:

'What sort of car is it?' We would ask.

There were few takers for the many Volkswagens but people with Mercedes had no problems. In times of trouble however, I prefer a small unpretentious car with a turning circle that can quickly get me out of trouble.

Next the big jets roared onto the longest runway in Africa. The airlift had begun…

The press corps was 'bottled up' in Léo (as we all called it) and could get no further than Njili airport. A week after arriving in the Congo I was over in Brazzaville with Bob Morse. He went to the American Legation and I went to the airport to 'ship' film. Bob's C.I.A. contact mentioned confidentially that American transports were due in Brazzaville that afternoon carrying helicopters to rescue American missionaries and others from the bush. The C.I.A. man was Frank Carlucci, later to become President Reagan's Secretary of Defense. Could this be our great chance to get out of Léo?

Bob and I enjoyed a good French meal and we returned to the airport. Sure enough, the transports were already unloading the 'choppers'. We contacted their commanding officer.

'I speak good French, am an ex-R.A.F. pilot and know the Congo well. Can I help you as your guide and interpreter?' I enquired.

'You bet you can,' he beamed back.

Not only were U.S. military helicopters about to operate illegally in a foreign land and without permission but they also carried tough, highly trained and well armed Special Forces personnel to guard the 'choppers' and crews. This was probably the first time in history that U.S. forces had operated in the heart of darkest Africa.

I had my large camera bag with me and plenty of film, but only the khaki shirt and trousers I stood up in. Bob was disappointed that they could not take him; space and weight were precious in the 'choppers' so he returned to Léo to collect a change of clothes for me. Members of the foreign press corps watched each other like hawks so, to account for my sudden disappearance, Bob announced that I had been taken ill in Brazzaville and was staying with Jack Williams, our Congo 'stringer'.

The next morning was Sunday. At dawn we took off on our first mission. A Harvard training fighter had been shot down by the Force Publique at Inkisi in the Thysville area. Then a Belgian military helicopter had also been shot down trying to rescue the crew of the Harvard. I warned our Captain, Lieutenant George Crawford, that Inkisi was a 'hot' spot. Guided by a Belgian civilian, Julien van Durman, we followed the Congo river westwards for an hour before turning inland. I was sitting by the open door getting my first view of the revolution outside Léo. Approaching Inkisi, we dropped to 300 feet and started searching for the missing planes. Glancing back, I saw streams of tracer bullets curving up towards us some 50 yards astern. I could not locate the guns but was surprised our Captain took no evasive action. Obviously he had not seen it and there was no intercom to warn him. To my horror he put the chopper into a tight turn and headed back over the guns. At this height we were a 'sitting duck'. I heard the rat-tat-tat and saw the tracers coming straight at us. There was a ripping sound as the bullets tore through the side of the fuselage. I immediately swung my legs back inside the cabin as everyone dived for the floor. It was like being shaken up inside a tin can full of pebbles.

I had a Nikon around my neck and the wide angle lens was already set for just such an eventuality. One frame caught van Durman a split second after a splinter nicked the side of his nose. I never remember taking that picture. I was as scared as the others, probably more so because I realized the imminent danger we were in, especially if we were forced to land. This time the pilot saw the tracer and flung the chopper into a steep turn, weaving out of trouble. The machine had been hit in many places, so we headed back for Brazzaville. On landing, Crawford inspected the damage, particularly where a bullet missed a vital transmission shaft by a fraction of an inch. 'We were lucky,' he remarked laconically.

At dawn on Monday we were finally off to rescue missionaries. Our course was east into the hinterland and to areas that hopefully would be more peaceful.

There was a strange finality about these evacuations with people forced to uproot themselves, often at a moment's notice and leave behind possessions collected over a lifetime. What to put in that one suitcase? Almost invariably items of sentimental value were given priority – wedding and other photographs, small African wood carvings, guitars and Bibles. More practically, most carried small transistor radios to keep abreast of the revolution. Children clutched their favourite dolls or toys.

At the end of that week I flew back to Brazzaville in the U.S. Embassy D.C.3 laden with overwrought and tearful women. I had been wearing the same clothes for a week in the tropical heat and contrasted unpleasantly with the clean, neat missionaries who sat around the floor of the cabin.

LIFE ran that story for a six-page lead and made it all worthwhile. It showed our readers a little of the horrors of the Black Continent.

On a Friday noon in late July 1961 I returned to the Memling Hotel from Brazzaville where I had shipped our film. I was enjoying a beer at the bar when there was shouting and screaming outside the hotel. Grabbing my cameras I ran out as two shots were fired and followed a throng of frightened, angry Africans down the road where we were confronted by another mob from a different tribe. Rocks started flying in our direction and fighting broke out. Promptly a truckload of U.N. soldiers drove into the middle of the melée and out stepped a very British-looking officer. It was General Templar Alexander, commander of the Ghanaian forces. All the time I was shooting pictures I kept glancing at my watch, because tomorrow was Saturday and around midnight the magazine would 'close'. The Air France plane was due off from Brazzaville in 45 minutes.

At this moment Alexander came over from where a man had just been killed, cupped his chin and gazed down on the body. I shot the picture, ran back to the hotel, grabbed a cab and told the driver to go like hell through the Cité to the small airport at Ndola where there was a Piper Pacer. There was trouble in the African city and the driver was not keen (neither was I), but a hastily negotiated large fee persuaded him.

It was my only hope. We entered the Cité where small groups of men stood on every corner armed with coshes. A bad sign. The next moment rocks were clattering against the side of our cab. There was a crash of glass and a rock came through the small fixed rear window. 'Lie down on the floor,' yelled my driver. I was already there. He kept his head, put his foot down on the accelerator and drove at high speed down the Boulevard Baudoin scattering groups that tried to stop us. The cab bumped over obstacles in the road and reached the airport. I decided to 'borrow' the Pacer if its pilot was not there but he was. After agreeing to be paid in dollars, he flew me the few miles over the Congo river to Brazzaville while I wrote the captions. We taxied up to the Air France plane where I persuaded the air freight man with a good tip, to open up the big red envelope I had given him that morning and which had already been cleared through customs.

The story closed two pages the next night in New York.

One minute a film can be worth thousands of dollars; the next, if a flight is missed, it can be worthless. It is a tough decision to break off at the height of a good story because of the clock. It is difficult to persuade the layman of the sweat, blood and often large sums of money that may have to be expended on film contained in an insignificant-looking little metal can. How simple is all this today with the transmission of pictures by satellite…

On another of our patrols in the white quarter of Léo we saw black smoke rising vertically in the air and heard screams. We approached cautiously. Already other journalists were running down the road. We drove through them and saw a group of four Congolese pulling an elderly Belgian couple out of a car. I shot the incident with a long lens then, with my colleagues, raced towards the car switching to a wide angle lens as I went. The Congolese ran off.

When these pictures appeared in the magazine I was criticised for shooting the event instead of first helping the old couple. However a news photographer is always 'on edge' waiting for the unexpected. When it happens his first reaction is to get the picture. He becomes detached from the event. He is a bystander, an observer. He is costing his company a lot of money to be there. His job is to record rather than to participate. Of course, in an event like this he does help.

Jim Bell and I worked closely with Arnaud de Borchgrave of *Newsweek*, our direct competition, but Arnaud had certain influential contacts which we did not have. On a trip into the riot-torn Cité we were rounding a corner when a ragged Congolese soldier fired at us from close range. I was in the back of our Jeep, with Jim and Arnaud in the front. Arnaud accelerated as the soldier ran after us, firing at close range. I dived to the floor but shot a very blurred picture of the soldier as I went down. This was another picture I never remember taking.

The New York office would often query us on stories that were purely fictional – something we found difficult to photograph. Therefore, I used to advise them on the reporters they could rely on and those that wrote more or less fiction. A reporter, particularly on British dailies, was often expected to produce exciting, colourful and readable stories, hopefully with some connection to current affairs. So, much had to be 'thumbed'. He did have his problems, however, as he was expected to file every day on the general, military and political situation as well as on local events. He dreaded the cable, 'WHY YOU NOT THERE QUARK.' He dared not roam too far from the telex room and this limited his activities.

Covering events as unpleasant as the Congo, one came to know one's colleagues well. You could clearly differentiate between the reporters who saw for themselves, and those reporting from the coolness of the Memling bar – even waiting in the lobby to catch photographers returning from a mission and debriefing them. The latter used to get wild stories from me, some of which I later saw in print.

Nevertheless, there was a powerful 'freemasonry' amongst regular members of the foreign press corps. Whilst a high degree of competition existed, pressmen felt that their jobs were difficult anyway so it was usual to cover for each other and to be tipped off about upcoming events. However, when outsiders joined the pack things could be different. One photographer I knew resorted to moving a rival's film packet on to a separate shelf in the air freight office so that it missed the first flight.

The office sent in my replacement to the Congo and I returned to Johannesburg. I had been home for 72 hours, just long enough to pull up all the pipes to our windmill, as Lesley had been without water for several days, when Fiona Ilic handed me a cable, 'You are

Jomo Kenyatta in prison at Maralal in Northern Kenya (April 1954)
Chapter X

The Bali volcano erupting (April 1963) Chapter XVII

Stuart Udal unconscious on Mt. Kilimanjaro (October 1953)
Chapter XVIII

A snarling baboon in Kenya (May 1964) Chapter XVIII

Gorillas in the forests of the Virunga Volcanoes (August 1963)
Chapter XVIII

*Terry in the little Radfan war
(May 1964)
Chapter XXII*

*Cuban airmen arrive in the
Congo (January 1965)
Chapter XIII*

Joan Miro and Terry, ready to dive off Antibes in the south of France (July 1968) Chapter XXVI

Miro's sculpture 120 feet down in the Mediterranean (July 1968) Chapter XXVI

Richard Branson in the bath on his Little Venice canal boat. The start of Virgin Atlantic (May 1984) Chapter XXXIII

Punk in London (May 1983)

Actor Tim Dalton at Battersea Park (August 1970)

Vietnam – Blast from a 155mm howitzer in action (May 1965)
Chapter XXIII

A Viet Cong prisoner is flushed out of a bunker by US 3rd Marines (May 1965) Chapter XXIII

Lake and Sampan

Vietnam execution. (May 1965) Chapter XXIII

A Viet Cong youth is led out blindfolded to be shot.

Seconds after he is shot — he crumples on the post.

Coffin is beside the dead body still tied to the post.

The body is carried off.

not going to like this one,' she said. It read, 'WANT YOU GO ELISABETHVILLE URGENTEST AS LUMUMBA TROOPS INVADING KATANGA.'

I phoned Lesley. Poor Lesley. She had only recently returned from a trip to England. We had hardly seen each other in months. 'Oh no!' was her only comment.

The fantasy of the reports of the fighting being filed out of Elisabethville was such that I cabled George Caturani, 'EYE FEEL THAT KATANGA POSITION AS FAR AS REPORTED FIGHTING IS CONCERNED SHOULD BE PUT INTO PROPER PERSPECTIVE FOR OUR REASONABLE PICTURE POSSIBILITIES. FRONT IS 400 MILES FROM EVILLE AND NOT A SINGLE JOURNALIST HAS SEEN ANY CURRENT FIGHTING SPENCER.'

It was obvious that we photographers had a serious problem in trying to cover this new war.

I buttonholed President Moise Tshombe after one of his daily press conferences and persuaded him to give me Katangese military accreditation and permission to fly up to the front in my charter aircraft but to return in his empty Dakota (D.C.3). This war correspondents' accreditation was to open many doors for me in the following months. It was the only one he ever gave.

Alan Kearns, a charter pilot from Northern Rhodesia, flew me the 400 miles north to the Katangese front. Tshombe's accreditation brought me full cooperation from his army on the Lualaba river. I was with them for three days and watched them mine the last few bridges. Horrific rumours were spreading of the imminent arrival of Lumumba's army but I never heard a shot fired along the entire front.

My next search for the war was with Arnold Lacagnina, a cameraman with Visnews. This time a Swedish U.N. army unit took us to Manono along 400 miles of road. We met countless road blocks guarded by a motley crowd of rebels, often drugged and drunk. Some were armed with bows and arrows and ancient flintlocks, a few with modern Sten guns. Manona was in chaos. Prisoners had been released from the jail and every house belonging to the Belgians had been ransacked; some burned. The Belgians had lurid tales of the horrors they experienced with these wild tribesmen on the rampage. Their witch doctors gave them potions and assured them that with these they could not be killed: 'Only water blows out of the white men's guns.' This gave them suicidal courage.

It was good to be relieved and allowed to return to Southern Valley, though I anticipated from Lumumba's antics that it would not be for long. I did not tell this to Lesley. Raina, my youngest daughter, was two years old. She hardly knew me and I sadly missed seeing her and Cara growing up.

Sure enough I was soon back in my old room at the Memling Hotel. Léo had not changed in the last four months, except that a new strong man was emerging. Colonel Joseph Desiré Mobuto had been appointed as Lumumba's Chief of Staff under General Lundula. Now it was Mobuto's turn to go on the radio and announce that the army was taking over.

The next morning Mobuto's men found Lumumba and Lundula together in a house which they surrounded and shouted, 'Lumumba must die.' Ghanaian soldiers saved his life but he had to make a quick escape. He had lost control.

Mobuto had the fire power to make his orders stick and that is what counted in the Congo. The most potent weapon was the press conference. It was announced that Mobuto was giving an urgent one at the Paracommando barracks on the outskirts of Léo. It was not an area we liked going to in daylight, far less at night. However, there were three cars loaded with journalists and we would stay together. Army barricades let us pass through.

The 29-year-old Colonel was impressive. Lean, clean-shaven, of medium height, he wore metal rimmed spectacles. The brass on his Sam Browne belt and his buttons shone brightly. He was wearing well-pressed shorts and a short sleeved uniform shirt. His press conference was to leave us in no doubt as to who was boss in the Congo. Furthermore, he said that he had arranged to go to Elisabethville to meet President Tshombe. This was big news. Reporters ran to their cars to file this seemingly impossible report.

President Kasavubu fired Lumumba and Lumumba fired Kasavubu, though neither was in a position to do so as Mobuto held the gun.

I received an assignment from New York to do a story on the United Nations civilian operation in the field. The U.N. naturally cooperated in full on such a story. They flew me to Luluabourg, some 500 miles to the east. It was the capital of the Kasai and the centre of tribal fighting between the Luluas and their better educated enemies of old, the Balubas.

The scene in the Luluabourg hospital was grim. There was little food or drugs. Two brave Belgian nurses stayed when the rest of the staff escaped. One of them, Adith Verhaegen de Meyer, introduced me to a skinny, pathetic four year-old-boy called Lukiku Badibaga. He had been rescued from nearby Bakwanga after seeing his parents murdered. Both his brothers had died of starvation in the room beside him. Somehow, Lukiku survived. He was so emaciated and in such an advanced state of kwashiorkor, a protein deficiency, that Adith felt his brain would be permanently damaged.

Maurice Frauchiger was a member of the International Red Cross. He invited me to join his convoy of lorries delivering precious flour and manioc to an area around Bakwanga. This was a particularly bad area. Any white face was Belgian and a target for immediate extinction. Maurice suspected we would find thousands of Balubas in advanced stages of starvation. He decided to take a patrol of Ghanaian soldiers to guard the trucks.

The Baluba refugees had gathered round the mostly deserted mission stations. Everywhere we saw ragged-clad skeletons, bones barely held together by sore-ridden skin like black parchment. In places this parchment looked like perished rubber where grossly swollen pot bellies, knees or ankles tried to burst through. Some blind people were being led by the hand while others groped and staggered around with no one to help them.

At Tshika, Maurice discovered that there was a serious situation at Mai-Mune mission, 40 km. away, where 2500 Baluba had gathered and were starving to death. He had to leave his U.N. Ghanaian escort behind to guard the main supplies. Knowing that our lorries could be threatened even with an army escort, I was not too happy accompanying Maurice but realised I was on to the biggest story in the Congo and had it exclusively. Also, I knew that the situation needed the power of LIFE magazine to convey to the world the horror and suffering that was taking place in darkest Africa. I took a set of pictures that was to show the death harvest of an anarchy that called itself 'freedom' in a land where laughter had long since vanished.

Maurice estimated that there were 250,000 Baluba refugees in southern Kasai of which 200 were dying every day. We were witnessing the worst famine the world had seen for 20 years. It was a tough decision to leave such poignant picture situations but, I had a deadline to meet. Also, I could a get a ride out of Luluabourg on an empty D.C.3.

Ed Behr of *Time* had told me about a King Lukengu. After Independence, democracy had taken a strange twist. The new Kasai government considered it undemocratic for one man to have 800 wives and ordered Lukengu to reduce his spouses to a mere 50. This sounded a good story but Lukengu's royal kraal was 190 miles north of Luluabourg at Muchengein through dense tropical forests teeming with hostile tribesmen.

The second morning I had been sitting out at the airport under the burning sun waiting for my DC3 when a Belgian charter pilot landed in a small single engined Cessna. I told him about Lukengu.

'Have you ever been to Muchenge?' I enquired.

'Yes. There is a short bush airstrip there near the royal kraal.'

'What about flying me up there?' I ventured.

'Why not? But you won't see the King unless you can bring him a bottle of scotch.'

We agreed on a high fee to be paid into the pilot's bank account in Brussels and I drove into town in search of an almost impossible bottle of scotch. After chasing three contacts and paying an exorbitant price I returned to the airport with my prize.

We were greeted at Lukengu's airstrip by a Bakubu missionary who spoke French and escorted us through the model village of

Muchenge. Its neat grass huts had geometric drawings artistically woven into the walls. They were surrounded by screens made of pressed palm leaves. We were introduced to Bope Mbelepe, the King's favourite son.

'I would like to talk to your father and I have brought him a gift of whisky,' I told him.

'Follow me.'

We entered a labyrinth of tattered sagging raffia screens and were passed on from one guard to another as we weaved our way through the maze. Leaving the bright sunlight, we stooped while entering a large room lined with bamboo. Straining my eyes to adjust to the darkness, I saw the large hulk of a man covered with a blanket. He was lying on a grass mat on the ground. With the help of a servant, Mbelepe struggled to get the King into a sitting posture.

There in front of me was the great and mighty King Lukengu, Nyimi of the Bakubam, powerful leader of 500,000 Bakuba tribesmen and their subject tribe, the Bakete. The King was naked to the waist except for a heavy bead necklace and brass bangles around his right wrist. The bags under his bloodshot eyes matched his drooping breasts. He looked as though he had just satisfied every one of his 750 departing wives. He appeared older than his 60 years, as well he might have been. He lifted his tired eyes when he saw the bottle of scotch and smiled.

'What brings you here?' he enquired in his native Busongo, through our missionary interpreter.

'I am from the American LIFE magazine. We did a story on you when you were at the height of your splendour.'

'Yes, I remember. Things are different now. Circumstances have given us Independence before we are ready for it. The authorities are undermining my authority. They have taken away most of my wives. I am an unhappy man.'

I took the pictures I needed and flew back to Léo elated. I knew I had two excellent and very different stories and both exclusive. This is difficult with a large foreign press corps all searching for 'that different' story.

Living Dangerously

A week later in Léopoldville I was handed some cables. One was from LIFE, "LUKENGU GREAT STORY CLOSED THREE PAGES." Another from *Time*, "EVERYONE LOVED LUKENGU CLOSED 69 LINES AND TWO PIX THANKS HARTSHORN." I tore open the third expecting my Kasai story had made the lead, only to read a mundane service message. I was wild, sick with anger. How could they use Lukengu and not the famine?

I forgot breakfast and rushed to Henry Tanner's room. Henry worked for the *New York Times*. I leaked details of the famine to him. I knew that our editors studied his paper and if they saw it in the *Times* they would sit up and take notice. It was a ruse I was to use many times in the future. LIFE never seemed to like exclusive stories though they would not admit it. I was always delighted when I received a cable, 'WHAT ARE YOU DOING ABOUT.....?' and to cable back, 'STORY COMPLETED AND DUE NEW YORK TONIGHT.'

Back home in Johannesburg for Christmas, I reflected that one minute you were involved in the beastliness of war and the next you were in the tranquillity of your own home. The Congo seemed another world.

I spent Christmas with my girls high up in the splendour of the Basutoland mountains at the Blue Mountain Inn. We rode sure-footed ponies up the craggy slopes and into the hills.

I returned to Johannesburg after our holiday to be confronted with a cable, 'WANT YOU PROCEED KASAI FOR STORY ON DISASTROUS FAMINE.' I immediately telexed, 'REFER MY EXTENSIVE TAKE ON THIS FAMINE SHOT LAST NOVEMBER.' Back came the answer, 'YES, WE WANT YOU TO UPDATE.' I learned that the U.N. had flown a party of journalists to Bakwanga to show them the situation.

So it was back to Luluabourg yet again. I hung around the airfield until a U.N. H19 helicopter agreed to fly me to Bakwanga.

Conditions had improved considerably since my November visit, though people were still dying and others still starving. Travelling around that area was now safer. Nevertheless, distribution lorries were mobbed on several occasions by frenzied, shouting, wailing mobs.

Men still fought women for food. Women screamed as they and their babies were trampled under foot. Tearful, frail and pathetic mothers with outstretched pleading arms had to be bundled back into the queues in an effort to maintain law and order. In the scramble, bowls of flour were overturned. Pitch black faces would emerge looking deathly white as they ate the uncooked flour straight off the mud.

To add to the famine difficulties World Health Organisation men discovered smallpox victims in outlying villages. Bodies were covered with small, grotesque bumps which made them look as if they had emerged from a squirming bed of soldier ants. The risk of a major plague was alarming.

I often heard whites say that when people live close to nature, they become hardened to starvation and death. Nothing could be further from the truth. These people experienced the same feelings, suffering, pain, love, sense of loss and lack of security as we do.

Returning to Léo I airfreighted the new updated packet to New York. Things were quiet in the Congo so I returned to South Africa.

I knew LIFE was laying out several pages on the famine because of the amount of checking queries coming in to the Jo'burg office, so it was not altogether a surprise when the final telex read, 'KASAI FAMINE CLOSED SIX PAGE LEAD STOP ALL HERE SEND CONGRATULATIONS ON A GREAT JOB - BERMINGHAM.' (Don Berminham was on the LIFE news desk).

All I could think of at this time was why it was not used two months earlier when we would have had an exclusive story that might have saved thousands more lives. A story like this, seen by ten million readers had an immediate and salutary effect, not only on the millions of dollars the public contributed but on the Senators who immediately originated aid.

Letters poured in to the magazine, some of which were reproduced, 'Never in my knowledge have wood and pulp and printer's ink been so combined as in 'Harvest of Anarchy in the Congo'. 'The story of the starving Congolese children was shocking and, as a mother, pained me deeply. With all the riches in this country it is hard to believe such conditions exist.'

Finally a cable arrived from the United Nations Secretary General which I was proud to receive: 'CONGRATULATIONS ON BRILLIANT HANDLING OF KASAI STORY – DAG HAMMARSKJÖLD.'

A DC3 from Léopoldville unceremoniously dumped Patrice Lumumba on the tarmac at Elisabethville. He was blindfolded, shackled and thrown into a van to the accompaniment of swinging rifle butts. That was the last time he was seen alive in public. A little later, on a chopper ride up to the front with Tshombe I remarked, 'The world suspects you of arranging the murder of Lumumba.'

'Let them prove it,' he answered with a grin.

There were racial demonstrations to be covered in Salisbury, Southern Rhodesia, in June 1961 when Africans entered 'white' hotels and 'whites-only' swimming pools. We followed them, to the angry reception of hostile whites who yelled at us, 'Fuck off, you bloody Commies and take your bloody Kaffirs with you.' A burly Afrikaaner took a swipe at me and only a swift kick to his balls averted a swollen face. Fortunately, a tough policeman came to my rescue.

We pressmen had few friends, certainly not amongst the whites. They shouted a criticism I had heard so many times in Africa, 'You bastards come to our country and think you can write all about it after only a few days here.' An experienced journalist can, in fact, do just that. Like a detective, he is a trained investigator. He has travelled widely and seen similar situations in other parts of the world. He will not write simply about what he sees but will be given contacts by his stringers and embassies. In the case of most American embassies there will be an overt C.I.A. man who can be contacted and will furnish him with 'off-the-record' information. Secret Intelligence Service (S.I.S.) people in British embassies are not so readily available and maintain a low profile. We usually knew who they were, however. The stringer will have contacts with the police and will introduce the correspondent to leaders on 'both sides of the fence'. He will be able to approach underground movements that are quite inaccessible to the local police. He will talk to politicians, bankers, tradesmen, the ubiquitous taxi drivers and bartenders. He will check controversial points from 'well informed' sources with people of totally divergent views. Finally, he will see through the intrigues and lies of some politicians, being aware of their desire of how to hoodwink the press and keep them quiet. The magazine photographer must operate the same way but express himself with a camera rather than with a pen.

We suggested to LIFE that we cover Bobby Kennedy's first visit abroad for the Ivory Coast celebrations but only *Time* picked it up, so I flew to Abidjan and soon realized that this was also a great LIFE story. I shot 1,650 pictures, sending LIFE a cable, 'SUGGEST YOU TAKE A LOOK AT THE BOBBY KENNEDY STORY IN NEW YORK WITH TIME MAGAZINE SPENCER'. Then a cable came asking me to cross the width of Africa to cover the release of Jomo Kenyatta from jail. The only way I could reach Kenya in time was to fly north to London and then south again to Nairobi, equivalent to flying from New York to Montreal via London.

My flight was three hours delayed which made me late for Kenyatta's release at Gatundu. I had not been to bed for two nights but had to start work right away. I used to adjust my body-clock mechanism by setting my watch to the destination time and readjusting mentally along the way. Using this technique, I rarely suffered from jet lag. Anyhow, I amassed sufficient material on 'Burning Spear' Kenyatta for the story to run.

Henry Reuter, our Kenyan stringer, handed me a cable to return to Southern Rhodesia for the capture of some rhinoceros. I spotted Eric Robins on the terrace at Salisbury airport. He was waving a cable. It was from LIFE, 'EVERYONE DELIGHTED WITH YOUR KENNEDY STORY WHICH MADE PAGE AND HALF PICTURE OF THE WEEK PLUS SIX PAGE LEAD STOP CONGRATULATIONS - BERMINGHAM.'

I heard later that Harry Luce, the boss of Time Inc., had asked the LIFE foreign news department, only minutes after my advisory cable arrived, what they were doing about the Kennedy coverage on the Ivory Coast. Someone answered, 'We have Terry Spencer there and his extensive take is due in New York tonight.' What Luce was not told was that LIFE had turned down our original suggestion and they would now have to go on bended knee to *Time* for the use of the pictures.

Living Dangerously

The United Nations decided to use force to make President Moise Tshombe of Katanga reunite his province with the Congo, so it was back to Katanga yet again in September 1961. We met Tshombe on the border. He was on his way to Ndola for talks with Dag Hammarskjold; talks that never took place as Dag was killed that night when his D.C.6B crashed on landing at Ndola. The reporters waiting for his arrival were kept clear of the airfield and could get no information. Because of the early close-down at the cable office, and uncertain telephone communications with London, most of them filed contrived stories of Dag's arrival. Some even filed quotes from Dag.

In the early hours of the morning news filtered through that Dag was dead! This was a hell of a story in itself. Correspondents woke each other and scrambled for the telephone to kill their previous night's stories and advise on unconfirmed stories that Dag was dead. There was one correspondent who had not 'played ball' with the foreign press so no one woke him. I imagine he had some explanations to make to his paper.

We had to continue to Elisabethville. Tshombe warned us that there was heavy fighting around the city so gave us a small gendarmerie military escort which we welcomed. We heard the gunfire many miles from the city but our escort knew the U.N. Gurkha positions and we were able to reach the Léo II hotel with minimal scares.

Elizabethville was a ghost city, The small press corps was huddled in the hotel not daring to venture out into the street more than a few blocks from the hotel.

I shared a room with Sandy Gall on the wrong side of the hotel, that is, towards the Katangese army's highly inaccurate mortars which kept up a ceaseless bombardment above our heads throughout the night. Thumps and crashing bricks indicated more strikes. The staccato rat-tat-tat of machine guns and irregular rifle fire complemented the mortars. Correspondents worked in the inside bathrooms, some typing on lavatory seats. The firing continued into the next morning. There was nothing for the photographers and T.V. cameramen in the hotel. We had to get out on to the streets. Spent rifle and machine gun bullets were dropping out of the sky and ricocheting off tin roofs. This was one of the rare occasions when I would have liked a tin hat. Four times we had to duck for cover when a small Fuga jetfighter, piloted by a Rhodesian mercenary, strafed us. The Gurkhas had the nearby 'tunnel' and the post office under fire, the latter being only one hundred yards from our hotel. That hundred yards became known as 'murder alley'.

The heavy firing continued most of the week. We expected an attack at any time from the tough little Gurkhas whose primary targets were the white mercenaries. Most of us pressmen wished we had darker complexions. None of us fancied our chances of coming face to face with a Gurkha and his kukri. We also tried to keep out of their gunsights. We saw enough people being shot in the streets without having any desire to be one of them. One youth was less than 20 yards from me when he was hit through the head by a sniper's bullet. White and black civilians had to dodge in and out of pillars in the Avenue Etoile to avoid the intensive U.N. fire.

One afternoon Ernie Christie, an N.B.C. television cameraman and I tried to get shots of the fighting around the 'tunnel'. We crept on our bellies along low walls and when in sight of the 'tunnel', all hell let loose. Bullets were whizzing and pinging past us in all directions. Brickwork joined in the melée. We knew they would mortar us any minute so we had no alternative but up and run for it. We heard the whine of a mortar and ran even faster, if that was possible. It fell between Ernie and myself when we were less than ten feet apart but it fell into the soft grass in the main square and failed to explode. We had some distance to go to reach safety. We were zigzagging and running faster than I ever imagined possible with bullets bouncing off the road around us. Neither Ernie nor I were hit, though we were two very shaken individuals.

A mercenary picked us up and we made a lunatic 70 m.p.h. dash in his Landrover across the city to collect a colleague who had been badly wounded. A brave Red Cross team went out under fire, carrying their flag, to bring him in. They need not have bothered. He was dead. Nearby, an African, Moise Msonda, had his left leg shot off as he waited in his ambulance.

That afternoon I was reminded that you cannot photograph bullets but you can catch the expression on the faces of those doing the shooting or, more effectively, on those being shot at. Alas, the latter means that you, too, are the target.

A photograph loses too many senses – the sense of smell; perspiration; noise; screams; pain and fear. If the photo is to convey the events dramatically, it must contain intense facial expressions and be boldly composed against a background of war and destruction. That is why there have been few really great war pictures. Probably the best remembered of them all, the famous Robert Capa's Spanish soldier at the moment of death, relies entirely on the caption. Incidentally, doubt has since been raised as to whether this was a genuine picture of death or whether it was merely a training picture. This strengthens my belief that a photographer is a bad editor of his own pictures because he has not lost these senses when he looks at them afterwards. I would add here that photography can be a 'con job' and totally distort the situation. Like paintings, few people really understand photography. Editors are invariably word men and if you produce one great picture (it might even have been suggested by your reporter) you are 'IN'. Editors remember that one picture. Several of the LIFE photographers agreed with me that some of their best pictures had been taken by mistake. Also, when you have a 'name', editors see things in pictures that you never knew existed.

By the Wednesday Elizabethville was virtually deserted. Food was getting scarce. Only Michels, the Greek restaurant, was serving anything vaguely edible. All the services had broken down, including electricity.

We were trying to cover a story where pressmen had to face five hostile elements. The Belgians hated us because we gave them a bad press; the Katangese thought we were U.N. spies; the Gurkhas tried to shoot us as white mercenaries; the mercenaries were scared of having their pictures published; and lastly, the tribesmen wanted our blood because we were white men. No one loved us and none of us loved the Congo. Indeed, it has remained to this day the most unpleasant assignment any of us have had to cover. This, despite the fact that press casualties, compared with Vietnam or Cambodia, were low.

I had returned to Elizabethville for the final saga of the civil war to do a story on the white mercenaries fighting for Katanga who were grimly holding out against the U.N's determined Gurkha and Dogra troops. Blacks and whites were nervous. I was covering a young mercenary as they retook the 'tunnel' from the Swedes when I felt a rifle butt in my back. A burly Rhodesian mercenary yelled, 'Lift that fucking camera and you're dead!' I knew he meant it. It summed up the problems of doing a story on the mercenaries.

The U.N. was in trouble. A unit of Irish soldiers was surrounded at Jadoville but managed to send out a brave message, 'Will hold out till last bullet but send whiskey.'

One afternoon we watched Swedish U.N. Saab jets rocket the nearby Lido Hotel. Ian Berry, a tall dedicated Magnum photographer (of Sharpville fame), Barry von Below, short and jovial, a South African photographer, and Sandy Gall of Reuters and I decided to take our small car and investigate. We had just turned the last bend through the trees leading to the hotel when we ran into trouble. Bullets ripped up the road around us and branches flew off the trees. I turned the car in its own length and zig-zagged back down the road at full speed. Barry had thrown himself on the floor by my feet and looked up plaintively, 'Hope I'm not in your way?' His calm eased my fear. Jim Biddulph of the B.B.C. was not so lucky the next day when, also in a car with three other correspondents, they were ambushed. Jim was shot in the head and seriously wounded.

There were rumours that the ceasefire had taken place during Wednesday night, though there was still a hell of a lot of firing in the city. I had to get down to Ndola to 'ship' my film as Thursday was my last day to meet the Saturday night deadline in New York.

Reporters had not been able to file their stories during the battle so there was a stampede to fill my car en route for Ndola. Donald Wise, now working for the *Mirror*, Ian Berry and N.B.C's Ernie Christie (he was later killed in an air crash in South Africa) and I decided to chance the direct route because of the time factor. This involved 80 miles through hostile rebel country before reaching the Rhodesian border. We loaded the car with countless bottles of beer and chickens and set course. We were stopped many times by trees felled across the road, some manned by irregular troops who were impressed with my Tshombe laissez-passé and let us through. One road-block was manned by drunken tribesmen steamed up on home brewed liquor and drugs. They were armed with bows and arrows. We handed out bottles of beer and chickens to these people. With the awkward ones, I took a polaroid picture and, while they were squabbling over the print, we made our escape.

None of us could hide our relief while driving into the Northern Rhodesian police post at Kasumbalesa. From there we drove straight to the airport near Ndola to 'ship' film; then phoned our stringers in Salisbury to tranship it to London and on to New York. My pictures of that gruelling week later made four pages in the magazine.

Relatively little of a foreign correspondent's life is spent on actual journalism. He has to hang around embassies for visas; air line offices for reservations; cable offices and airports. In West Africa he will rise at unearthly hours to catch a flight, often delayed. Equally he could miss the flight altogether if his taxi runs out of petrol. African drivers often asked for cash in advance to put a few pints into the tank. Flights in Africa in those days tended to go north and south towards their old colonial masters, so one could wait two or three days for flights travelling east or west. If airlines had insufficient passengers to warrant a stop at your out-of-the-way place, you could wait for a few more days.

Working the African continent, we became expert at reading airline time tables since we could not rely on the majority of the African information clerks. In fact it was vital for us to know most of the schedules for 'shipping film.

So ended 1961, a year I was not sorry to leave behind.

LEFT: *Congo revolution, July 1960. One of many occasions when our car was held up by Congolese soldiers. Many of them were drunk.*

CENTRE: *Congo Revolution. A soldier fires at our Jeep. I took this picture as I dived for cover on the floor of the Jeep.*

BOTTOM: *Congo Revolution. This elderly Belgian couple were dragged out of their car by rioters. As we ran down the road the rioters escaped and left them.*

Living Dangerously 129

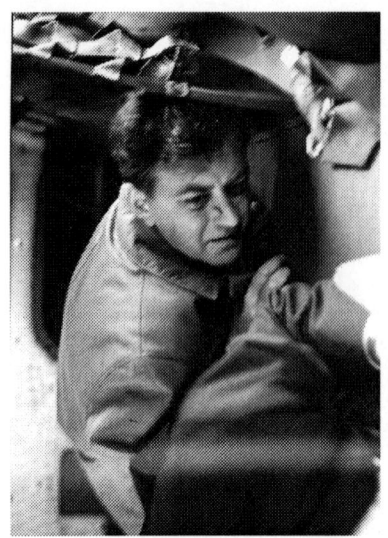

Van Durman man whose nose had been nicked by a machine gun bullet a split-second before this shot was taken

The Irish UN camp near Leopoldville blows up

A Katangese soldier ready to confront the Lumumba troops.

The much-feared Gurkha soldier attached to the UN forces.

Living Dangerously

Congo Revolution, Sept 60: a very scared father and son.

Jan 1961: the dreadful famine in Kasai Province.

A father and his desolate children in their wrecked house.

Living Dangerously 131

Congo Revolution: President Moise Tshombe of Katanga, Sept 1960

King Lukungu, Nov 1960, after losing 650 wives (see text)

Louis Armstrong ('Satchmo') at Leopoldville in Jan 1961

Scrambling for food at Katanga, September 1961

Ivory Coast, Aug 1961. A young girl carries many pots on her head.

Girl reflected in mirror

Living Dangerously

CHAPTER XIV

Lesley's last days in South Africa

When the troubles first started in the former Belgian Congo at the beginning of 1961, it meant Terry and many of our journalist friends being away from home for weeks on end. Communications were bad and I would go for days or even weeks without any news. My nerves were stretched to the limit. One day I called at the Time-Life office in Johannesburg hoping the secretary would volunteer some information, but in the event I was too proud to betray my anxiety.

Unfulfilled on this occasion, I went straight round to the main post office and sent off a cable to a chap called Don Bermingham on the foreign desk in New York. It read, 'PLEASE TRACE TERENCE SPENCER (signed) LESLEY SPENCER'. Back came the reply, 'WE WOULD ALSO LIKE TO KNOW WHERE HE IS – BERMINGHAM'.

After an absence of five and a half weeks Terry sent a cable to say he was leaving the Congo and going for a few days to Lourenço Marques (then a favourite holiday resort – always known as L.M.). This was too much for me! It later transpired he had sent two messages explaining the situation but neither had arrived.

I decided to take Cara out of school and drive the 300 miles to L.M. After packing up the house we left rather late and arrived in White River, close to the Portuguese border, after dark. The roads were so badly signposted, I began to feel nervous, wondering if we would ever find our way to Plaston where we had friends. It was a relief to turn into the gates and up the drive of their lovely farm where Barbara Jager made us really welcome with hot drinks, sandwiches and comfy beds. We soon turned in, having to leave again early next morning.

We had slight misgivings on reaching L.M. as to whether we were at the right hotel. We walked in to the vestibule of the Polana and there was Terry…

So began a short, much needed holiday.

I would like to say here and now that I am not the independent type by choice. I used to dream I would marry a man some ten years older than myself, serious and silent with steely blue eyes who would care for me as if I were made of porcelain. Terry does have blue eyes but there the dream ends.

At a Battle of Britain reunion 25 years later, we met 'the love of my life.' 'Lesley looks pretty good', he said sweetly. 'So she should', said Terry, 'she's been so well looked after'. Survival of the fittest, I say.

The Congo revolution, long drawn out as it was, finally came to an end. After that the news scene moved nearer home. When the treason trials opened in Pretoria, it began to be painfully obvious that this was not a country boasting a free press. Our friends were finding it more and more difficult to write up what they saw and heard.

Gradually, the news scene was changing and journalists started to move out of South Africa; this was also happening with members of the clergy and the legal profession. One brilliant barrister, Abraham Fischer, with whom we have sat over the dinner table, was sent to the infamous Robben Island prison and only released a month before he died. Jimmy Kantor served 90 days under house arrest and wrote of his experiences in his book *A Healthy Grave*. He was fortunate to be able to leave the country – in another way, so were we.

With the message that the treason trials had taught so many of us, we decided to put the farm up for sale. This was to be a slow process, mainly because it was too far out of the city to appeal to families as a residence and was not large enough or sufficiently developed to be a really commercial farm. After many frustrating weeks of waiting and hoping, Terry made a suggestion: 'Try and think up some story or gimmick – now is your chance'. I took it. Perhaps there has always been a latent journalist in me. This was my story. During our stay in Honeydew I was so often homesick for my own country. All I wanted in life was to live on the edge of an English village where I could walk down the street, say 'good morning' to the vicar and buy a bottle of gin at the local store.

So, Terry had built Southern Valley for me, a village with its 13 thatched buildings. All that was missing was the store, the bottle of gin and the church. We were selling because we were returning to England to live in Chiswick Village! In Ernie Shirley's best journalese my story appeared, together with a large aerial photograph, across two pages of the Johannesburg *Sunday Times*. Within a month the farm was sold.

After the removal men had been and gone (the load was light as I had not meant to settle permanently), we ourselves went down the drive for the last time. I never once looked back at Southern Valley, the scene of so much happiness – and of tragedy.

Not quite the way we left South Africa.

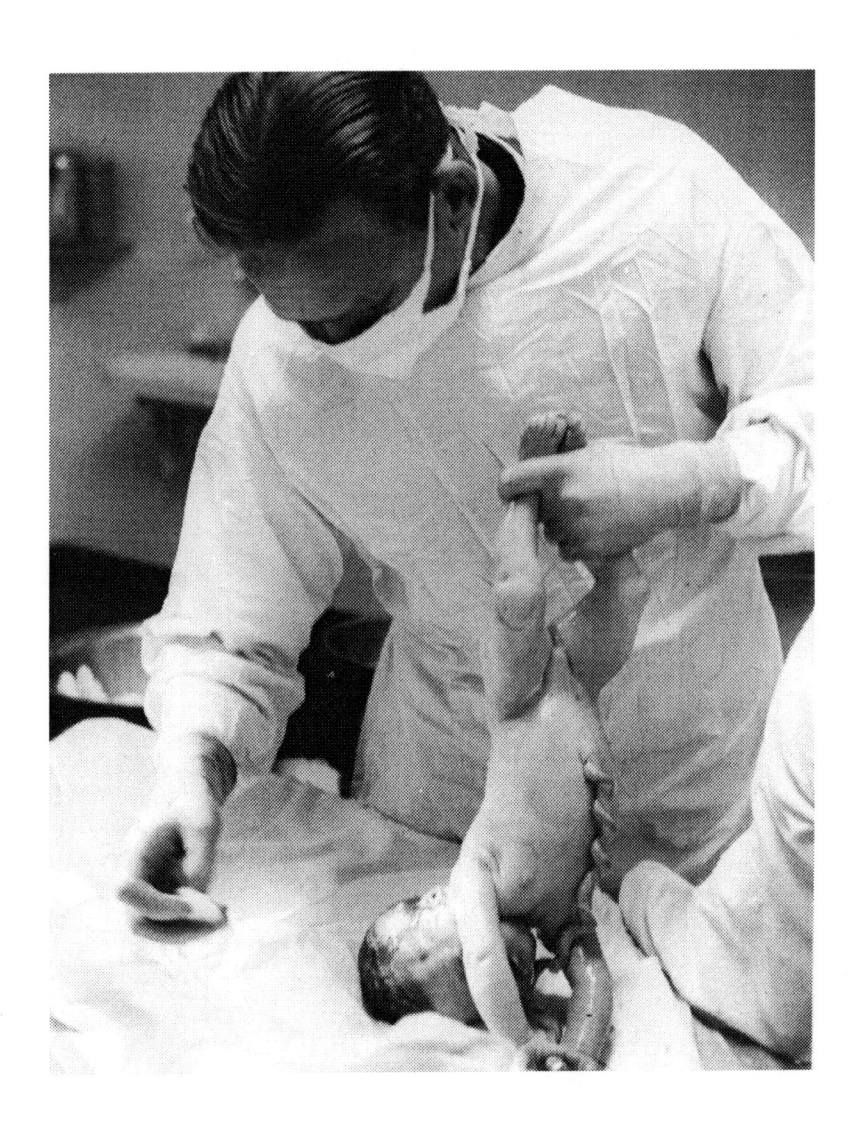

Our daughter Raina is born, August 1958.
Such pictures were barely acceptable just 40 years ago.

Open boat whaling in the Azores, July 1962.

Skakel joins the old timers in a cup of black coffee in the small cafe at Varadouro where they await the cry of 'Baleia" (whales).

CHAPTER XV

Terry goes whaling off the Azores

The year of 1962 started off for me with a real change-of-pace South African story to show up apartheid (segregation) for what it was, an economic barrier rather than a question of colour. Wherever one looked, 'apartheid' was relaxed when it helped the white man to maintain one of the highest living standards in the world. White families hired black nannies and had their food prepared by black hands. How much more intimate can you get? Yet black craftsmen were severely restricted in white areas until such time as the whites could no longer cope; then they used blacks. In January 1962 trade was booming. As already mentioned, the Japanese were declared 'white'. Not so the Chinese who, generally speaking, held down only menial jobs.

I had noticed that news seemed to veer away from an area after five years. Thus Africa's time was nearly up. We decided to leave and return to Europe. It was not a good moment for such a decision as LIFE had started 'firing' photographers for the first time. Bob Ajemian, our Paris bureau chief, had told us that the magazine was losing money and that assignments were to be curtailed. When I told Bob that we planned to leave Africa he warned me to stay on as it was unlikely that my contract would be renewed in England. We decided to go anyway.

In February I received a cable from Roy Rowan summoning me to New York. Roy was assistant managing editor in charge of foreign news. I had no doubt what it was about, but promised Lesley I would not change my mind.

Within minutes of getting in to the Time Life building in Rockefeller Center in New York and seeing Roy, I was hurrying down into Fifth Avenue to add another camera to the large coverage of astronaut John Glenn's cavalcade through the city. On 20th February Glenn had been the first American in space when he made three orbits of the earth. It was an exciting arrival and my first 'ticker-tape' parade.

Every time I went to New York I discovered new marvels. Few sights are more beautiful than the jewelled city at night with its millions of lights sparkling like some gargantuan tiara with the Empire State building rising up to form the centre-piece.

On Saturday nights when the magazine was being 'put to bed', LIFE hired a top New York restaurant to produce a lavish dinner on the 49th editorial floor and supplied copious quantities of liquor 'on the house'. Glamorous researchers tripped in and out of the elevators, each carrying a sheaf of copy in one hand and a full glass in the other. It was fun to meet the faces I had been dealing with in cables for so long.

George Karas, head of the photo lab, showed me around and introduced me to some of the finest photo technicians in the world. Fifty two of them processed 60,000 rolls of film a year and made 250,000 prints. I once remarked to George, 'I don't know how you get such great prints out of those contrasty African negs I send you.'

'Of course you don't,' he answered, 'You're a photographer.'

I had been wining and dining around New York for a week and had seen Roy briefly on several occasions, but nothing was ever mentioned about why I had been summoned to fly 11,000 miles to see him. On the tenth day I made my way down endless corridors to Roy's office. 'I believe you wanted to speak to me about something?' I asked. 'Oh, it was about your position in Africa;' he answered with disarming casualness. 'I gather you have had enough of the place and Lesley has already moved to London. I don't blame her. Would you be prepared to stay on in Africa, based in Nairobi, if we give you a return flight to London every three months?'

'Yes, I most certainly would,' I answered with almost too much enthusiasm.

Returning to London a phone call from the office said that Bob Ajemian wanted to see me in Paris the following day to discuss my new contract. He had invited four other photographers to dinner with him and his wife Betty in their elegant apartment overlooking the Eiffel Tower. There was the always amusing Loomis Dean who had started life in the circus, Hank Walker and Paul Schutzer. John Launois of the Black Star agency had just arrived from Japan.

Most cities of the world have a bar where foreign correspondents gather. In Paris it is the Crillon, in Saigon it was the Caravelle, in

Aden the Crescent, in Nicosia it used to be the Ledra Palace and in London it is El Vino's in Fleet Street. You could be sure of meeting a colleague in these bars who would update you on current affairs and supply contacts.

As I was now in Paris, I met many old friends in the Crillon bar the next morning, including the suave John Rich from N.B.C.; the gruff-voiced, fiery red-headed George Gale and Dick Killian, both from the London *Daily Express*. We drank several glasses of Ricard before I had to leave for West Africa on a story of great hotels of the world and then travel on to Johannesburg.

I was not quite finished with the horrors of Africa. I had been waiting a year for a visa into Angola. It arrived at the height of yet another civil war. After luscious lobsters in Luanda, the capital of Angola, I joined a Portuguese army commando unit in two well armed Jeeps. We drove 400 kilometres through troubled territory where a 'scorched earth' policy had been in practice. At Bembe, terrorists had laid waste the village. They had placed a white woman on a saw bench and cut her up the middle so that she fell apart like one of the red lobsters I had recently enjoyed. Although the woman was almost certainly dead before being sliced in two, this single incident created more fear in the hearts of the whites than anything else in that war. It emphasised that the quintessence of a terrorist campaign is not what it achieves but what it might achieve.

My next cable sounded weird. 'WANT YOU PROCEED LISBON SOONEST FOR A WHALING STORY. STOP MEET SKAKEL RITZ HOTEL MONDAY AND GOOD LUCK – AJEMIAN'.

A tall bronzed American came up to me as I checked in to the Ritz Hotel in Lisbon. 'You must be Terry Spencer, judging by all that equipment. Good to meet you. This trip looks like being fun – IF it ever comes off.'

'You're Jim Skakel? Great. I want to hear all about it.'

'Hasn't LIFE filled you in?'

'Not a word.'

Living Dangerously

'My God! Well, we are going to try and harpoon a 50 ton whale from a flimsy canoe off the Azores. I came over last year with a LIFE team to do the same thing but we couldn't get permission. 'Strings' have since been pulled and we hope to be more successful.' Jim, it turned out, was Bobby Kennedy's brother-in-law and a multi-millionaire. He was tall, powerfully built and sun tanned. For a week I, too, lived like a millionaire as Jim chased up contacts. We ate well at Tavares in Lisbon, gorged the seafood at Muchaxos in Estoril and visited Sintra.

By the time we reached the islands of the Azores, Jim and I were pretty apprehensive about the trip. We had heard lurid tales of a 52 ton whale reducing a canoe to matchwood with a single whack of its mammoth tail, and the injuries and death suffered by so many of the pathetically poor fishermen. I persuaded myself that it is the fear of the unknown that is the worst. Anyway, we were committed.

We left the little fishing port of Angra aboard the Ponta Delgada for Horta where we were met by Captain Rui Castro who told us that he had received news from Lisbon that he should help us. This was good news.

Rui had acquired a vintage Austin 7 for our use and the three of us drove around the island to the village of Varadouro. Steep, volcanic peaks dropped nearly vertically to the sea far below, forming a jagged, rocky coastline hammered continuously by Atlantic rollers. Wild flowers and roses abounded, with hydrangeas bordering the narrow roads. In places, the countryside resembled patterned carpets of varying shades of blue. A general atmosphere of tranquillity pervaded the island. A steep, winding track of lava dust led down to the tiny whaling village of Varadouro with its few houses and a café bar. Two whaling canoes were drawn up on the small sandy beach beneath towering cliffs.

Rui introduced us to José de Jesus, the Master of our canoe, and unfolded our plan. His fellow whalers gathered round to listen but were not enthusiastic. The language barrier made our task difficult. Anyway, for two days we joined the men drinking copious cups of coffee (Jim was an ex-alcoholic).

Slowly, and mostly by signs, we managed to communicate. I took their photographs with a polaroid camera and gave them an immediate print. They thought it was magic. They had never seen anything like it. José showed Jim how to throw the heavy, rough wooden-handled harpoon and was impressed with his strength and enthusiasm. Jim towered a full 12 inches above the whalermen.

Rui had hired a house for us in Areeiro, high up on the hill above Varadouro, and a woman to look after us. Our view from the terrace was spectacular. One evening Rui brought José to join us over a few glasses of Pico wine. 'You realize the problem of getting two of you into one of those boats. When things happen, they happen fast. There is a tall mast and no keel and the canoes are unstable. Absolute teamwork and co-ordination is needed and at times it can be dangerous. However, de Jesus is prepared to drop one crew member and take you if you will agree to compensate them should they lose a whale due to your presence. This could cost you $3,000.' We immediately agreed though I hoped I would never have to tell LIFE magazine.

Rui went on, 'You will have to spend many weary hours 20 to 30 miles out in the rough Atlantic before there is a hope of seeing your first whale. Only about 50 are caught off Horta each year and about ten canoes are lost or damaged trying to harpoon them.'

Open boat whaling is a game of patience. Every morning we rose at five and joined our men in the small café below for black coffee, chicken and cheese. 'Jaimie', as the men called Jim, grew a dark stubble over his sunburned face. He wore an old cloth cap pulled across his head at a jaunty angle. His coat and shirt were ragged and his trousers threadbare. He seldom wore shoes and a cigarette hung out of the left corner of his mouth. He even chewed chicken legs along with his soup like his fellow whalers and daily grew more like them.

Early in the morning of 9 August 1962 as heavy rain clouds floated low overhead, Jim and I were sitting outside the café-bar when suddenly a rocket was fired from the launch and a shout of 'Baleia! Baleia!' (Whales, whales) rang out through the village. Everyone sprang into action. Sleepy men grabbed their bundles of clothes and red kerchiefs containing bread and cheese, racing for the beach where the two canoes were dragged into the water. We jumped aboard H-21-B, Jim making his way to the bows while I remained amidships. We rowed feverishly out to the motorboat, joined by our second canoe, and were towed out into the Atlantic. Similar activity was taking place in ten other villages. The race was on.

Our stroke oarsman was Norbeto Matos. The previous October he had spent 22 hours on the upturned bottom of his canoe fighting off sharks after the canoe had been dragged under by a whale. Two of his colleagues were drowned that night. On rare occasions a whale, after being harpooned, can run out the full 500 metres of nylon line that links it to the canoe. Skippers are usually loath to cut the rope, trusting that the weight of the canoe will be too much for the exhausted creature.

For two hours we were towed further out to sea. The canoe tossed about like a cork in the wake of the motor boat. José was standing in the stern steering with a large oar. Suddenly, from under his wide brimmed hat came a shout which startled us all, particularly Jim and me, as everything aboard was strange and with the language barrier we knew little of what was going on.

'Oooowsh,' sounded from the crew. José had spotted a school of five whales nearby. We cast off our tow, hoisted the mainsail and jib and were under sail. All was deathly quiet.

Canoes from other villages joined the hunt and tension mounted. Competition between villages was intense.

José Silviero Rafael was the most experienced harpooner in the Azores. He was lean and muscular. His finely chiselled face was gaunt against his high cheek bones covered by dark stubble. Though only 40, he had a wrinkled brow and deep creases fell away from his eyes. He wore a cloth cap and often had a cigarette dangling from the corner of his mouth. José stood in the bows and handed Jim the heavy harpoon.

At one critical moment, when we looked like losing the race for the nearest and largest whale, everyone grabbed their Indian paddles and rowed feverishly as though their very lives depended on winning.

Jim glanced at me. 'If I could do it, I would blast those other goddamned masts right out of their boats.' I am sure every member of our crew felt the same. I certainly did. My heart was pounding in this most exciting race of my life. José shouted, 'Forca! Forca!' (faster, faster) as our canoe surged forward, and we gained on our neighbours. The whales 'sounded' (dived) as we approached and remained submerged for some 15 minutes. José had to decide which course to steer to bring the canoe over one of the whales as it surfaced. Whales cover considerable distance under water and so make this judgement difficult.

Our race was getting desperate. De Jesus remarked later, 'It's everyone for himself out there.'

Jim remained outwardly cool. He leaned over and whispered, 'I'm not throwing this harpoon until José shouts 'AGORA' (now) and then I'll go into the whale's mouth if that's what he wants me to do.' I knew he meant it. Jim had to allow for the deflection of the water as he threw his harpoon into the vast side of the whale. He had been warned that a second attack on a wounded whale is exceedingly dangerous.

We were some 20 miles out from Faial in the deep swell of the grey Atlantic. There were no life jackets aboard, no flares nor any form of life-saving equipment.

The final approach for the attack is best made under sail when the Master has better control. It is more silent and after harpooning, the get-away is quicker and smoother. Silence is all important if the whale is to be stalked and attacked before it realizes the danger.

Jim was in position in the bows. His knee steadied in the cut-away portion of the gunwhale. There was a considerable swell on the water and I was having difficulty steadying myself for the picture. José Raphael was standing just behind Jim, propped against the 37 foot mast. The harpoon line was coiled in two tubs towards the stern with a turn around the loggerhead beside the Master.

I was scanning the sea a mile ahead when it happened. The tenseness throughout the crew sent a shiver down my spine. A few feet ahead of us, like an enormous submarine surfacing, was the massive creature. Water swirled off its black, shimmering back. It seemed bigger than anything that could be driven by a living heart.

José de Jesus ordered the tack and jibed the boom. I had to sling myself to the bottom of the canoe, trying to keep four cameras out of the water that was pouring in over the gunwale. The boom hit the back of my head as it swung across and in that blurred instant I heard Jose' scream, 'Agora!'

Jim was standing ready to harpoon to the right but as the canoe lurched over the top of the monster he had to swing across to the left. In that split-second Jim lunged the harpoon into the side of the whale only five feet away. His aim was perfect. My head was still reeling yet I somehow managed to capture this absolutely vital moment.

In a flash, Jim Skakel had become the first amateur sportsman ever to harpoon the mighty sperm whale. He remarked afterwards, 'At the moment of attack, I experienced what matadors call " the moment of truth" as they lean over the horns of the charging bull and lunge the death sword.'

The harpoon has to be thrown with tremendous force, as it has to penetrate a full three feet and must land in flesh. If it hits a rib, it can bend and the harpoon will pull out. Once properly embedded, a small wooden peg breaks and the head splays out at right angles, securing the harpoon.

Once the harpoon had lodged securely, there was bedlam aboard. Men shouted and rushed around the canoe, more water poured in. Ropes were released and both the mast and mainsail collapsed simultaneously. The whale struck the bottom of the canoe with a thud. Once again, I found myself slushing along in the water trying to extricate myself from under canvas and ropes as I fought to record the bedlam. Meanwhile, the whale was diving fast. He made violent and convulsive efforts to escape as his mighty tail lashed the water alongside us.

The harpoon line was screaming out. We had to be careful not to get tangled in it. A foot carelessly placed could lead to disaster. This is the moment when most of the whaling casualties occur.

Slowly, order was restored. The sails were furled, the oars were checked and the men began to relax. Strain was gradually applied to the line by de Jesus who poured water over his hands as he did so to prevent being burned. Eventually, the line was fully 'snubbed' and the canoe was in tow behind the whale. Speeds of up to 30 m.p.h. have been known but usually it is around 10 m.p.h., as in our case.

We sat back and enjoyed our 'Nantucket sleigh ride', as it used to be called, while we watched another drama being performed by our fellow canoe from Varadouro. It went in to harpoon the mate of our whale which was now fully alerted and dangerous. It 'sounded', but resurfaced quickly. The two whales sought each other's company for mutual protection. Meanwhile a canoe from a 'hostile' village was bearing down for this valuable prize. Everything depended on our colleagues getting the harpoon in first. Two whales in a day from one village would be a very profitable achievement.

Our friends went in for the second attack but, again, were unsuccessful. The whale was too smart. The competitor was closing in for his attack. The tension was unbearable. For more manoeuverability, our colleagues dropped their sails and took to oars. This put them at a speed disadvantage over their rivals who were still under sail in a fair breeze. Both canoes jockeyed for position behind the two whales which were swimming side by side. At that moment the breeze dropped as if by magic and our exhausted friends closed the last eight feet to lodge their harpoon into the second whale with the other harpooner also poised for the attack. A great cheer went up from both canoes.

Our excitement was not over, however. The whale swung round and tried to ram their canoe. They had no time to drop the mast and were thus dangerously top heavy. For a moment the canoe actually rode on the back of the whale and was lifted a few feet out of the water. Another bump and it would have capsized. The canoe being attached to the whale they might all have ended up in disaster.

We were in tow for another 45 minutes while our colleagues in H-24-B took off in another direction behind their conquest. When the two Josés decided our whale had tired sufficiently, they began to haul in the line and close the distance separating us. Preparations were made for the final kill. We were now alone about 23 miles from land and de Jesus was taking no chances.

For the second time we closed to within a few yards of the whale. The Master was keeping us well clear of the tail. The mammal was still very much alive and, like a Spanish bull filled with bandeleros, dangerous. Lancing is done from about 12 feet away. Raphael's unerring skill found its mark straight away. To be quite sure, he made a second attack, this time aiming for the blood-sack. Again, his aim was true. The sea slowly turned into an ocean of deep red blood. The stricken whale made a last and desperate attempt to attack us but the crew swiftly back-oared out of danger. A powerful jet of blood – the red flag or the chimney of fire according to the ancient whalers – shot vertically out of the whale's blow-hole.

Whales are unpredictable, except that they always turn towards the sun to die. Ours was no exception.

Almost two hours had elapsed since 'Jaimie' had harpooned the monster. Communications with our crew were still minimal but their reaction to Jim's feat did not need words. Each in turn embraced him as we rode the Atlantic waves and then wine jugs were emptied as they toasted their Yankee hero.

The wind strengthened and the waves rose. We tossed about alongside our monstrous prey for ten long hours while our men fought off sharks as they tore off large pieces of flesh from the floating whale. Norbeto, our fellow crewman, actually rode the body of the whale as he beat off the sharks with a flensing knife, killing five of the brutes.

It was almost dark when we saw the welcome light of the motor boat, which had spotted us, and almost 18 hours after leaving Varadouro, we were back and walking up the beach in the dark. On our first trip out we had caught and photographed two whales being harpooned. We invited the two crews to our house and drank wine well into the night by the light of an oil lamp. Jim stuck to his black coffee.

The next morning Jim and I went to the whaling factory and watched them drag his prize slowly out of the water. It weighed 45 tons, about three quarters the size of a Boeing 707 airliner.

We caught two more whales with our crews over the next few weeks before we sadly had to bid them farewell and I returned to London to write 25,000 words of text and captions over a two-week period. So much effort went into these major stories that the feeling of euphoria as the packet finally winged its way to America was always great.

Open boat whaling: TS in a whaling canoe, July 1962.

CHAPTER XVI
Southern Africa again

I was in London for the month of September 1962 and helped out the bureau on several minor stories. During that time our furniture arrived from South Africa. The customs man was at our house and asked me to produce the Colt automatic I had declared. For measure of good discipline I cocked the weapon and fired it into the air to ensure there was not a round up the breach. But there was a hell of a bang – much to our mutual surprise. He had been a Captain in the Indian army and took it in good spirits. I hate to think where that bullet landed.

Then it was back to Johannesburg yet again. Ernie and I boarded an ancient DC3 Dakota and flew to Windhoek in South West Africa. We had a rough ride for 90 miles in a Jeep running along dried river beds winding their way through the desert and sparse bush country to a lonely farm run by a 60 year old German woman, Frau Hedwig Aston. Frau Aston managed a 3,500 acre farm alone. She was too poor even to hire an African farm hand but, she did have Ahla.

Ahla had arrived on her farm seven years earlier as a baby. She was brought up with the 100-strong goat herd where she found love and companionship. Eventually, she took over the job of looking after the herd. But Ahla was no ordinary goatherd: she was a fully grown baboon.

Due to four years of drought, finding grazing for the herd was no easy task. Each morning at dawn Ahla drove the herd out of the stockade and took them for three or four miles over rugged terrain, crossing deep river beds that had not seen water in years. The banks were lined with dead and dying trees, and leafless branches stretched out in mute appeal to the cloudless sky to bring them rain.

Ahla also had to contend with marauding, half-starved leopards, jackals and wild dogs. Even so, every day she found new pastures for her flock. Baboons cannot count but Ahla personally knew every goat in her charge and never lost one. Frau Aston told us that one evening after Ahla had returned to the farm, she realized a kid was missing. She searched all night and returned triumphant in the morning carrying her charge in one arm. Ahla slumped exhausted for an hour before taking her herd out to graze for another hot day.

We watched Ahla helping kids to find their mothers. If a reluctant mother baulked at feeding, Ahla gave her a slap or a gentle bite. If the trouble was a swollen udder, Ahla sucked each teat in turn until the milk flowed again. As a result of this remarkable baboon, Frau Aston managed to keep her farm going.

On my return to Johannesburg there was a cable in the office, or what was left of it, to phone Bob Ajemian in Paris. I say, 'what was left' because the Government had refused visas for American correspondents of *Time*. Herman Nickel was kicked out, in effect, but managed to return many years later as the American Ambassador to South Africa!

Bob wanted us to go ahead with a story we had suggested about house arrests.

The South African Government could detain or place people under house arrest without taking them to court. Some were held under 12 hours detention meaning that they could go to work between the hours of 6 a.m. and 6p.m.; others were under 24 hours house arrest and could not leave their homes at all. Such was the case with the Hodgsons. Rica was under 12 hours and Jack was under 24 hours in their Hillbrow flat in Johannesburg. They were not allowed to discuss politics or their case with anyone. Rica could not even talk to the girl sharing her desk at the New Age office where she worked. No one, other than the Hodgsons, was allowed to enter their 'prison'. They were closely watched.

Ernie Shirley and I knew this story would take us into direct confrontation with the Special Branch police and increase the already large size of our dossiers at their Gestapo-like headquarters at the Grays in Jo'burg.

We discovered that the flat above the Hodgsons was occupied by a correspondent from the South African Press Association. While other residents were scared to let us even enter their apartments, the S.A.P.A. man had no objection.

Ernie and I met Rica in the her office and outlined our plan. We would photograph 24 hours of their lives without entering their flat.

Living Dangerously 151

We would soon have been arrested had we done so. We gave Rica a long mirror, two powerful quartz iodine flood lamps and a loaded motorised Nikon camera. She was to place the mirror at a 45° angle on the balcony so that I could see into her flat from the apartment above. The camera was to be mounted on a tripod, previously set and focussed, and I would drop the remote control lead for her to connect to the camera. I told her where to place the equipment.

We knew that their telephone was being tapped but reckoned there would be some delay before the police would replay the tape. We decided, therefore, to direct the operation on the telephone and leave hastily as soon as we had our pictures. It was also unlikely that the police could trace the telephone calls. It all worked perfectly.

The next evening we planned to shoot the night sequences of the Hodgsons incarceration from the top of a nearby building, using a powerful 1,000 mm telephoto lens. We knew that the evening performance would not be so easy, especially as we had to make the final arrangements over the telephone and only afterwards realized that we had talked about starting to shoot at 8 p.m. which would, in itself, somewhat startle the police.

At 7.30 p.m. Ernie and I, with another colleague, arrived near the flat. We nearly collided with Colonel Spengler, head of the Special Branch and one of the most feared men in South Africa. We did not think he had recognized us. Early in the afternoon we had bribed a house 'boy' in an apartment block across the road to leave the door to the roof unlocked. As before, Ernie remained in the street below to keep watch. If he put on his cap it was the signal that we had been spotted. With our other colleague (I will not mention his name as he was a prominent journalist in South Africa), we lugged the heavy equipment into the lift for the sixth floor and climbed through the unlocked door to the roof.

Exactly at eight o'clock Rica switched on the powerful lamps. It looked as if a beacon had lit up Hillbrow. The Hodgsons performed as in the film Rear Window. All the time my colleague was watching Ernie in the street far below. Nothing happened. I had time to change to a second camera and complete our programme. We were packing up the gear when Ernie calmly put on his cap. I unloaded the two rolls of film, put them into the well padded bag we had brought for the occasion and threw it down to Ernie. Figuring that the police would come up the lift, we escaped down the iron fire escape and joined Ernie with his car at the prearranged rendezvous. We celebrated appropriately at the Hide Away and a girl flew the film out of the country the following morning.

The story never ran. Perhaps New York knew that it was too hot and that we would all have been thrown out of the country.

My days in South Africa were over. Jo and Ernie Shirley drove me to Jan Smuts airport and, with a magnum of champagne, I was finally saying 'goodbye'. I was happily leaving behind the strain of living in a country where, because I worked for *Time* and LIFE, I had become the target for hostility even at private dinner parties. I was saying 'goodbye' as well to the tensions of ten years evading the Special Branch and suffering their intimidations while trying to do my job.

A cable sent me north to the Mediterranean to photograph Phillippe Cousteau's new diving bell. I arranged for Lesley to meet me at the elegant Negresco Hotel in Nice. It was lovely seeing her again after 12 weeks. With Paul Ress, the *Time* stringer in Antibes, we dined at 'La Trappa' in the old port. Paul suggested we try the 'specialité de la maison' but Lesley does not like offal so she had devilled chicken. When our main course arrived and looked delicious, she asked to try one, 'You're right, Paul, they are good, she said. What are they?'

'Testicules,' Paul replied in French.

'What!' exclaimed Lesley with exaggerated horror, 'Whose?'

I returned next morning to the Negresco to clean up after working in the diving bell and joined Lesley for a late breakfast on the balcony in the warm December sunshine. Corsica was 150 miles away and beyond lay the vast continent of Africa. It seemed a long way off to me at that moment. A green velveted 'flunky' disturbed my day-dreams with a cable served on a silver tray. It was from Bob. 'YOUR WHALING STORY CLOSED NINE PAGES IN B/W AND COLOR STOP READS AND LOOKS TERRIFIC STOP COMBINATION OF COLOR AND B/W VERY STRONG

Living Dangerously 153

STOP YOUR BYLINED ESSAY IS ONE OF HIGHLIGHTS OF SEA ISSUE STOP SUGGEST YOU PROCEED LONDON AFTER COMPLETING COUSTEAU BEST AJEMIAN.'

An exciting Christmas present and now at last I was in the London bureau.

House arrest in South Africa, November 1962.

The Hodgsons under house arrest in their flat in Johannesburg (see text). This picture was shot with a 1,000mm telephoto lens from the roof of a building across the street.

A baboon shepherd, Nov 1962. A poor widow used this baboon to look after her flock of 100 goats in South West Africa. He is seen here looking tired out after a long day in search of grazing for his herd.

Ahla the baboon shows a tender solicitude for her flock of goats. If one of them strays from the main flock she gently brings it back again.

Living Dangerously 155

CHAPTER XVII

Terry in Indonesia

Early in the New Year of 1963 I was given the chance to do a major essay in a country on the other side of the world, one I had never visited – Indonesia.

Since the Time-Life organisation was banned in Indonesia, arrangements had been made for me to represent a French magazine. I was also going alone so would have to file lengthy text pieces on many aspects of the country.

Minutes before the Indonesian embassy closed in Singapore for the weekend of 30 March, a plump and smiling little Javanese man came over to Raffles Hotel with a telex message: 'Mr. Spencer, welcome to Indonesia. I have your visa, valid for three months.' This was a relief after seven days of waiting. even though it had enabled me to explore the magic worlds of Hong Kong and Singapore.

John Shaw, the Singapore stringer, arranged for me to address film packages to the French magazine and send them clandestinely out of Indonesia in packets belonging to one of the international news agencies. Their Singapore office would inform John who would airfreight the package direct to LIFE magazine.

Within hours I was aboard an Indonesian Garuda Lockheed Electra plane for the comfortable one and a half hour flight across the Malacca Straits to Djakarta. It was once suggested that the beautiful archipelago of lush green islands lying in a crescent 3000 miles across the Pacific was the result of some land that God had left over. He slung it into the air as one might sling chaff and down landed the 10,000 islands that comprise Indonesia – the 'lovely islands of dancing and flowers.' With over 100 million people then speaking 114 dialects, I had plenty of material to investigate.

There was an air of degeneracy and disrepair at Kemayoran airport, combined with utter chaos, as thousands of little people clamoured to get aboard the limited flights that would take them to their far-flung islands. It was clear that law and order barely existed in Java.

Just as I was wondering where and how to start my story, I heard that a volcano had erupted on the fabled island of Bali and that thousands of people had been killed.

I spent my first night on a couch in the Shell representative's office at the airport. By 4.30 a.m. the next morning there were 400 people fighting, scrambling and arguing to get aboard the Bali flight. Trying to watch all my cases as I, too, scrambled and fought, was no easy task. Having bribed everyone in sight I was eventually given a ticket with a confirmed seat but on reaching the check-in counter I was told that the plane was more than twice overbooked and that my name was not on the list. Another hefty bribe and I staggered out to the plane, sweating and lugging my gear with me. I knew none of it would have arrived had I checked it in. Seeing the pilot, I told him I was an ex-Spitfire pilot and he allowed me to stow my equipment in the cabin, inviting me up to the cockpit for the two hour flight to Bali. He circled to within a few hundred feet of the smouldering, belching volcano on Mount Agung, allowing me to get excellent aerial pictures through his open window.

In Bali I was greeted by Prince Agung who acted as the Information Chief for the island. He drove me to the Bali hotel in Denpassar, a tin roofed single storey building. Making my way up to the bar I received a hard and unexpected slap on the back. It was Horst Faas of the Associated Press.

'How the hell did you get here?' He knew that *Time* and LIFE were banned in Indonesia. Glancing anxiously at the Prince I answered, 'I've come for *Paris Match* to cover the volcano.'

'That's funny,' he retorted, 'I've just received a request for pictures from them myself.'

'They obviously did not think I could get here in time,' I cracked back.

Horst got the message.

I hired a taxi to take me up to the village of Sebudi on Mount Agung, only eight kilometres from the centre of the volcano. Sebudi had been obliterated. One thousand one hundred people had died in their beds after being engulfed by the sudden flow of steely blue lava that slithered down the steep slopes of Agung, accelerated by the heavy rains. The devastation everywhere was appalling. Three thousand homeless people, many of them badly burned, hastened to safety carrying their meagre possessions tied to bamboo poles. Buses loaded with dead rolled in to Klungkung.

The casualty list alone warranted a story. Add to this the romance of Bali and it was a 'must'. We hate to admit it but our media ratings of disasters went something like this – one American or British killed compared to three French or Dutch to 25 Spanish or Italians to 50 Greeks or Turks to 500 Arabs to 1000 Asians or Africans.

At Denpasar airport I met an attractive Garuda air hostess called Nyomon Sukert who told me she daily made the run to Djakarta. We had an enjoyable lunch together and she promised to take my packet to the Hotel Indonesia and deliver it personally. I knew my colleague would appreciate such a glamorous messenger.

President Soekarno flew into Bali to see the carnage for himself. I teamed up with Kim Thung from Intara, the Indonesian news agency, and together we drove to Soekarno's house at Tampaksriring. The drive gave me the opportunity to enjoy the island scenery and to photograph the reflections of palm trees in the paddy fields whose contours resembled Picasso designs. We passed exquisite bare-breasted girls working in the fields or gracefully carrying pitchers of water through picturesque villages with large palm trees languidly shading wooden houses. We watched small boys scampering up lofty coconut trees with the ease of monkeys. They threw down the nuts, the milk from which sated our thirsts in the sticky climate.

The next morning we drove to Bug-Bug and waded across the swollen river. Carrying heavy equipment in sweltering heat we walked the six miles up the side of Agung to Subazen where 200 people had been killed. A helicopter landed and out stepped a gaudily uniformed officer who introduced himself as Colonel Sabur, Soekarno's Chief of Security. Soekarno had been unable to come, he informed us. Kim and I spent that night in a 'doss-house' at Klungkung where we attracted our fair share of bed bugs.

The time came for me to leave Bali. I had a confirmed booking on the flight to Djakarta and Nyomon said she would put me in the seat next to Colonel Sabur. Once again, I lugged all my gear on to the plane only to be told that Soekarno's dancing troupe had to travel and there was not a seat for me. Nyomon agreed to watch my equipment while I went to phone the Governor whom I had met. In ten minutes I was back aboard and settled down next to the Colonel. By the time we reached Djakarta we were firm friends. He drove me to the Hotel Indonesia in his staff car and promised he would send me an invitation to the ball at the Mardeka Palace to meet the President.

This association with Colonel Sabur opened the almost impossibly closed doors to Soekarno and led me to spend three weeks with him and accompany him throughout Indonesia and its many islands.

When I arrive in a strange part of the world without contacts I agonize, wondering where to start and whether I will even see a picture. There was a saying on the foreign press corps that the only thing you were likely to get in your hotel bedroom was sex – so get the hell out in the street, hire a taxi and go somewhere – anywhere,. talk to the cab driver, to strangers in the street, to tradesmen, dock workers and policemen. Returning to the hotel in the evening there is the hall porter and the barman. Local businessmen visit the bars of most big hotels and often enjoy talking to foreigners, especially if you buy them drinks. I tended to avoid mingling with military personnel as they seldom contribute much and can lead to suspicion.

In Djakarta we had to tip the telex operators the equivalent of a month's pay to have our messages transmitted or they never went. Not important, as the black market rate of exchange was astronomical against the U.S. dollar.

For confidential, inside information, there are the embassies and legations where you can expect thorough briefings strictly 'off the record'. They give valuable background information about the local situation. In certain embassies around the world it is possible, in dire circumstances, to use their diplomatic bags to 'ship' film and sensitive stories and even to use their communications. It is a practice strongly discouraged and never admitted.

Dealing with embassies and legations I had the best of both worlds. I could visit the British and American ones and in Djakarta even the French. I soon learned seldom to bother with the British as they could rarely compete with the Americans. Also, in sensitive areas, and Djakarta was such a place, British correspondents seemed to be viewed as an embarrassment by their embassy and staff.

Two days after checking in to the Hotel Indonesia, I was approached at the bar by a man who told me he was from the American embassy. 'You're Terry Spencer, I believe. We know who you are and what you are doing here. We will keep track of you.' He gave me his card. 'If you need any help or information, don't fail to contact me.' This was a considerable comfort to me as I felt very much alone and had no wish to 'disappear'.

You could not move in Indonesia without sheaves of paper, such was the red tape, endemic in their society, so I had to visit the Information Department for the press pass representing my French magazine and for a host of other permits. Garnis Harsona, head of the department, asked me, 'Why is your magazine so interested in our country after the big story you did on us under a year ago?' He tossed me over a copy of the relevant issue with the 'top' blaring out, 'Soekarno, le grand seducteur!' I knew I had problems.

With my new press pass I took the precaution of getting a re-entry visa into Indonesia – just in case.

True to his word, Colonel Sabur arranged an invitation for me to attend and photograph a diplomatic function at the Merdeka Palace. He introduced me to the President who greeted me warmly in French and invited me to the big reception he was having the following week.

I went to the Merdeka Palace for the ball. It was a crowded, glittering occasion. Four orchestras from outlying islands entertained the guests who danced throughout the night. Beautiful girls, exquisitely dressed in handmade batik, wore long skirts slit to above the knee and cut to show the contours of their finely curved bodies. Flowers in undreamed of quantities decorated the room. In the adjoining banqueting hall long tables groaned under the weight of food.

There was champagne and wine for the guests but the Indonesians, being mostly Muslims, drank only exotic-looking fruit drinks.

Soekarno hardly missed a dance. At one stage he invited me over to his table. We discussed what I was trying to do. 'I think you will enjoy next week's ball better than this one,' he said, 'It is at my Palace at Bogur, 55 kilometres from here. It will be less formal and more fun.'

He was right. The music, the flowers and the girls were all the same but there was also an air of relaxation. People were enjoying themselves. Towards the end of dinner, Soekarno again called me over to his table. 'Wasn't it your magazine that once called me "le grand seducteur"?'

'Indeed it was, Monsieur le President,' I answered in French, 'but you know the implication of the word "seducteur". It is not like its crude English counterpart. In France it implies a man who is attractive and successful with women. Soekarno seemed pleased. I breathed a sigh of relief and was glad I'd had time to think out that answer.

'What do you think of our Indonesian girls?' he asked with a friendly smile.

'I think they are beautiful.' I answered truthfully.

'Who do you think is the most beautiful girl here?'

I hesitated, pointing out one in his party; then singled out another girl I had spotted. Soekarno called his aide and had her summoned over to our table. He took my arm. 'I cannot understand Westerners and their attitude towards women. Most of your men seem to enjoy liquor rather than beautiful girls.'

'That's sometimes true, Monsieur le President but I am not one of them.'

'You are English, aren't you?'

'Yes.'

'How is it that you are working for a French magazine?'

'I am a freelance photographer and take on any assignment I am offered, especially if it takes me to Indonesia, a country I have never been to before. Also, I spent much of my early life in France.'

Living Dangerously

'Ah, France. That accounts for your love of women. You must be very famous to work for that magazine. Do you ever work for American magazines?'

I was longing to meet the girl Soekarno had ordered to our table. She was standing patiently behind us and the President took no notice of her.

'Firstly, Monsieur le President, I am not famous and yes, I have worked for American magazines.'

'Do you know any *Time* and LIFE people?'

'Yes, I know several of them.'

'They write bad things about me and my country. The next *Time* and LIFE man who comes into Indonesia will do so over my dead body!'

'Quite right, Monsieur le President.' I answered nonchalantly. Despite this conversation I enjoyed the evening.

The girl, Lestari, never left my side. We watched dancing troupes representing many of the far-flung islands and we danced to unusual music. We feasted off the long banqueting tables and afterwards strolled through the immaculate lawns in the cool evening air. I had not had an alcoholic drink all night and around four in the morning began to appreciate what the President had said to me.

I came to know Soekarno well over the next few weeks. He invited me to attend most of his public functions and personally arranged my press facilities. This alone saved me countless hours of frustration.

Soekarno was taller than most Indonesians despite having a Javanese father and a Balinese mother. His hair was receding and grey, though one seldom noticed this as he never appeared in public without wearing a black 'forage' cap. He looked younger than his 62 years. He was always immaculately dressed in a freshly pressed, well tailored uniform bearing row after row of ribbons below a pair of pilot's wings. He carried a Marshal's golden handled black baton.

Soekarno tolerated only the best. He lived in medieval splendour in one of his five palaces inherited from the Dutch. He owned

21 automobiles, mostly American, and his personal Lockheed Jet Star whisked him around his Paradise islands. He used a fleet of helicopters for local gadding about. Girls I spoke to at his palaces found the President handsome, charming and easy-going. He certainly exuded a warmth and sense of good manners towards his guests whom he obviously enjoyed entertaining. He once said, 'I hope I never lose interest in women, not even in my grave.'

My next invitation was to a another ball, this time in Bandung in central Java. Being higher, it was cooler than Djakarta. There was trouble with the Chinese and riots were breaking out all over the town when I got there. This made me late for the ball and I arrived after Soekarno. As I made my entry, he silenced the orchestra and announced to the 400 assembled guests, 'Voila, le grand seducteur lui même.'

I could have died a thousand deaths but produced a sickly smile as I bowed to the President. He summoned me to his table. 'You will be glad to hear that Lestari is here from Bogur.' I was. She was still at my side as dawn broke. She accepted my compliments as if it was the greatest thrill of her life. It was an experience to be in a land where women seemed to have been put on earth to please men, instead of the reverse being the case in our part of the world.

One of my greatest journalistic breaks occurred that night or rather at daybreak when Soekarno invited me to join him on his extended tour around some of the islands, culminating in the West Irian Independence celebrations. West Irian was the former Dutch New Guinea. Soekarno added, 'I will arrange for you to travel with me on my Jet Star and to sail with me on my cruiser.' I could not believe my luck.

About this time I was befriended by a reporter from Intara, the Indonesian news agency who, pleading lack of money, anxiously wanted to accompany me wherever I went. I had no illusions that he could be tuned in to the secret police but he would be a guide and interpreter. In any case, I liked him.

Two days later at 4 a.m. I was woken to be told a car was waiting to take me to the airport where I joined Soekarno on the first long flight to Makasar. There we were given a lavish reception before flying on to Ambon to join the cruiser, Irian. While pulling out at dusk I was arrested by two naval security men who told me that the ship was packed with secret electronic equipment and I had no right to be taking pictures. I told them that the British even had pictures of the bottom of the ship thanks to Commander Crabbe. (Crabbe had lost his life examining the hull of this ex-Russian cruiser while it had been visiting Portsmouth harbour many years previously.) I persuaded their officer to take me before the President as I was his guest. Soekarno told them I could photograph anything I liked.

During the long cruise eastwards to West Irian I had several lengthy discussions on deck with Aidit who was the boss of the ten million strong Indonesian communist party, the third biggest communist party in the world at that time after China and Russia. The all-powerful Aidit was little known in the West and was later murdered during the anti-red uprisings. People seldom think that photographers are interested in words. They will divulge to them intimate details they would hesitate giving to reporters. Aidit appeared delighted to have someone with whom he could discuss his favourite topic — his Party. Fortunately, I have a good memory over short periods and soon had all the details of these talks down in my note books.

Even aboard ship Soekarno was accompanied by two attractive women. The crew were envious when he publicly danced with these women after a concert on the large after-deck. I was photographing this event when an officer grabbed my arm and told me such pictures were not allowed. Soekarno noticed this and admonished the man, 'I want the world to see me with some of my beautiful women!'

During the three-day cruise, and without a drink, I was glad to meet one of the Russian engineers aboard who seemed to have unlimited supplies of vodka in his cabin. The ship was otherwise 'dry' so we had to be careful.

Eventually we steamed proudly in to the overbearingly hot and humid little bay of Kota Barnat in West Irian. Outwardly enchanting, I later found the town to be dreary and fast decaying as it nestled against the thick tropical jungle.

The Governor entertained us to a buffet lunch at his residence and there was another late party that night. After a few hours sleep I joined Soekarno in the cockpit of an air force C120 troop carrier. He took over the controls for the benefit of my camera as we flew over dense jungle and mountains for another ceremony in the south of Borneo, before returning to Biak to join the Jet Star once again. Soekarno had stunningly glamorous air hostesses aboard whose prime job seemed to be to sit with the passengers on the long, otherwise boring flight back to Djakarta. They cared for us as only Javanese women know how.

Returning to the Hotel Indonesia, I was depressed to find no cables nor letters from home but there was an ominous note to see Harsona.

I completed the captions of the tour, batched the film together and enclosed all my used note books. A television reporter was flying to Singapore that evening and agreed to take my packet with him. I took him out to the airport and after checking that his plane had taken off, I went to see Harsona.

'You work for LIFE magazine, don't you?' he queried menacingly and produced a copy of the recent sea issue containing my whaling story.

'I have done a lot of work for LIFE,' I answered. 'I am a freelance photographer and work for anyone who commissions me and that includes you if you pay my fee – in dollars.' He was not amused.

'Look,' I went on, 'you have an embassy in Paris. They can verify that I am indeed working for that Paris magazine.'

I left the Information Department and went straight to the American embassy and told them of my fears. These fears were compounded the next morning when I went to the Merdeka Palace to see my old friend, Colonel Sabur, and asked him to arrange a final portrait session with Soekarno. He refused to see me.

I was joined that evening at dinner by my colleague from Intara who told me I was under suspicion. I had to complete the contentious side of my story without delay.

Living Dangerously

One of the embassies introduced me to a girl who was well connected with the underground and opposition. Francoise in turn introduced me to the leaders whom I interviewed and some of whom I photographed. She also volunteered to show me some of the worst slums in Djakarta.

I collected her with my 'tame' taxi driver at six the next morning. We drove down the well-tended Lumumba Avenue leading directly to the slum areas. The pavements were crowded with small mobile shops. Their owners had carried them to the site on long bamboo poles precariously balanced across their shoulders. They provided food, cheap clothes, shoe repairing and tailoring. Some erected crude hessian shanties and sold hot satés and tjemedol. Filth and poverty dominated the scene.

I had problems shooting pictures in these areas as people shouted and screamed at me every time I lifted a camera. Some openly threatened me. Even in these conditions of poverty, people have their pride and dignity.

In the afternoon I went to the dock area carrying only a sub-miniature camera as photography was strictly illegal. The dockside was piled high with cases, mostly Russian, and in such chaotic fashion that they must have lain there for months, containing millions of dollars worth of much-needed equipment that no one seemed to know existed. I had to be extremely careful when surreptitiously taking these pictures, especially knowing that I might be under surveillance. If caught I could be arrested as a spy.

My task in Java was nearly done. I visited four embassies for last minute briefings. At the French embassy the ambassador remarked to me, 'It seems funny that an Englishman is working for a French magazine in Indonesia.'

'Much funnier,' I thought, 'if he had known that an Englishman was working for an American magazine which was banned in that country.'

I had just returned to the hotel and was enjoying a cool Danish lager when an embassy official came up to me, 'Terry, they are going to arrest you! Get packed quick. I have a car outside.'

I packed in minutes, slapped down a load of travellers cheques at the cashier and we were on our way to the airport. In the rush I mislaid my inoculation certificate without which you could not leave the country. My embassy friend took me to a senior official at the airport health office and in return for 1000 rupiah I had a new book with all my 'shots' fully updated.

Once aboard the Malayan Airways Comet I needed a stiff gin and tonic to return my pulse rate to something like normal.

Liz and John Shaw met me at Singapore airport. It was good to see them. John had booked me into Raffles again. I was desperately tired. The strain of leading a double life for seven weeks had caught up with me.

I still had work to do in Northern Sumatra and was glad I had taken the precaution of getting a re-entry visa. I was not keen to return to Indonesia in the circumstances but working on my old African adage, 'always underestimate your enemy', and in this case being confident that the right hand knew little of what the left was doing, I reckoned I had a week before the central government could catch up with me.

From Singapore I flew to Penang before crossing the Maluccan Straits to Medan. I was met by an official from the U.S. Consulate who organised a car to take me the 100 miles south east to Kasaran. The road ran through miles of rubber plantations to the one owned by my host. I was ushered into my room where a young, very pretty Javanese girl asked me, 'You like geen and toenick?'

'Thank you,' I happily answered in the sweltering heat.

'You like one or three ices?'

'Three please.'

Sri left the room. She had laid out a clean set of white cotton clothes on my bed. In moments she was back with a long glass dripping from condensation and topped up with a large slice of lemon.

'Please to sit down.'

Sri sat down beside me on the bed as I sipped my drink. She unbuttoned my sweaty shirt and took it off.

Living Dangerously

'You stand up.'

She unzipped my trousers and removed them together with my underpants and led me to the shower. Under the refreshingly cool water she washed me down; not a part of my body escaped the soft touch of her small, delicate hands.

It was a hectic party that night at a neighbouring plantation and when we returned to the house in the early hours of the morning, Sri was in my bed. She immediately got up and left the room only to return a minute later with a glass of G & T and three pieces of ice.

She undressed me and I slipped under the single sheet. Sri loosened a button at her slender neck and her short white nightdress fell to the floor.

I understood then why the Dutch gave up Indonesia only after a fierce struggle.

Kim Tung of the Intara news agency and TS in Djakarta.

Indonesia, May 1963: President Soekarno delivers a passionate speech

April 1963: Mount Agung erupting, causing thousands of deaths

Bali, Indonesia, April 1963.

Djakarta slums.

Living Dangerously 169

CHAPTER XVIII

Gorillas and Mount Kiliminjaro

I returned westwards to New York via Tokyo, allowing time to wallow in the strong surf on Waikiki Beach in Honolulu. Imagine my excitement when I walked into the Warwick Hotel in New York to find LIFE had flown Lesley across the Atlantic without even telling me. We had a fabulous reunion after so many months apart, though I had to wade through 5000 Indonesian pictures with Peggy Sargent and Barbara Brewster in the LIFE office.

Our New York visit was abruptly cut short when George Hunt, the managing editor, sent Lesley and me south to Miami for a 'cloak and dagger' story into Cuba. We were booked in to the luxurious Key Biscayne Hotel.

At the Jolly Bar on the outskirts of Miami I met two of the principal characters involved in our adventure. Johnny Martino was a real life Mafia figure. He wore dark glasses, had a cigarette permanently hanging out of the corner of his mouth, with a long ash curling down and dropping on to his jacket. He had spent three years in Cuba and knew it well. Little, tough, curly-haired Eddie Bayo was to lead the team of ten men into Cuba. He had been there several times on clandestine operations. Johnny outlined the plan: 'Two Russian officers, involved with missiles, have defected to our guerillas and it is your job to go in and bring them back here.'

At midnight on Friday 7 June 1963 our party was taken to a remote corner of Miami airport used by the C.I.A. where we were locked into a central compartment of one of their PBY amphibian planes. After an eight-hour flight, we landed on the sea off the southeast tip of Cuba where we transferred into two rubber dinghies. The weather was breaking and a violent squall blew up. Waves crashed over our boats and I had my time occupied trying to keep cameras and film dry. Things looked serious when the other dinghy sprang a leak and started to deflate. We secured it alongside us as a ship loomed up out of the storm and took us in tow. It was the C.I.A. raider ship, the Rex, which had been sent to our rescue by the PBY.

We landed on a small island and dried out. By nightfall the Flying Tiger II had found us and we went aboard. There were three C.I.A. agents on the boat, including Rip Robertson, if that was his real name, whom I was to meet on another bizarre C.I.A. Cuban operation in the Congo 18 months later. The agents were not at all keen to see me, being British, on such an operation. Guns and ammunition littered the boat.

The next night we sailed for Cuba, making landfall at midnight. We had only one scare, when we narrowly missed a Cuban gun boat on patrol. We cut our engines and let them pass across our bows. We had a 20mm anti-tank gun for such an encounter but I was glad we did not have to use it. We could have come off worst.

We reached our despatch point a mile off the coast and again switched off our engines to listen...

We were satisfied we had not been spotted. Guns, ammunition and equipment were loaded into a rubber dinghy and the ten Cubans jumped in. I photographed all this using infra-red equipment. At that moment it was decided I did not look Cuban so could not accompany them, a decision I was not altogether unhappy about.

We wished them luck as they rowed away quietly into the night. When they were well clear we started engines and headed slowly back out to sea. We hove to near an atoll 100 miles east of Cuba. We returned each night to the agreed rendezvous and hung around for a couple of hours but they never appeared.

We were getting worried about our own safety and the atmosphere on the Tiger II became increasingly tense. Finally, on the third day, another PBY landed beside us. They told us that despite intensive searches they had not been able to locate our boys and that the search had been called off. We were to return without them to Miami. I had been allowed to photograph freely on condition that the film was handed over to the C.I.A. for processing and editing.

I heard many years later that all ten of our Cubans had disappeared. There were theories that they had been captured on landing and, because of the sensitivity of the Russian missiles in Cuba at the time, their deaths had been covered up. In addition, it was rumoured that they never reached the shore from the Flying Tiger II but I could not agree with this.

I filed 20,000 words on Indonesia before I was back in Kenya in July to work on a major LIFE essay on primates. We had to mount a major operation to photograph gorillas in the Congo. Tony Irwin had my Landrover overhauled before George Schaller arrived. George had already spent a year with gorillas and was the world's leading zoologist on these intriguing beasts. Gorillas were one of the few species of wild animals that frightened me. Blood-curdling tales had been woven around these near human creatures. Anything I could do, they could do better. I could visualise no escape if they attacked me. George assured me otherwise. In the crowded Long Bar of the New Stanley Hotel, this normally serious American suddenly bent over, raised his arse towards us and looking back said, 'If attacked, this is all you have to do. It is an act of submission they understand.' He was serious. I could see myself doing that in the face of a 400 lb charging male gorilla!

It was August 1963 when we started the 10,000 feet climb to Kabara in the Virunga Volcanoes lying to the north east of the Congo bordering Rwanda. The Congo troubles were still much in evidence with hostile bands on the rampage so we took an armed guard with us. From Kabara we spent several days breathlessly lugging heavy camera equipment up to 13,000 feet as George followed gorilla spoor. At dawn one morning our efforts were rewarded. For four and a half hours we sat up a tree in the thick forest and watched a troop of 14 gorillas a mere 40 feet from us. They performed like any human family might. Mothers lifted their babies admiringly before showing them to others while the magnificent male stood erect beating his chest as he let out a chilling roar. George assured me later that this was not intimidation but a release of tension.

We took the first-ever colour pictures of gorillas truly in the wild and were to photograph several other troops in the days that followed. We watched the boys and girls engaged in love-play while the younger males openly played with themselves. I must say that after watching gorilla family life in the wild and seeing them enacting so many of the dubious habits I had long been ashamed of, I left the Virungas feeling very normal.

Back in Nairobi I received a cable to go south to climb Mount Kilimanjaro with Stewart Udall, then the U.S. Secretary of State.

We set course from Marengu in Tanganyika on the slopes of Kilimanjaro with five guides, 20 Chagga porters and Otis Imboden of *National Geographic* magazine. We covered 16 miles on the first day to Peter's hut at 12,000 feet and another 11 miles the following day, taking us up 15,000 feet to Kibo. So far it had been a foot slog, mile after mile through stunning scenery along a well-worn track but it was tough going for Udall and Otis. I felt rather smug as, after the Virungas, I was fit and enjoying every step. However, at Kibo the nights were bitterly cold and for two nights we were unable to sleep, suffering from headaches seeming to blow our brains inside out. The lack of oxygen was telling on us.

We left Kibo soon after midnight on Friday the 13th of September and I now found the climb exhausting. I dared not think what Udall and Imboden were suffering as we slowly plodded ever upwards. Though Otis and I had porters carrying our equipment, the final 1500 feet to the summit must rank amongst the most Herculean tasks of my life. Loose gravel scree covered a 60° slope. One agonising step upwards seemed to result in two slides backwards. We were able to make about ten paces before having to lie down for three or four minutes to recover our breath. It became a mental battle trying to decide whether it was less tiring to move one foot ahead of the other or to lie down knowing that somehow you would have to get back on your feet again. On one of these many rests Otis turned slowly to me and whispered, 'Why the hell are we doing this?'

'Because we are being paid.' I answered.

'No,' he blurted out, 'I've come to get a picture of LIFE photographer Terence Spencer unconscious on Kilimanjaro'.

'That's funny,' I retorted, 'I thought that about you and I have my caption written already – Mr. Otis regrets…' (after Elisabeth Welch s famous song). Neither of us laughed; it was too much effort.

Living Dangerously

Three hundred feet from the crater Udall passed out. With the towering glacier just above and after what we had gone through, I knew we must make the summit. Without Stewart there was no story. With the guts and will power I am sure even Stewart did not know he possessed, and with the help of two guides, he made the crater at Gilman's Point. But this was not the actual summit.

The Tanganyikan government had assigned 28 year-old Captain Mirisho Sarakikya, who had made the climb on several previous occasions, to lead our expedition but, at Gilman's Point he was obviously in a bad way and had to lie down. Emmanuel, his No. 2, led us around the crater to Uhuru Point at 19340 feet. To be amongst those tall glaciers almost on the equator and to experience the aerial view across Tanganyika to Mount Kenya to the north is a memory I shall long cherish. For a few moments I even forgot my nauseating sickness and excruciating headache, only alleviated a little when I was violently sick.

I had to force myself to take the summit picture, by which time Udall looked the fittest of us all.

Back at Gilman's Point it was obvious that Sarakikya was now in a serious condition. The others descended for help and with two guides I remained with him, but after 45 minutes I noticed his eyes had started to glaze over and he was dying. It was impossible to lift his body at that altitude and the first part of the descent was over rock. We had no alternative but to drag him down like a sack of potatoes. Fortunately, he felt nothing. Once on the scree it was like a fast toboggan ride.

We met the stretcher party above Kibo and they rushed him down to Peter's hut where he regained consciousness eight hours later and where we spent the night. Returning to Marengu the next morning, we were garlanded with the small 'everlasting' flowers of Kilimanjaro. In three and a half days we had walked some 60 miles apart from the actual climb itself and almost without sleep.

Then I travelled from Kenya to Nigeria where I had a story to do on the Sultan of Kano and only mention this because of the crazy cable I received from New York, 'WANT SULTAN LAZING ON

ANIMAL SKIN COUCH WATCHING MOVIE STOP ALSO WHAT CHANCES OF SAME IN HAREM?'

I cabled back: 'SULTAN IS MOST RELIGIOUS LEADER AND LIVES IN REASONABLY AUSTERE CIRCUMSTANCES STOP ONLY WOMAN PHOTOGRAPHER CAN ENTER HAREM OR POSSIBLY EUNUCH STOP NOT EVEN FOR LIFE MAGAZINE AM EYE PREPARED MAKE SACRIFICE NECESSARY FOR LATTER BEST SPENCER'.

TS and US Secretary of the Environment, Stuart Udall are 'crowned' after reaching the summit of Mount Kilimanjaro.

Cuban Raid, June 1963 on our Atoll off Cuba.

Cuban raid, June 1963. Landing our Cuban exiles into a rubber dinghy close to the island of Cuba. Shot by infra-red film.

CHAPTER XIX

The Beatles

I returned to England at the end of October having been away for most of 1963 and on almost continuous assignment for a year. I was overtired and did not react too favourably when my daughter, Cara, greeted me, 'Dad, you must do a story on the " fab" Beatles.'

'The Beatles? Ugh!' I uttered in horror. 'What next?' I little suspected then the phenomenon they were to become.

Bob Ajemian, still my boss in Paris, flew to London in November to have lunch with us in Rules where I tried to 'sell' him the Beatles story. At that time they had a few numbers at the top of the charts but were little known in the United States. Rather unwillingly, New York gave us the go ahead for a 'spread' (two pages). With Frank Allen who was the LIFE driver and lighting expert on the bureau, we set course for Bournemouth where the Beatles were performing at the Winter Gardens. We had been unable to contact their press agent, even if they had one in those early days. Anyway, we decided to go along and introduce ourselves.

Ringo Starr thought he had seen a copy of LIFE at the dentist. 'Something like Melody Maker, isn't it?' The other three had never heard of the magazine which did not help our entrée.

The scenes we witnessed that night left us in no doubt that we were experiencing a phenomenon. Even the music, which we did not understand, was electrifying, shattering, unbelievable – but it was clean and happy.

As the curtain went up, four glossily-clean and spruce long-haired boys dressed in black with high buttoned collarless jackets, stood on the stage. Two thousand kids, mostly girls aged between 12 and 17, let out frantic shrill screams such as I had only heard in wild African tribal ceremonies. As Ringo hotted up the drum beat and John Lennon, George Harrison and Paul McCartney pounded out their guitars, so the decibel rating mounted and blared out from gigantic loud speakers. Despite the deafening crescendo, the music could barely be heard above the orgiastic, ear-splitting screams. If it was humanly possible the screams became even more intense as the Beatles hit the high notes of 'She loves me. Yeah, Yeah, Yeah.'

Frank Allen and I had often to work close to the speakers and felt we would be permanently deafened. I had brought back powerful quartz iodine hand lights from New York. Somehow Frank managed to plug them in to mains points and follow me into the holocaust of screaming girls. The strong light sent the kids into wilder gyrations of passion and exhibitionism. Great for pictures.

Police lined the front of the stage to prevent the audience storming it. As a young girl leapt out of her seat, a burly cop went up and whispered something in her ear. She passively limped back to her seat in tears.

'What did you say that made her sit down so promptly?' I asked the 'bobby'.

'I didn't say nothing. I just trod on 'er bleedin' foot!'

The theatre foyer at the interval looked like a makeshift field hospital with small, over made-up girls slumped in lines as St. John's Ambulance men knelt over their sobbing, shaking bodies, trying to revive them.

After the show the Beatles escaped from the theatre in a police van. We tracked them down to a quiet Bournemouth hotel where they were staying, but they would not see us. We hung around outside most of the next morning, then tailed their Austin Princess car as they headed north towards Coventry. They stopped at a truck drivers café. 'If you are that persistent, you had better join us for lunch and we will talk,' they told us.

We needed more than talk and subjected them to a form of journalism they never knew existed. They understood nothing about the demands the media were to make on them in the years to come and which would change their life styles.

Over the next month we rode with them in their cars while they tried out many of their great hits. We ate with them in small wayside cafés, safe from their fans, and we followed them to recording studios. I photographed their every move, both in their dressing rooms and on stage. Eventually I became part of the scene and they hardly noticed my presence.

These young Liverpudlians were fun in those early days. The zany Ringo chirped back at reporters when asked why he wore four rings on his fingers, 'Because I can't get them all through my nose.' Ringo was the jester and the lark. John Lennon was more serious and generally considered leader of the group. He had a quick and witty answer to questions and was not bothered with class. At his first Royal Variety performance in London before the traditionally glittering, formal audience, John stepped up to the microphone and announced in his lilting Liverpool accent, 'Those in the cheaper seats please clap. The rest of you rattle your jewellery!'

George was the quietest and I thought the nicest of the group. Paul had an angelic face and with John wrote the songs. His young female fans loved him.

By the end of 1963 the Beatles had set a cult throughout England – Beatlemania.

While we were with the Beatles in Coventry I asked them to record a message on my tape recorder to my daughter, Cara, who had originally suggested the story. They spoke to Cara at length, 'We've been boogered around by yer 'ole man.' The rest was punctuated by four letter words which flowed naturally to them. Each then sang a verse of their favourite number and ad-libbed words for Cara.

Lesley was a little dubious about giving it to Cara, although she would have heard the vernacular before, but the tape was such a unique souvenir at the time that we handed it over. Cara played it on top of the bus going to school while the conductress came over to listen and forgot to charge her the fare. She played it clandestinely at her school where it became a listening 'must' for most of the 600 girls. A few months later I was taping a long cable over the telephone from Paris and left the machine on 'record'. Cara played it later for the umpteenth time – and erased the tape! She cried for days over this terrible loss.

A few days later at the Apollo Theatre in Manchester which seated 2000 people, there was pandemonium in the auditorium even before the curtain went up. So Frank and I used the disturbance to erect four large Ascor 600 strobes capable of lighting the entire theatre and recording the wild scenes during the performance. The management thought that Frank, up the ladder erecting the lights on either side of the stage, was a Beatles engineer.

The screams, the swoons, the antics and the deafening noise were now familiar to us as was the foyer, again looking like a field hospital. I had no problem walking around the stage during the performance with a long lead attached to the strobes and 'shooting' the Beatles on stage with the audience in the background. People just thought I was part of this incredible spectacle.

I was to spend four months on and off with the Beatles and shot 5,000 pictures. They went on to fame and fortune and we went on to other stories.

'The Beatles as never seen before'.

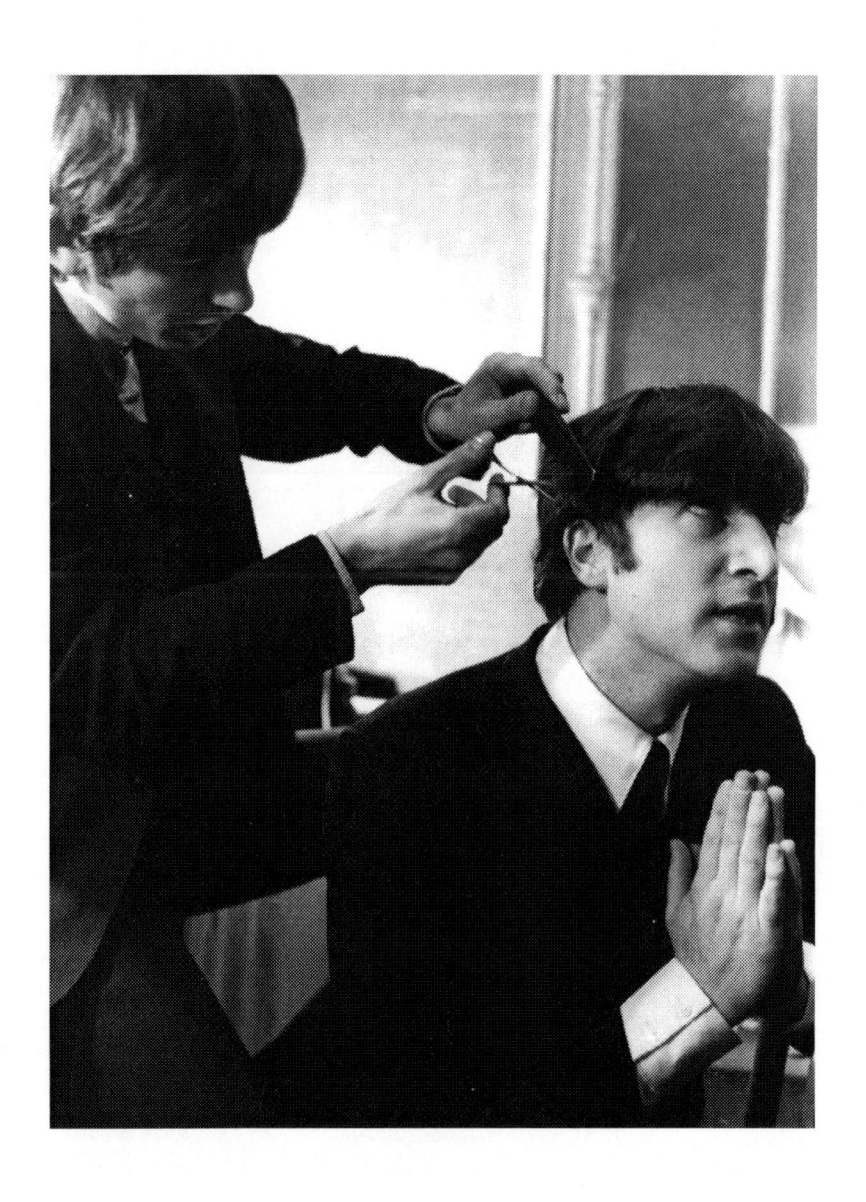

*John Lennon says his prayers while George cuts his hair.
Sadly, these two are not with us any more.*

Living Dangerously

Beatlemania, December 1963.
Girls go crazy during a concert in Manchester.

Brian Epstein with The Beatles.

CHAPTER XX

Lesley's return to England

Chiswick Village here I come! It is difficult to describe how I felt about being back in England. Just the ordinary everyday experience of living the way I had been used to before going to South Africa was balm to my soul. No hermit or recluse would ever understand the pleasure I derived from the lights of the Chiswick flyover shining in my kitchen window at night time. I never once regretted exchanging life on a High Veld farm for the continuous hum of London traffic.

It may seem as if we had had no family life at all, with Terry away so much on assignments – however, this was not altogether the case. It was perhaps worse in Africa where we had difficulty making any plans for entertaining though we had numerous barbecues and tennis parties involving numbers of friends and acquaintances.

We came back to live in England in 1962. My mother had found us a house in Chiswick Village with separate floors above for paying tenants – a useful income. She bought the house next door, ensuring good company for me.

My father when he died had left me the princely sum of £400. I had the bright idea of buying a caravan trailer so when we stayed with friends we could be exempt from offering to help with the washing up! However, Terry had different ideas and the money went instead to buying Careana. This was a 21 foot sloop which we were able from time to time to park on the courtyard of our Edwardian house. Sometimes we towed it to Pangbourne and launched it on the Thames. Here we would have parties on board and drive it rather than sail it.

Our furniture, such as it was, arrived in due course and once the alterations were made to the house, we became comfortably settled. Not Terry, of course. He was soon off to Kenya, the Seychelle Islands, Indonesia, the Radfan war and whaling in the Azores. Once a call came from New York just as we were going out to dinner, telling him to leave in the morning for Vietnam. We little thought the

Living Dangerously 183

assignment would drag on and on, reminiscent of those awful Congo days and that we would not see him home for six months.

When this trip came to an end LIFE demanded his presence in New York. They gave me a ticket, so at last I visited the metropolis housing the greatest of glossy magazines – to grace the cover of which was the secret dream of every publicity-minded actor and actress. They had looked after my husband enormously well, financially, and only expected his soul in return.

Plans were made for me to join Terry on his arrival in the U.S.A. and I was fortunate in finding a good, long suffering friend, Melanie, to move in with the children.

My brother Roderick was working for the British Motor Corporation as it was then, and we eventually stayed with him in his delightful New York apartment overlooking the Hudson River and the George Washington bridge.

It is no good pretending my first visit to America was a success. I just could not get acclimatized to the pace.

We did not have long after Terry's arrival back from Japan to enjoy ourselves before the office sent us both down to Miami. Here I was left on my own in a luxury hotel in Key Biscayne while an abortive Cuban landing was attempted. I may seem ungrateful but frankly I would rather be at home with the chores than alone in foreign parts, however sumptuous the surroundings.

When Raina was five years old she and I accompanied Terry on a wild-life story in East Africa. We covered 4,000 miles in a hot uncomfortable Landrover but, since our five year old refused to grumble, how could we? She sat in the back on top of our luggage, cameras and blankets, where she created, I am sure, some small world of her own. She once overheard me boasting how good she had been and confessed in a whisper that she had really rather enjoyed it.

While Terry and George Schaller sought out their gorillas in the Virunga Volcanoes, Raina and I would sit by the Landrover with our picnic lunch quite oblivious to the danger from elephants and other wild animals which we only learnt about later.

We spent a memorable night in the Murchison Falls game park. Our little rondavel was some way from the main building. We put Raina to bed with misgivings and went over to the restaurant for dinner. Half way through the meal who should appear but our small daughter! Walking back to the rondavel after dinner we noticed huge imprints in the turf where a herd of elephant had passed through the camp. What if she had been confronted by an elephant on her lonely trek in the dark?

Next day she and I took a trip down the Nile on a tourist launch. There were dozens of crocodiles on the banks and slipping into the river, but sadly only a brief glimpse came out on my film when I showed it later. We drove through the game park on our own and came close to a herd of elephants. The rather amusing sign posts stated that 'Elephants have right of way'. It was certainly awe-inspiring.

For three weeks on end Terry and George disappeared into the forests photographing gorillas. Raina and I were left in a comfortable modern hotel in the Mountains of the Moon, a long way from Kampala in Uganda. But what to do? We walked on the golf course. The library was inadequate. I am ashamed to say I was bored to tears. How did our friends keep their sanity on Robben Island?

When my mother died there seemed no reason to stay on in Chiswick. Coupled with that, our XV century cottage in Berkshire had been ruined when six huge pylons were erected, virtually obliterating our lovely view across the valley. What we now wanted was a house in a country town combining the advantages of Chiswick with the charm of the cottage. We were away in Austria with Terry working on the film *Chitty Chitty Bang Bang* when we heard there was a house for sale in Windsor. I could not believe our luck! I had walked along Kings Road and knew those elegant Georgian houses. I can say now it was the loveliest house we have ever lived in and at the last count, that is twelve! But it was even harder to believe that we could ever sell it. It seemed a crime but airport noise from nearby Heathrow nearly drove Terry out of his mind.

From suburban London where we lived for three years we would escape to the west coast of Ireland. The film *Ryan's Daughter* led us there and we built a house on an inland creek that was magical.

So now for our holidays, it was not Florida nor Lourenço Marques or Kenya or Basutoland but Lowertown, Schull in County Cork set beneath Mount Gabriel. We would stop the car as we arrived in the summer so that Freddie, our Boston Terrier, could have his usual run along the farm road; in the spring the tides often cut us off for two or three hours in the day. Perhaps we would meet Jackie Daley, our neighbour, with his horse and cart on their way to the creamery.

The swans are back, Heliose and Abelard, nesting on the little island. The heron, which we christened Pompidou, is there in his usual place and Raina's piebald pony is grazing in the old meadow. Across the water is Jamesy O'Regan, the fisherman in his little white cottage where he has brought up eleven children, and beside it the farm and imposing old house in the trees, somehow reminiscient of a Brontë story. Here in the evenings we would watch the cattle walk in single file along the edge of the creek and then we might see Jamesy bringing in his catch from his small boat or from his lobster pots. The pace is slow, the people friendly and just sometimes we could understand, our immediate neighbour, Jackie Daley s broad dialect. On we would drive past the honeysuckle and fuschia hedges up the drive bordered by escalonia and red pillar roses to Seanacluian.

We eventually decided to ship Careana to Ireland where it was docked in our little harbour next to the Shamrock. This old wreck had a sad history. Some years before two brothers were out on her fishing when they had a fight. One of them fell overboard and was drowned. The boat was never taken out again and nobody went near it. The remains are still there today.

It was quite a challenge for little Careana to take part in regattas. On one such occasion at Baltimore, as was my wont, I chose to drive over there with the necessary supplies (i.e. gin and whiskey) and watch for its arrival. It was blowing half a gale and I was standing on the jetty a long time before I saw a little red sail struggling round the distant point. When Terry and my brother, Rod, finally made the mooring I had to break the news that the regatta had been cancelled and everyone was in the pub!!

After LIFE magazine folded Terry came off news and when Time Life became Time Warner, a lot of the old enthusiasm was lost to a more commercial world. We decided reluctantly to part with our house in Ireland as our girls were growing up and had other ideas for their summer holidays. It also seemed a pity to leave England at its best time weatherwise. The alternative in this case was Spain.

The delightful Ard na Greine hotel in Schull was run by Charles Rogers and Harry Medhurst who lived in Southern Spain from October until April during which time the hotel was closed for the winter. How wise, we thought, so in due course we bought a pleasant little villa just outside Nerja on the coast. Here we escaped the English winters for some three months each year. Alas, the area sadly changed and grew and grew with hotels and pueblos everywhere. The beautiful countryside became enveloped in plastic under which the locals grew fruit and vegetables.

Again we were on the move and followed Charles and Harry 3000 feet up into the Sierras some hundred miles north of Granada where they had a charming little cottage. They subsequently found one for us almost next door.

Seanachuian.

CHAPTER XXI

The Pope's Middle East tour and war in Cyprus

In January 1964 I was off to cover the Pope's tour of the Middle East. My first task was to get a second passport to visit Israel, otherwise with an Israeli stamp in my original passport, entry into most Arab states would not have been allowed.

Most of the LIFE team of 18 under Hugh Moffet, who had taken over the Paris bureau from Bob Ajemian, were already in Jordanian Jerusalem. In an endeavour to control the 1,800 men and women of the world's media who were there, the Jordanian Information Department held meetings to allocate press tickets for the various functions. Hugh Moffet and Lee Hall had never ending arguments over our photo positions. *Paris Match* had a team twice the size of ours, with 20 photographers and 37 others. They had rigged up their own Caravelle jet aircraft as a laboratory and planned to fly daily 'takes' to Paris with the film being processed en route. It was alleged that they had paid large sums of money for certain privileged camera positions. They certainly seemed to be getting preferential treatment. Maybe we were just jealous. It was rare for LIFE to be outbid by Paris Match.

Before the Pope arrived we had time to see the exciting places we knew only from the Bible: the Holy Sepulchre, the Garden of Gethsemene and the Mount of Olives. Here an Arab guide pointed out an indentation in a large stone and remarked that it was the foot print of our Lord as he ascended into Heaven.

'Jesus Christ!' a colleague blasphemously remarked in disbelief.

'Yes,' answered the little man.

We strolled through the ancient, narrow streets of the old city and were horrified at the commercialism and prostitution of religion. Pieces of wood were being sold 'From the original cross'. Judging by the amount being sold, the cross must have weighed several thousand tons. With the shambles and disrespect witnessed over the next three days, it was difficult to experience any form of religious excitement.

After a press conference in Jerusalem given by the young, pleasant and jovial King Hussein wearing a smart army uniform, we visited the lowest spot on earth, the Dead Sea, 1,292 feet below sea level.

The Pope arrived on Saturday, January 4. We drove the 60 miles to Amman to meet him at the airport and on his return he stopped at the Jordan River to dip his hand in the water. What should have been a touching scene was ruined by an Italian R.A.I. television cameraman holding his large camera a few feet from the Pope's nose for every step he took. Any other vacant spots were filled by paparazzi photographers. They acted with total disregard for the rest of the media. Okay, if that was the way they wanted to play the game, we would play it their way. Fighting broke out between photographers and cameramen around the Pope and this was the pattern of the coverage over the whole tour. As these cameramen walked backwards in front of the Pope a sharp kick on their ankles sent them reeling. T.V. men who behave this way can be dealt with. They are restricted with their umbilical cords attached to battery packs and sound recordists. Heads in front of their lenses and unspeakable vernacular shouted into their microphones make life difficult for them. One colleague carried a pair of wire cutters and simply snipped their battery cables.

Outside the Damascus Gate the army had to disperse the mob, mostly cameramen, by bringing in armoured troop carriers and machine guns. After being hit across the back by a police swish and seeing soldiers using rifle butts on their fellow Arabs, I moved to an overall position and set up a camera on a tripod for dusk colour shots. A burly R.A.I. man spotting my situation planted himself firmly in front of me but, by now, I was carrying a lead weighted cosh for just such an occasion. I only had to threaten him with it and he knew I meant business. Moffet had also organised personal bodyguards to help us maintain our sites and take our exposed film to waiting motor cyclists. That evening people and the media fought to get in to the Basilica. They banged on the closed doors and shouted obscenities. Inside it was so jam-packed that a pygmy could not have squeezed in.

Photographers were clinging perilously to windows trying to shoot at slow shutter speeds in the dim light, using only one hand. As usual the R.A.I. men surrounded the Pope even at the altar and blinded the rest of the media with their lights. I had a commanding position up a tall ladder, high above the congregation, until the surging mob knocked the base of the ladder and I came crashing down, my fall cushioned by people. One camera fell and hit a man on the head. He picked it up and apologised! I broke another during this incident. We were shooting in both black and white and in colour and I was carrying six cameras with different film and lenses.

At midnight on Sunday we crossed through the Mandelbaum Gate into Israel, the first time the border had been opened since the start of the Arab/Israeli troubles. We drove through the night to Tel Aviv and Nazareth and on up to the Sea of Galilee where again T.V. crews and photographers ruined an otherwise moving ceremony. Swarms of photographers plunged into the water ahead of the Pope who had left St. Peter's church to go down to the water's edge. Like the others I had to drop off my vantage point on a rock into the water up to my chest. I carried my gear high above my head struggling to get near the Pope. Arguments and foul language broke out with the tough monks who tried to protect the Pope.

When I returned to England to tell Lesley how I had jumped off my rock into the Sea of Galilee and got drenched, adding, 'That parable about walking on water is a fallacy,' she answered, 'Who do you think you are?'

Lesley and I decided we needed another 'honeymoon' at a romantic old pub, the Royal Oak at Yattendon in Berkshire. The inn was noted for its good food. We finished dinner when I was summoned to the telephone . It was Tim Green, our new London bureau chief.

'Terry, I have mixed good and bad news for you,' he said. 'New York plan to close the Beatles on Monday as a big lead and need more shots of them against typical Paris backgrounds where they are off to tomorrow. Can you meet me at London airport at 9 a.m. in the morning?'

Good news about the story but, oh dear! How to tell Lesley?

My gear was always ready in the boot of the car. We left the pub very early on Sunday morning, to the astonishment of the publican.

The Beatles were not happy when we asked them to accompany us to the Eiffel Tower and other well known spots in Paris but, in the end, they did cooperate.

The following morning back in England Lesley and I returned to Yattendon to continue our 'Lost Weekend'. This time we survived dinner but no sooner had we got into our big bed than there was a knock at the door.

'Sorry to disturb you, Mr. Spencer, but there is an urgent call from London for you.' It was Tim again. 'You're going to murder me! New York urgently want a cover and pictures of the Cavern in Liverpool where the Beatle story all started. We have two days to get the film into New York.'

I returned to bed for just an hour. We began to wonder, 'Was it all worth it?' Then we dressed, packed up and went down to pay the bill. The look received from the publican suggested we had either had a terrible row or were mad. 'We'll try again next weekend,' I said mournfully.

Tim and I caught the early morning train to Liverpool. The smokey Cavern reverberated with jazz even in the afternoon, so we had our pictures and returned to London to find the office had laid on an elaborate set at the Astoria in London where the Beatles were performing and had persuaded them to give us a few minutes before the show for our cover picture. They failed to turn up until minutes before the curtain was due up and made it impossible to shoot the cover material required.

Months later we received a 'blast' from the Beatle's press agent saying they would never again do anything for LIFE after they had given up their valuable time for a cover that never ran. Alas, many famous showbiz people treat the media as an intruding menace to be used at their convenience only. Where would most of them be without us? Unfortunately, showbiz is big business for magazines so we have to put up with this sort of behaviour, knowing that when it suits the stars they will be back for more. The Beatles were no exception.

The story closed as an eight-page lead and made it all worthwhile except that the Cavern and Paris pictures were never used... Alas, on the 17th August 1967 Brian Epstein, the Beatles' manager, died of an overdose of drugs in his bedroom in Chapel Street, Belgravia, London.

I flew back to Kenya at the end of January 1964, this time to cover the army mutiny. For five frightening days it looked as if the three newly formed East African governments would be wiped out in a wave of anarchy. A bloody revolt on Zanzibar had already toppled that regime. It looked like the Congo all over again except that this time the British forces took control.

Two weeks later I was back in London and had hardly entered the door of our house when the phone rang. It was Lee Hall from the Paris office, 'We want you to go to Ghana, leaving tomorrow morning with Hal Wingo.' I hopped on a taxi straight to the Ghanaian embassy and was being stone-walled whilst trying to get an immediate visa when the London office contacted me. 'Forget Ghana. New York now want you to go to Cyprus. Hal is flying over from New York. Join him at Heathrow for the Athens flight in the morning. We'll have your tickets.'

The foreign correspondent must be a professional traveller, always ready to move to the other end of the world at a moment's notice. Injections must be kept up to date along with a first aid kit. He often travels with morphine and a syringe in case he is wounded in remote places. He keeps check-lists of equipment, not forgetting lead bags to protect film from airport X-rays, and clothes for climates ranging from -35°C below freezing to tropical heat. He updates passports, documents and contact addresses, and maintains large stocks of travellers cheques, money, film and credit cards.

It is important to know plane schedules. He needs to know how to get on fully-booked flights at the last moment by trying airline press officers or, if that fails, buying someone off the flight and taking his ticket.

More trouble had broken out on that lovely Mediterranean island. Correspondents were rushing in from all parts of the world. One I bumped into on the tarmac at Athens was my old buddy, Don

Wise of the London *Daily Mirror*. He had decided to head for Ankara in anticipation of the Turkish invasion of the island. It is the sort of gamble a correspondent takes which, if it comes off, gives him a good scoop but if it does not, then a fast cable from his office asks, 'Why the hell…?'

It seemed almost impossible that any pressman could operate in Cyprus without the help of Savas. Savas was the concierge at the Ledra Palace Hotel in Nicosia. He seemed to know everyone who mattered on the island. When trouble broke out he knew immediately and would wake us up in the middle of the night, having already laid on a driver willing to take us to the trouble areas. He supervised our every need. No correspondent ever felt better covered than when in the hands of Savas. Not least, he was a good friend of the foreign press corps and received his rich reward accordingly.

Cyprus was the oddest war I ever covered. We photographers could raise a white handkerchief, hold our cameras high above our heads and walk across from Turkish-held positions to Greek strongholds and vice versa in reasonable safety. Nevertheless, it was an eerie experience, especially when wildly fired bullets were cracking past in all directions, ricocheting off masonry and throwing flying fragments into the air. I had long since learned that bullets can hurt and have to be treated with respect. The more inaccurate the firing, often the greater the danger. Mortars, too, are unpredictable, though they were not used when I was in Cyprus.

We had no problems entering the Turkish-held round-towered castle of St. Hilarion with its massive stone walls and a stupendous view of the island and the sea far below. The castle and the well armed, motley-clad, rough-looking irregulars looked more suited to a film set than real life killers.

We met Greek EOKA fighters in villages like Ayios Theodorous just off the Nicosia to Limmasol road and joined them behind the barricaded doors of their farms or houses. We watched these sturdy, weather-beaten men shooting it out across the village street with Turks who had been neighbours all their lives.

There was fear and uncertainty throughout the island. Our problems were navigating the long winding and lonely roads where a

B.B.C.T.V. crew and other correspondents had been fired on, killing one of them and wounding others. Night driving was even more hazardous.

Back in London I glanced at the weekly magazine contents and was horrified to see that I had no pictures in the big lead on the Cyprus war. That was bad news indeed. We struggle; we try; we experience the variety and uncertainty of life and often its dangers for one purpose and one purpose only: to see our pictures in print. Few of us were in this odd business for money alone.

I spent much of March and April working with Dorothy Bacon on an essay about British witches. The rituals were conducted in the nude. Photographing a beautiful body in the nude for a family magazine is a delicate enough business but paunchy, middle-aged men and women with drooping 'boobs' were a severe test of ingenuity. At times Dorothy was on her knees inches from our subject throwing deep shadows from a spotlight across vital parts. Witchcraft here was essentially the same as I had seen in South Africa and in New Guinea in that you had someone who 'rolled the bones', foretelling the future, the medicine men who healed and those who cast spells or practised 'black magic'.

Tim Green and I also fitted in a story on Shakespearian striptease at the Casino de Paris Club in London's Soho. They had Lady Macbeth stripping and Romeo and Juliet performing acts that could only have been envisaged in the mind of the great dramatist whose 400th anniversary was being commemorated. I shot the artistically produced show from the auditorium through rows of glistening bald heads.

Soon I was in Stockholm where the King of Sweden opened a new section of the subway underground system. In perfect English the King invited me to join him in the driver's cab. Working for LIFE gave one the privilege of hobnobbing with royalty and beggars, so much so that it was difficult to be impressed by the great or feel any particular reverence in their company. Often, the more famous, the more human they are.

I enjoyed working in England where I felt a sense of competition never experienced in Africa. There I had it all my own way. I had no illusions about my limitations in photographic techniques, especially in the art of lighting, which I seldom had to use in Africa where, I sometimes felt I was just an animal photographer: some had white skin, some black, and the rest fur.

It was pleasant working with writers and photographic assistants and having travel arrangements made for me by pretty secretaries instead of having to do everything myself. I never experienced the loneliness I felt in Africa or South East Asia. Work on the London bureau covered the spectrum of photography from topless dresses to copying priceless paintings; to wars and dreadful tragedies; to the setting up of complicated lighting jobs. I flew supersonic in the stratosphere and worked thousands of feet underground in coal mines and even dived a hundred feet under the sea, all in the pursuit of spectacular pictures!

Cyprus Civil War, Feb 1964. Out of his cave on the way to the attack.

Cyprus Civil War, Feb 1964. British troops find a dead body on the road.

CHAPTER XXII

The Radfan war in the Yemen

In May Lee Hall phoned me to say I was to go to the little war in the Yemen with Jordan Bonfante. Jordan and I were to do many stories together even before he became LIFE's London bureau chief. As with Rudy Chelminski, Jordan and I worked so closely together that we instinctively knew what the other was thinking and where and what we would do in an emergency. LIFE teams became almost a 'marriage'. Hardships and danger, frustrations and privations breed a lasting and deep friendship so that most of my best friends today were working colleagues. Journalism must be the last of the great comradeships. Few people work harder or play harder than foreign correspondents.

Trouble in the Yemen had started two years earlier when the feudal ruler was toppled in a coup backed by President Nasser. The Egyptians then poured in 40,000 troops armed with Russian weapons. Nasser also armed the Radfani to fight the British in the mountains to the south of the Yemen and block the Dhala road, the only lifeline to the south.

The very nature of this little war posed impossible problems for the media. The only safe way up the mountains was with the R.A.F. and, as always on this sort of operation, the British forces felt that the less they saw of the press the better. Furthermore, there were only a few helicopters and these were carrying water and ammunition to the front line troops and were certainly not going to transport unnecessary correspondents.

I discovered that the squadron operating the 'choppers' was 26 Squadron, one of my old wartime units, so Jordan and I had no trouble being picked up at Thumair by a banana-shaped Belvedere and lifted to Cape Badge high in the desolate Radfan mountains overlooking the sensational Wadi Thame, thousands of feet below. To our dismay we discovered that nearly all operations against the rebels occurred at night, thus offering little chance for pictures.

The Air Marshal commanding the R.A.F. in Aden was Johnny Johnson, the Allies' top scoring fighter pilot of the last war. I had been one of his squadron commanders. Johnny did not let me down!

We watched brave men going up into the mountains to parley with Radfani chiefs and we saw patrols of the elite Special Air Service going off on more clandestine operations but for me there were few pictures. So back to Aden we went, to the Crescent hotel. Many of my old buddies were in the bar that night, including Dick Beeston of the London *Daily Telegraph*, Peter Younghusband of the *Daily Mail* and George Clay of N.B.C. We had plenty of catching up to do over a lot of Scotch while they filled us in on the war.

Much as we enjoyed the next few days sunning and swimming in Tarshyne, it was not our reason for coming to Aden. Things were happening in the mountains and the army did not want us there. Furthermore, they were giving us 'bumsteers' or misleading information, but when determined members of the foreign press corps gather together in a bar and start swopping the snippets of information they have gleaned, the jigsaw starts falling into place. Someone will have a contact he can pursue. With information so gathered, a few innocuous questions posed to police or others can confirm or deny a story. It is almost impossible to hide the facts from the media. Their means of investigation are infinite and there is always the cheque book to help make people talk.

I had reason to believe there was going to be a daylight attack against the Radfani, so it was vital to get back up to Thumair in the mountains. By air was impossible at that moment so with Denis Neald and Brian Calvert of the Associated Press and Nuys Thomas of the *News of the World,* Jordan and I hired a clapped-out old Landrover and decided to make the drive on our own.

We laid in supplies and set course. After two hours of bumping along the first dried-up wadi (river bed) past the village of Sheik Othman, steam started rising through the bonnet. The radiator had almost fallen away. We had no tools but unwound a piece of wire which seemed to be holding the rear axle in position and secured the radiator.

We had no maps, and anyway one wadi looked much like another. We tried to follow vehicle tracks but many had been obliterated by wind and sand. The thought of taking the wrong wadi and ending up with our balls sewn inside our mouths, a favourite Radfani torture, was not encouraging. The possibility of mines and snipers along our route seemed mild in comparison, though the thought of an ambush did scare us.

We were unequipped to cover a war, other than having the water bottles we all carried. This was so often the case in our job. We usually had to leave at a moment s notice, possibly to the Arctic or the tropics, when preparations were impossible. The British army in the Radfan was not interested in our problems. In Vietnam the situation was different as we were able to buy the latest Special Forces equipment on the black market in Saigon. Aden had no such facility.

Luck was with us, as we were overtaken by an army convoy which allowed us to follow them. The heat and dust were unbearable. We looked like men who had been dragged through bins of flour. The dust forced its way into our ears, our teeth and every crevice of our bodies, and worse, into my cameras despite being wrapped in thick plastic bags. The track became even rougher as we climbed into the dark red satanic volcanic mountains before coming to an open scarred plain. Though barren, it was dramatic country.

We reached dirty, dusty, waterless Thumair in the evening and, having no bedding, played cards late into the night, in fact, until the table was rudely upset as we dived for cover when a machine gun opened up uncomfortably near our tent. Major Don Clarke remained in his chair and said with a chuckle, 'If I were a newsman I would have a good headline for this: "Fire stopped play!"'

Jordan and I hitched a ride in an army Landrover north to San'a where Arabs with large ugly knives in their belts and ancient rifles slung across their shoulders wandered through the colourful market. Camel trains brought in supplies to traders while men who looked more like smugglers and drug traffickers, lounged around narrow street corners. An army patrol took us across the border into the Yemen to visit a quaint turreted, gleaming white fort appearing like a scene out of Arabian Nights.

The following night we were back in Thumair. The desert gets surprisingly cold at night, especially when you have no bedding. We were bothered by sand flies and slept little.

At dawn I contacted a 26 Squadron pilot who agreed to smuggle me aboard his chopper and fly me up to the 3rd. Parachute battalion, the famous Red Devils. On arrival I met Colonel Tony Farrar-Hockley who commanded the Paras. He welcomed me and promised I would accompany the leading sections during the forthcoming daylight attack on rebel positions.

The Radfan was very much Lawrence of Arabia country with its Beau Geste forts and chieftains swathed in bandoleers loaded with cartridges. The Radfani had been fighting among themselves for hundreds of years. Their houses were forts and often connected to each other and to the main forts by underground tunnels. This made life difficult and hazardous for the Paras. The terrain had been converted into a natural fortress over the centuries. Now the Radfani were trying to overthrow British influence in Aden Province.

At dawn the following morning I set out with a section of a company detailed to descend the steep rock face into the wadi thousands of feet below. Though covered by the company remaining on top and by Hunter jets screaming overhead rocketing the forts and other pockets of resistance, we were still badly shot up by the deadly accurate fire of the Radfani. They used ancient flintlocks and muzzle-loaders dating back to the XIX century, but backed up by modern Russian automatic weapons. The Radfani are traditionally good marksmen. They have had plenty of practice.

The Wadi Ligne was perfect terrain for guerillas, but almost impossible for a modern army, even when the battle is being fought in the unorthodox fashion favoured by the Paras. We were probably the first white men ever to venture into this hostile country that has been under siege for centuries.

The Paras stormed the forts under heavy covering fire and brandished revolvers as they hurled grenades down the thick walled passages. Within minutes of leaving a fort the rebels returned and opened fire on us again. In one fort the company commander decided to leave two men behind to lie in wait and asked if I would like to stay with them. I could hardly refuse. For half an hour we lay silent. The slightest noise sent a chill down my spine but this time the rebels did not return.

The climb back up the rock face was arduous, but being in full view of the rebels we did it after dark. At times the dead and wounded had to be hauled up with ropes. I had only my cameras to carry whereas the Paras had heavy equipment, albeit little ammunition. I was 25 years older than these highly trained men and had been worried about keeping up with them but adrenalin urges one on in such circumstances. Rock or no rock, I slept soundly for the rest of the night.

Another dawn I was attached to a section of 'C' company which was going to make a frontal attack on one of these film-set forts. The action that followed was no make-believe skirmish. Once again we experienced the accurate fire of the Radfani. The steep rocky lands around the mountain had been contoured over the centuries for agriculture and held together by low stone walls about 18" high. We crawled along on our stomachs behind these walls and felt safe but when we reached gaps blown out by rockets we had to make a dash to the next wall. Within seconds the area was alive with bullets and flying splinters of rock. No film production could ever recreate the look in men's eyes or the action of their limbs as they raced for cover while bullets cracked around them.

In this operation I found the ideal way of getting these pictures. My section commander allowed me to race across the gaps ahead of his section. Even before I had completed the skid on my belly behind the safety of the next small wall, bullets were hitting the rocks around me. We waited a few minutes and then, one by one, the men of my section ran the gauntlet. Except for the flying pieces of rock I was reasonably safe and could concentrate on the faces and actions as each man dived for cover beside me.

Alas, my still camera could not record the noise or the smell of cordite, nor could I record the uncertainty we all felt. During such moments men seldom speak. It is only afterwards that one hears the

Living Dangerously

oaths and curses. Miraculously, no member of our section was hit, though the overall casualties of the battalion bore evidence to the accuracy of the Radfani marksmanship.

The midday temperature in the mountains soared to 120°F and was intensified by the reflection off the rocks. Men collapsed from heat exhaustion. Water was rationed to two pints of water a day for all purposes. I was permanently thirsty but realised the supply problems when told that one of our chopper pilots had made 48 flights in five hours.

In the afternoon a bullet pinged a few inches from my ear and smacked into our section radio set beside which I was cowering. I had brought my two small 'walky-talky' sets with me and left one at company headquarters so that I could be directed to a section engaged on an interesting operation. This became our only means of communication. I dreaded being ordered to leave one section for another, as it usually involved crossing uncertain terrain alone. On this occasion we made the frontal attack on the fort across open ground only to find we were unopposed. The jets had done their work and the defenders had fled. I still have an old hookah pipe I found in this fort.

That night Farrar-Hockley sent me on an ambush patrol. I went armed with infra-red film. We spent a cold, spooky night on the roof of a captured fort, alerted by every sound, but the rebels probably knew we were there and did not return. A chopper piloted by Lt. Colonel Ian Graham-Bell picked me up at dawn and inadvertently flew too low up the Wadi Misr. A machine gun opened up on us from a 'deserted' fort and bullets ripped through the flimsy structure. It was one of the few moments of my life when I would rather have been killed than taken prisoner.

We arrived back at headquarters on the mountain top during a service for those killed in action. As usual during my years with LIFE I refrained where possible from 'shooting' dead bodies as they contributed little to the story. I felt that on this occasion the very setting was dramatic and poignant and conjured up much that I wanted to show about this little war and its consequences for those involved. So I took a shot across a body laid out and covered with a groundsheet,

'Blimey, mate,' a voice blared out at me, 'Why do you want to take that sort of picture? What do you think his missus will feel when she sees it?' I explained to him, as I had done so many times in the past when attacked for intruding into personal tragedies, that the more these sort of pictures were shown, the closer it brought home the stark realism of what war is all about to people leading their safe and comfortable lives. Little did I suspect then the way it would be done in Vietnam a few months later.

At the end of the month I was sitting on the edge of an almost sheer drop of thousands of feet to the valley below as with a long telephoto lens I photographed rocket attacks on the forts below whilst jet after jet screamed a few feet above our heads. My orchestral accompaniment was my small transistor which was interrupted to announce that Nehru of India had died.

As far as I knew Jordan and I were the nearest LIFE team to New Delhi, so I bade a rapid 'goodbye' to my parachute friends and returned to Aden. Sure enough, there were urgent cables from New York and Paris, 'GO DELHI URGENTEST FOR NEHRU FUNERAL.'

At the airport Jordan was handed another cable, 'DO NOTNOT GO DELHI AS NOW PLANNING A RADFAN LEAD AND BURROWS EN ROUTE DELHI.' In fact, Nehru made the lead in the magazine that week and we were worried about our story. However, it ran eight pages in the following issue.

A month or so later I received an office memo from Tom Carmichael, a LIFE editor in New York, which read, 'I think the Radfan is the best story of its kind since Dave Duncan's Korean pictures. I plan to lay it out and enter it for the Missouri School of Journalism contest.' Dave's pictures concentrated on telling the horrors of war through the expression on men's faces, so I took Tom's memo as high praise. The story won second prize after Eddie Adam's immortal picture of the Saigon police chief shooting a young Viet Cong suspect in cold blood.

Jordan and I returned to London in time for the office party at the Derby and the hot summer of '64. For the next few years London was to become the swishiest, zazziest, naughtiest city in the world.

It almost outdid Las Vegas for gambling and certainly Paris for nudity. It was a new social trend which was to spread like a bush fire across the Atlantic to the United States. It was the youth revolution. The Mods and Rockers showed that it was also youth versus youth. Boys showed the girls who wore the 'plume feathers' and the girls retaliated with the mini skirt and even the topless dress. We were very much part of this scene.

About this time Hugh Moffet flew over from Paris. Hugh missed nothing. He saw an advertisement for the opening of London's first topless restaurant. 'Let's try it out, Terry.'

This was fun, not business. We descended the steps of the restaurant in Soho and standing coyly by the door was a young girl holding a brass tray under her ample naked bosom

'Are they on today's menu?' Hugh enquired with a glint in his eye!

Topless dress fashion, June 1964: a sixties fashion. Two girls see themselves in the dress from a shop dummy in London's Oxford street.

204   *Living Dangerously*

Kathie Keaton checks her dress in the mirror

LIFE's Tim Green looks on somewhat aghast at the dummy.

Living Dangerously

Radfan War, May 1964. Service for a dead paratrooper seen covered in foreground.

Radfani tribesmen, May 1964.

CHAPTER XXIII

The Vietnam war

In November 1964, New York contacted me in a restaurant 30 miles out of London, 'We are planning a big lead on Vietnam. Can you possibly leave in the morning? It's very urgent.'

I was becoming inured to the casual cable or telephone call sending me to the other end of the world at a moment's notice where, often for long periods, I would be called upon to witness tragedies, blood, killings, executions and men behaving in utterly degrading ways. But crises were our way of life and it surprises me on reflection how calmly we came to accept these instructions. For Lesley it was different. I was on duty 365 days a year. Even on our holiday on one occasion I was contacted with a cable saying, 'HATE TO DO THIS TO YOU BUT COULD YOU GET DOWN TO SOUTH AFRICA SOONEST?' It did not make for an easy social or domestic life. It is tough on a woman.

It was good to be back in South East Asia. Air Vietnam flew Jordan Bonfante and me to Phnom Penh in Cambodia before the final half hour flight into Saigon. John Flynn from LIFE met us at Tan Son Nhu airport and took us into Saigon in a rattle-trap old taxi where we checked in to the Caravelle Hotel, the headquarters of the growing foreign press corps in Vietnam. We had quite a party that night with the *Time* & LIFE teams, comprising Bob Morse, Larry Burrows, Marshall Smith and John Shaw, after a dinner aboard the floating Chinese restaurant on the Saigon River.

Horst Faas was now based in Saigon for the Associated Press and took me into the black market where I kitted myself out with the latest Special Forces equipment, including jungle boots fitted with steel linings as protection against spiked booby traps. Vietnam was the only war I covered where I was properly equipped. In Saigon as in the Congo, there was a flourishing black market in currency where dollars or, better still, travellers cheques could be exchanged for nearly double the going rate of 73 piastres to the dollar.

We later met Lee Hall at the airport accompanied by two more photographers, John Loengard and Henri Daumon. LIFE now had four teams in Vietnam. Larry was to cover the Special Forces, John the Junk fleet, Henri the Buddhists and I was to cover the 'Quiet War'. This was the covert war being waged south in the Mekong Delta to win the hearts of the peasants in that Viet Cong stronghold.

The man we were to work with was Rob Warne, a 27-year-old ex-army officer working for the U.S. Operations Mission (U.S.O.M.). He was well built with a mop of dark brown hair and wore horn-rimmed spectacles. He chain-smoked for reasons I was soon to discover. His pretty wife, Susie, and young daughter lived with him in Phu Vinh some 60 miles south of Saigon.

John Flynn and I flew in to Phu Vinh by helicopter and as I jumped out, carrying two heavy camera bags and my kit, I knocked out the bottom vertebra of my spine. I lay on the ground writhing in agony until taken on a stretcher to a filthy Vietnamese hospital and X-rayed to the accompaniment of bats, lizards and mosquitos. What a way to start a story!

The army press information office immediately despatched another chopper to take me back to Saigon where I was left lying in the lobby of the Caravelle Hotel for most of the afternoon, putting up with the jibes of my colleagues as they went in and out. That night I was taken to the naval hospital where everything was spick and span. Stainless steel shone from every corner and American nurses in freshly laundered uniforms moved cheerfully about the airy wards. Quite a change from Phu Vinh.

However, Naval doctors straightened me out and had me back in room 802 at the Caravelle in four days. I could walk but only with great difficulty. It did not prevent me struggling across the square to Brodards where Horst and I enjoyed a lobster lunch for less than a dollar. I also managed to reach the Romeo and Juliet bar on top of the Caravelle.

I spent the next two weeks with Rob Warne in the Delta suffering hell with my back as I could neither lie down, stand up nor sit down for more than short periods at a time. I was in a sorry state for this assignment.

Our first trip was to take much needed supplies to My Long. The V.C. (Viet Cong) had cut the road and our only way was by water. We sailed down the narrow Tra Vinh canal in a landing craft (L.S.T.) of the Junk Fleet and out into the wider Co-Chien River, both sides of which were held by the V.C. The countryside was open and flat and not ideal for guerillas except that the V.C. were well dug in and in small groups. We travelled by night and the superior fire power of our Vietnamese marines soon silenced the few attempts made to fire on our boat.

As dawn broke the following morning we sighted My Long and made our way slowly past fishermen in primitive craft. My Long must once have been an attractive fishing village with its palm trees lining the beach, but now it showed every sign of decay and poverty. Sweating villagers plodded out to our boat through the mud and lugged heavy bags of flour, sugar and salt and four gallon cans of cooking oil back to their village. They seemed to have plenty of rice, fruit and vegetables. They were poor but I never saw the poverty in Vietnam that I had seen in Africa.

Back in Phu Vinh the next day John Flynn announced he had stomach trouble and was returning to Saigon. I was angry as this now meant I had to write the story as well as take photographs. In my painful condition I really needed help.

I set off on another trip with Rob in the L.S.T., this time northwards to Tra On. We went in daylight and received several bursts of automatic fire. On each occasion I dived for cover but noted how calmly Rob and the Vietnamese accepted these attacks. The Vietnamese had grown up from birth with this war and these incidents were an every-day occurrence to them.

We were eleven hours on the L.S.T., towing two barges loaded with supplies, making for slow progress. Again, the countryside was flat. We passed frail-looking houses covered with banana leaves and perched precariously on spindly poles sticking out of the water.

We reached Tra On at midnight in the middle of a mortar attack. Rob decided to spend the rest of the night on board as he wanted personally to supervise the unloading and distribution of supplies. Pilfering, like the war, had become a way of life in Vietnam.

At dawn Rob and I went over to the market and had breakfast in a café he frequented. Our meal was interrupted by the arrival of a U.S. military adviser saying that a woman had been arrested nearby. She had a U.S. fragmentation grenade hidden under some spinach leaves in her basket and had already drawn the pin.

Mrs. Tran-Thi-Can was a small, pathetic little woman looking much older than her 27 years. She had left her two children asleep that morning and set out in her sampan across the half mile wide river from Thanh-Bassac My-Hung to Tra On. Her island was predominantly V.C. controlled. She travelled with an old lady and entered the market, but was recognised by an alert security man, who grabbed her basket.

Outwardly, Mrs. Can looked composed as she sat in a chair answering questions put to her in local dialect by Ly Duc, the District Chief. 'Who sent you here?'

'My chief,' she answered calmly.

'Are you Viet Cong?'

'Yes, I've been a communist for ten years.'

Ly Duc ordered that she should be taken to Saigon for trial. Her fate was certain death.

When I asked her after the interrogation, with the help of an interpreter, why she carried that grenade in her basket, she glanced round casually at the two U.S. military advisers and ourselves crammed into the small hot office and answered slowly and quietly, 'I hate Americans. They are here to kill us with their airplanes and bombs so I came to the market place to kill Americans.' I wondered if Rob and I had been her targets that morning.

Ly Duc asked her, 'What do you feel about the communists who give guns to the V.C. to kill fellow Vietnamese?' She remained silent. I asked her what would happen to her now.

'I will be killed, of course.'

These small vignettes brought home the horror of this war more poignantly than anything I saw in the fighting. What of her two small children?

After Mrs. Can's arrest, large concentrations of V.C. were reported gathering in the village across the river. Ly Duc wanted to see their Chief. Accompanied by the two U.S. military advisers and some soldiers he decided to cross over in our landing craft. He discovered the V.C. were hiding in a clump of trees 200 yards from the village and called up on the radio for a 4.2" mortar barrage which ripped into the trees. Rifle and machine gun fire erupted everywhere. It was impossible to tell from which direction. The Chief had fled and when we reached the plantation the V.C. had melted into the forest as usual.

I was happy to get back to Tra On in one piece.

I stayed that night with the two U.S. officers and felt a lot safer in their camp. However, on the way out we stopped short of a bit of the gravel road that had been disturbed and discovered two electric mines a few inches below the surface. The officers cut the firing wires.

Rob was stricken with a fever and temperature of 101° so had called up on the radio for a helicopter to take us back to Phu Vinh which pleased me as I did not fancy the return journey by boat after the trouble we had stirred up. It was pouring with rain at dawn the following morning and impossible for a chopper to land, so Rob had no alternative but to return with the L.S.T. We made our way down the interesting but dangerous Mang-Thich canal where the thicker vegetation made sniping easier for the V.C. The few times we were fired on were casually answered by our machine gunners.

Rob decided to leave the boat at Tan An Luong. The local District Chief volunteered to drive us the last 36 km. into Phu Vinh. It was dark and his car was a 'marked' vehicle in this area, almost totally controlled by the V.C He drove fast and well along the narrow, lonely dirt road. At one bend he remarked, 'This is a bad corner. I've been sniped at many times on the bridge.' I sat in the front expecting bullets to rip into us at any moment but nothing happened.

'About eight vehicles are blown up every week on this stretch of road,' he went on just to add to our fears.

Susie was obviously excited to greet Rob as we entered their house at midnight. By 1 a.m. her two Vietnamese servants had produced a delicious Cha Cio consisting of lobster, crab, pork and bamboo shoots cooked up together and served with rice. Susie looked

Living Dangerously

strained. Although her house was guarded it would have been easy for the V.C. to lob a grenade through an open window and disappear undetected.

The next day was Friday the 13th. I was shot down during World War II on a Friday the 13th and it is one of the few superstitions I have. When Rob wanted to leave at dawn for Vinh Binh in his well sandbagged Jeep, I hesitated, knowing it was not advisable to be the first vehicle along lonely roads, regularly road blocked and mined by the V.C., so I asked Rob if we could first visit a small hamlet I wanted to photograph.

I was glad to see Rob slip a sub machine gun into the Jeep beside him as we made our way to the hamlet of Phu My. There was sporadic firing when we arrived so we did not hear the explosion down the road we were about to follow. A fully-loaded 30-seater bus was blown up by a concussion mine, causing carnage and killing six passengers. We came upon the bus soon afterwards as it lay upturned in a sodden rice paddy beside the road.

Once again, it was a small incident that imprinted itself upon my mind and on my camera. Here it was the sight of an old man scratching around in the murky water further discoloured by blood, trying to rescue some of his precious rice from the burst bag that lay under the distorted wreckage. He seemed oblivious to the plight of his fellow passengers. I was relieved we were not the first down that road and yet tinged with guilt. These conflicting senses often bothered me in wars and at times of personal danger.

The next day we were on a flight south to a small hamlet called Long Toan when Rob leaned over to me and said, 'This is really the heart of V.C. territory.' I listened as he gave instructions to our pilot. 'Fly in high over the post, lose height rapidly in a tight spiralling turn and land to the south. The north is unsecured.' The machine gunner next to me braced himself for action.

It was the same at Long Khanh but here we had the District Chief with us as the morale in this hamlet was particularly low.

I had the impression in these hamlets, and indeed later, throughout the countryside of Vietnam, that these peasants did not give a damn who ran the country as long as they could get on with their own lives. They gave their loyalty to whosoever controlled their area and gave them supplies. In the Delta this could be the V.C. one day and the Saigon government the next. It was usually the former.

I spent most of the day photographing these remote hamlets while Rob sent off our two choppers to bring in ammunition, plus urgent food and equipment. As they took off He said, 'There go our only lifelines with the outside world.'

I returned to Saigon to complete captions, write the text and ship the packet to New York. All four LIFE teams joined up for a farewell dinner at Cheap Charlies before going their respective ways around the world. Larry Burrows, Bob Morse and I were going to Bangkok and had an early plane to catch. In fact, when we looked at our watches in the darkened Romeo and Juliet bar of the Caravelle Hotel, we noticed it was 5 a.m. None of us had packed and the flight was due off in two hours. We need not have worried. As usual our Air Vietnam DC6 was two hours delayed. We had a leisurely breakfast in the airport restaurant and discovered later that the place had been blown up by a preset time bomb an hour after our departure, causing many casualties.

Bangkok was famed for its massage parlours. After those weeks in the Delta and with my back giving me a lot of pain, I thought a visit to a renowned massage parlour behind the Erawan Hotel was a good idea. I was not disappointed. We sat out in the elegant garden drinking iced beers in the sultry, humid heat while some 20 girls dressed in immaculate white uniforms paraded round the tables. We chose our masseuses and were taken off to small cubicles where I was undressed and thoroughly washed down under refreshingly cold water. She dried me, oiled me all over and laid me on the table for the serious massage. She knelt on my back until I thought it would break and went on until every bone seemed to crack and every fibre tingle. She then rolled me over and performed the same delightful operation. It was terminated with a vibro massage. After that experience I had no problem sleeping through the long night flight to New Delhi, despite the agony of my back.

I returned to London but was back in Vietnam again early in 1965 in time to greet the first U.S. Marines to land on the beach south of Danang.

Living Dangerously

I joined the 3/4 U.S. Marine Battalion on patrols out of the ancient city of Hue before returning to Danang. Being the first correspondents there, Jordan Bonfante and I reserved a large room for Time Life people in the Marine press centre It had been a local brothel and our little girl who looked after us and our room had been one of their top models. She was only about five feet tall but beautifully formed, and treated us all as if we were the only men in her young life. She used to wake us up at dawn by putting her delicate little hands under our sheets and caressing us gently. A pleasant way to be woken up. Don Wise, who joined our room, soon christened her 'Mini Blow'.

On 27 April I attended an evening briefing for the first all-American helicopter offensive deep into Viet Cong territory, set for dawn the following morning. I did not sleep too well that night. It is always the fear of the unknown that is frightening. I had asked Colonel Dave Clement, commander of the 2nd Battalion 3rd Marines, to take me with him in the lead chopper so that I could photograph the arrival of the rest of the force as they followed us in.

Our pilot found the landing area. I had butterflies in the pit of my stomach as he cut the engine and I felt a warm draught of air from the exhausts drift across my face. We started the rapid descent into God knows what. Tracer started coming up at us. The machine gunner beside me stiffened, grabbed his weapon and opened fire at the ground below. Other Hueys flying alongside also opened up and started rocketing the ground as we went in to land. Most of us had leapt clear of the chopper before the wheels even touched the ground. With four cameras around my neck and a heavy bag, this was not easy. Men ran and stumbled as they took up firing positions. I spent the first half hour dashing all over the landing area trying to get near the other choppers as they disgorged their Marines in an endeavour to capture on film the tension as men went into action for the first time in their lives.

Fighting my way through the coarse, tall grass in that oppressive heat almost exhausted me before we even started the punishing patrol through dense jungle. Trying to keep ahead of my platoon so as to photograph faces and not backs needed every bit of willpower I could muster. I actually passed out during the first rest stop and was brought round by a gentle boot in the ribs: 'You can't stay here, Buddy.' Somehow, I found my second wind. I had to resist drinking water as the excessive sweating was even more debilitating. Besides, I only carried a quart for the whole day.

At 47 I knew I had a lot of training to do if I was going to keep up with these tough, young and well- disciplined Marines on lengthy patrols in temperatures exceeding 100° and humidity near 100%.

We returned to Danang in time to cover what was undoubtedly the most unpleasant job I ever had to do – to photograph the execution of a young man. Le Dau was 24. He had been caught ten days earlier with a transistor packed with explosive in the local Grand Hotel frequented mostly by Americans. A military court sentenced him to death. When we arrived at the sports field soldiers were checking an area around a thick pole backed by sandbags. They were using mine detectors in case the V.C. tried to thwart the execution. A lorry drove on to the field laden with Vietnamese military policemen and a small figure was helped to the ground. A black bandage was tied across his stark, staring eyes and he was led staggering towards the pole to which he was roped. His complexion had turned an ashen, pallid grey. The military policemen, fearing retribution, gave the photographers a hard time. I felt quite sick looking at the pathetic figure knowing that within a minute the warm blood flowing through his veins would spurt out as a volley of eight bullets tore into his chest. The body crumpled, held up only by the ropes securing him to the pole. An officer fired a 'coup de grâce' into his temples and he was unceremoniously bundled into a roughly hewn box lying nearby. John Flynn said it was all over in three minutes. It felt like a lifetime to me.

I accompanied the Marines for a total of 18 foot and helicopter patrols, all were selected for Viet Cong areas where trouble was most expected, yet I saw little action. A typical foot patrol lasted from dawn till dusk and covered some 12 miles. We had to fight our way through bamboo forests, 12 feet high elephant grass and through jungle so thick that you could pass within a few feet of a V.C. unit and see or hear nothing.

Trying to keep cameras dry as one jumped out of choppers into muddy rice paddies or wading chest deep through invitingly cool rivers was a continual problem. Polythene bags helped a little. Film was kept in inflated rubber bags which floated if necessary. We were sniped at on most of these patrols with bullets hitting the trees around us but rarely saw the enemy or even knew from which direction he was firing. On a patrol near the hamlet of Nghai Thay a Marine beside me was hit in the head by a bullet fired at close range but was miraculously saved by his tin helmet. It made me think, as I never wore one nor a bulletproof vest, since they were too cumbersome for taking pictures.

Such songs as 'King of the Road' and 'Red Roses for a Blue Lady' blared out from every service mess and PX store. I still get a lump in my throat when I hear these tunes played. Vietnam in those early days, before the big build up of American servicemen, was fun and exciting for us journalists. The Vietnamese people were friendly and the military cooperated with us. I was even given the use of a Bell helicopter when I needed it, but as the number of the foreign press corps escalated above the 300 mark, much of this sort of service evaporated.

An odd character arrived up at Danang claiming that he worked for a British publication we knew could not have afforded to send him to Vietnam. There was little doubt that he was an intelligence agent for some government and we resented his pose as a journalist. Many years later he was arrested in China as a spy! Unfortunately, the work of foreign correspondents is made more difficult by the amount of C.I.A., M.I.5 and M.I.6 men who travel round the world affiliated to well known publications. It is an obvious cover for them and one that is accepted liberally by communist countries but it opens all journalists to suspicion.

I was expending a lot of energy with the Marines and getting few results. I suggested to New York a story on the exciting air rescue operations into North Vietnam to rescue shot-down U.S. airmen. This was turned down with the instructions to 'Stay with the Marines.' Then there was a good story to be done on the naval air operations flying off carriers in the China Sea and this too was turned down.

The frustration became almost too great. Foreign correspondents are a special breed of people. They are prepared to work long hours, sometimes days on end with little sleep, lead a life of uncertainty, experience discomfort, drink dirty water and eat foul food, to catch ameobic dysentry – all for the satisfaction of getting into print. Except for Vietnam they normally have to cover wars and expeditions ill equipped, and accompany young Commando-trained soldiers on long arduous sorties. They select special operations to lead them to the action. Accordingly correspondents and especially photographers often see more action in a few months than a soldier sees on his whole tour of duty.

Boredom, inactivity and frustration punctuated by short bursts of action, summed up much of the life of the fighting man in Vietnam and of the photographers covering them at that time. The reporters did not have to hang around waiting for things to happen, as they could pick it up afterwards and anyway had to return regularly to Saigon to file their stories.

Bob Morse contacted me with the news that Bill Eppridge had arrived from New York to relieve me, so I was not keen to stick my neck out on another operation when the Co Be River to the north west of Danang was to be crossed for the first time. It was known to be an active V.C. village well protected with thick jungle on three sides of the river to the south. Anyway, I went.

We had to land in a saucer beside the village, making us vulnerable to attack from every direction . It was just beginning to get light as we flew up the river and swooped down on Nam Yen, landing in a murky paddy field. Firing was going on all around us. We leapt out and ran for cover behind an irrigation ditch. I noticed the Marines had fixed their bayonets. Within minutes we were followed in by 25 other choppers while Hueys strafed the woods around us. We had taken the village only partly by surprise. Most of the V.C. had fled into the surrounding mountains, but some had taken cover in deep dugouts. They were forcibly flushed out, first by shouting and then by lobbing hand grenades down the holes. If this failed, flame-throwers were used. Some VC escaped across rice paddies, arms and legs working like flails as they tried to weave and run even faster. It was a terrible sight to see them picked off with rifle shots. Some crumpled and fell, others ran on like wounded animals, struggling to keep on their feet, before collapsing in screams of pain. Others just stopped dead in their tracks without a murmur. Alas, little of this could be captured meaningfully on film as the distance was too great without the long telephoto lenses which we could not carry on these operations.

War is sickening. Every time I looked at a man killed I had a flash of a youth who loved his life, his girl friend, his wife, his mother, his ambitions. For his existence to end like this always seemed such a tragic waste.

Television was better able to bring these scenes into people's homes in far away peaceful countries than the still camera that lost so many of the senses earlier described. Unlike other situations I covered, the Vietnamese encouraged photographers and cameramen to 'shoot' acts of indescribable horror and so the Vietnam war was brought forcibly home to people as never before. It eventually contributed to breaking the will of the Americans at home to continue this war.

I sometimes wondered about myself. I had been able to witness many horrific sights through the view-finder of my camera. Like a doctor, I suppose, one is able to disassociate oneself from the emotions. Today, I cannot even watch a violent film.

As I learned during the last war in moments of great danger, one's adrenalin takes over to a degree that one is not scared any more and yet it allows the mind to function clearly and rationally. Also I never think anything will happen to me.

I had another execution to cover on my return to Saigon which was as revolting as the first. This time the authorities were considerate enough to ask photographers if the light in the market place was better at dawn or in the evening for the event!

T.S. in Vietnam during the war, May 1965.

Paratroopers landing on the beach south of Danang.

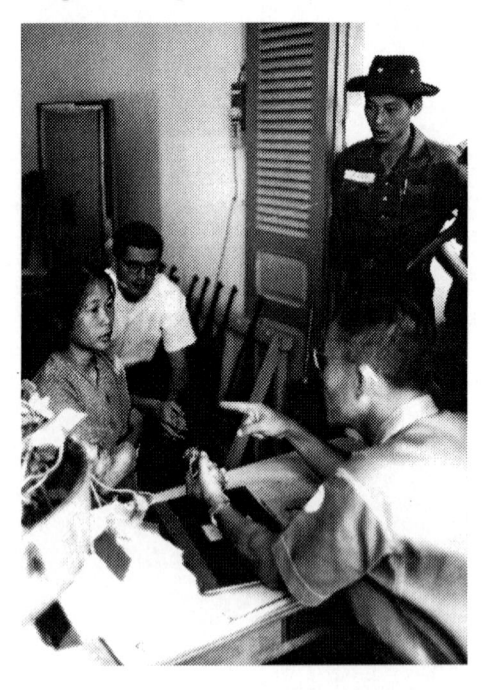

A Vietcong woman is caught carrying a hand grenade in her basket in the local market place. She was shot, no doubt, the following morning.

CHAPTER XXIV

Riots in Algeria, Greece, Southern Rhodesia; Crossing the frozen Baltic in a Unimog; and the IRA.

Back in London there were interludes to photograph the great 'bon viveur', oil magnate, 'Mr. Ten Percenter', Nubar Gulbenkian, at the Ritz Hotel with his famous London taxi, 'which can turn on a sixpence, whatever that is!' Then a trip to Gibraltar to cover the dispute between Britain and Spain over the sovereignty of the Rock.

At the end of November 1965 I heard the distressing news that George Clay, then working for N.B.C. News, had been killed by a bullet through his head while accompanying a mercenary convoy near Stanleyville in the Congo. The renewed troubles there soon had Rudy Chelminski, Jordan Bonfante, photographer Don McCullin and myself winging back to that revolting little war for a story on Cuban mercenary pilots flying B.26 bombers, supposedly for the C.I.A. After flying three aerial operations with them against the rebels, an urgent cable sent us all back to London for Churchill's impending death. Funerals for great men attended by heads of states invariably make for a big story. We had planned the funeral coverage over the previous three years.

Thirty photographers and writers from all over the world arrived in London for the LIFE magazine coverage. We had only five days to wait as the Great Old Man died at 8 am. on Sunday 24 January 1965.

Hyde Park Gate, where Churchill lived, was closed to the public and to the press that Sunday morning but Dick Beeston of the *Telegraph* lived in a rented house on the corner. From a window we had a perfect view of Churchill's house, No.28. An 800 mm telephoto lens brought everything into close focus from 420 feet away.

That night Frank Allen and I set up four large Ascor 600 strobes inside the shutters of the windows and hidden from view. We only had to open the shutters to direct these powerful lights towards No.28. At the crucial moment a French freelance photographer climbed on to the wall in front of our view and refused to move. We threatened him with a rope but this was not necessary as the commotion caused the police to look up and he was arrested. He could not speak enough English to give us away.

We peered through the shutters and around 9 pm a hearse drew up, the door opened and the coffin was carried out. Frank threw open the shutters and a blinding flash startled the police and everyone else in that quiet street. We had recorded the only pictures of that historic event.

LIFE 'went to bed' at midnight on Saturdays in New York and the funeral being the following Saturday could not have been worse timing for our deadline. In order to get a 20 page colour essay into eight million copies and away from the printers in Chicago on Monday morning, LIFE equipped and flew to London a chartered Boeing 707 jet. It carried a complete colour processing laboratory and technicians, film editors, senior editorial writers, the art director and lay-out men.

Each photographer for the funeral was assigned one or two positions along the route and a 'Rocker' with his fast motor cycle to rush the film through the traffic to London Airport and aboard the 707 where it was processed and edited.

My first location was on the terrace overlooking Old Palace Yard in Westminster where Churchill had lain in state. The 800 mm lens gave closeups of the frail Lady Churchill veiled in sombre black and supported against the buffeting cold wind by her son, Randolph, as her husband's draped cortege left on a gun carriage for St. Paul's Cathedral.

Frank did not have a permit to join me on the terrace but this was no deterrent to him. He had the charm and determination to get himself almost anywhere at any time. He took my film to our 'Rocker'; then we fought our way through the crowds to Waterloo Bridge, lugging the heavy equipment, and set up a position from where we were able to 'shoot' the coffin being taken off the boat after it had been brought up the Thames to Festival Pier.

This massive operation was to be the last of the really costly LIFE stories.

It was mid June 1965 when I was on my way again; this time to Paris. The office usually checked me in to the chic Elysée Park Hotel in the Champs Elysée but I preferred the smaller, more intimate and French atmosphere of the Bradford Hotel in the St. Phillippe de Roule. My destination, however, was to be Algiers after the Boumedienne coup. Jordan met me in his M.G. sports car and we joined Curt Prendergast on the Air France Caravelle jet. The glamorous Dita Champey, who used to be Bob Ajemian's secretary, met us at Maison Blanche Airport and despite the chaos of the coup we passed through customs and immigration with minimum bother.

We immediately started patrolling the streets of Algiers looking for trouble and soon found it in the newly renamed Didouche Mourade, formerly Rue Michelet, where left-wing students demonstrated and marched to the Forum. Shouting slogans in unison seemed to be the hallmark of communist agitators who used it as a means of raising the adrenalin level of their supporters much as the beat of the African drums excited warriors to war. They marched to 'Ya-ya Ben Bella,' and 'Boumedienne assassin,' all the time blowing blasts on whistles as they lit bonfires in garbage cans. When the police arrived with water cannons and tear gas to break up the march, they retaliated with stones. Jordan and I were soaked to the skins and choking with tear gas when finally feeling safe to leave the streets at 3.30 am.

Patrolling in Algiers was infinitely more pleasant than in Léopoldville as everything happened nightly in the main street. We could sit comfortably at two or three pavement cafés sipping campion or citron pressé or eating couscous, blik and tadjin at el Cacour while waiting for the riots to start.

I was glad to see Arnaud de Borchgrave of *Newsweek* in Algiers, remembering his unbeatable French contacts in the Congo and, once again, we teamed up with him.

On our second day Jordan and I were having lunch with Arnaud beside the hotel pool. Our large and expensive Lobster Thermidor had just been served when Arnaud was called to the phone. He rushed back, buttoning up his shirt. 'Hurry! We must go. There is a snap news conference being given by the Chinese at the Club des Pins.' To the

Living Dangerously

amazement of the French around us we leapt up, paid the bill, left our lobsters untouched, threw on some clothes and battled our way through road blocks out to the club where the Afro-Asian conference was being held. The Chinese merely told us what we were to learn an hour or so later – that the whole conference would end in disarray before it even started.

I returned to a lovely peaceful story in the Yorkshire Dales with Dorothy Bacon to illustrate an article written by J.B. Priestley. The Dales are remote and sometimes bleak but always picturesque. One evening at a pub called the Rose and Crown at Bainbridge we met the water bailiff who was obviously glad to see new faces.

'Where do you come from?' he asked cheerfully.

'London,' we answered in chorus.

'London! I don't know what people find to do with their nights there.'

I returned to our XVth century thatched weekend cottage and had hardly entered the door when Jim Hicks was on the phone: 'We are off to Greece in the morning. The young King Constantine has fired the 77-year-old leftist prime minister, George Papandreou, and it looks like trouble.'

Our stringer met us at Athens airport and within 45 minutes of clearing customs we were in the middle of riots in the heart of the ancient city. The stringer took us on to a balcony of the Grande Bretagne Hotel overlooking Constitution Square. In safety and comfort we were able to get overall pictures as hundreds of thousands of students and workers carrying red flags and shouting slogans in unison crammed in to the square below. It was a terrifying sight. No force could control this mob. The police were on hand but did not interfere. I was not relishing having to go down into this melée for close-ups. Jim and I hung around until 3 am when most of the demonstrators had departed.

The next day Papandreou announced that he would drive the 15 miles through the city. Students organised a large meeting to coincide with the drive. We selected a student who seemed to be the leader and spoke a little English. He introduced us to his cronies whom we hoped would look after us when the trouble started.

Delirious and hysterical people mobbed the car shouting, 'PAP-AN-DREO! PAP-AN-DREO,' clapping out the rhythm at the same time. Jim and I fought the mob for three hours in the oppressive heat as stewards forced a way for the car through the packed streets.

More members of the foreign press corps arrived at the Hilton Hotel where we were staying. Hugh Moffet came from Paris to supervise the LIFE team, also Jordan Bonfante and photographer Loomis Dean. We used to meet around 10am for breakfast by the pool and swop news. There was nothing for us to do during the day but laze and swim and glance enviously at the lithe, suntanned bodies of Greek-American-girls visiting the land of their forefathers.

At 6pm we went in to Athens. Our 'boy' was already addressing a large gathering of students on the university steps. He was gesticulating and rousing the fire of revolution in his audience by getting them to repeat in unison anti-capitalist, anti-establishment and anti-American slogans. The meeting broke up at 9.30 pm and the crowd streamed into University Avenue, led by our student. The march was well organised, student leaders insisting upon absolute discipline. This was well illustrated later when the clash came with the police. Stewards either ordered students to leap on to police vehicles, throw stones, break shop windows and loot the contents or they were able to restrain and control them at will. Their authority and control was remarkable.

Suddenly, the situation changed. Tension and fear filled the air. Ahead stood a solid phalanx of grey uniformed police wearing steel helmets and carrying long batons. They were reinforced by several riot trucks protected by metal screens and by two armoured water cannons.

Still the advance continued.

Jim and I were beside our 'boy' and knew we would bear the brunt of the police attack. Journalistically speaking, we were ideally positioned. Ironically, photographing the tenseness of a situation like this can be misleading as faces are often wreathed in smiles to hide fear. Arriving face to face with the police the students immediately broke up on instructions from their stewards and leapt on the police vehicles, attacking them with their flag poles. The shouting and screaming was deafening and spine-chilling. The police attacked ferociously, beating bodies and heads with their long batons. Sharp cracks rang out as they fired tear gas cannisters and riot vehicles rolled into the mob.

I was 'shooting' in colour and had two electronic strobe lights mounted on the camera, making the outfit unwieldy. Additionally, I had two more cameras round my neck and carried a large camera bag. Protecting this equipment was a problem in itself. Then I had the continual fear of a police baton landing on my skull each time I let off a powerful flash. Police the world over do not like this sort of action being recorded. Somehow, Jim and I managed to keep our student in sight. The power of the water cannons and the choking effect of the tear gas was too much for the rioters. They broke into a run down Stadium Street.

The police knew our 'boy' was the leader and were after him. With about 100 of his 'lieutenants' he was cornered by a barrage of powerful water jets and tear gas. The police surrounded them and in the chaos Jim and I managed to escape into the police lines.

As the tear gas haze lifted slightly we were confronted with a scene out of Dante's Inferno. Sprawled across the pavement was a pile of heads four or five deep belonging to bodies lying in layers on top of each other. Water was dripping off their faces which were twisted in fear and pain. Open mouths strove for breath that crushed lungs and tear gas were unable to provide.

The acrid fumes had penetrated my throat. My eyes were running so hard that at times I could see nothing through the view finder. I was choking and coughing violently. Another water cannon drew up and directed its jets of water at the piled up bodies, sluicing them across the pavement. Most limped to their feet and painfully escaped, but five forms remained, still awash with blood and water. They were surrounded by odd shoes, handbags and pieces of clothing saturated in water and vomit.

The police disappeared as quickly as they arrived.

Jim and I examined the forms on the pavement as people ran out of looted shops. One of the bodies belonged to our 'lad'. Froth oozed from a corner of his mouth. His puce coloured face and bulging eyes left us in no doubt that he was dead. He had suffocated at the bottom of the pile.

Later Jim and I were somewhat subdued as we sat over our meal at Dionysos under the floodlit Acropolis. It was 2.20 in the morning. Drenched, bedraggled and stinking of tear gas, we must have looked an odd pair to the elegantly dressed diners in the restaurant.

The next morning we discovered for the first time the name of our lad. He was Sotiris Petroulas. His death, far from being the end, was just the beginning of an extensive propaganda operation that was to make him a martyr and whip up the enthusiasm of his supporters to even greater levels of hate against the King and the new government.

Jordan pulled off an exclusive interview with the beleaguered King Constantine in his palace. The King sat at his desk surrounded by photographs of his family and throughout our interview worked overtime on his worry beads. He asked us if we had been injured in the riots and added, 'I think my people are democrazy!'

After almost three weeks in Greece I returned to London and that night Lee Hall phoned from Paris: 'Can you possibly leave in the morning for Kuwait? I know it is tough asking you.'

For only the second time in the 13 years I had worked for LIFE I said, 'No. Impossible. I only returned home this afternoon and start my three weeks holiday with my family in the morning.' I knew it was more than my marriage was worth.

Two weeks later, when we were staying on our boat in the Isle of Wight, Lee managed to contact me and asked, 'Hate to do this to you but could you go to Kashmir? It really is urgent.'

Again, I refused. Then, just before the end of our holiday there was a note to phone Jim Hicks in London: 'TIME want you to go to South Africa for a month on an extensive colour essay entitled "This is Apartheid" – what it means to live in that country if you are black.'

This time I relented, though I knew it was a dirty story to have to do. In fact, I was in trouble before I had even arrived in South Africa on the flight south. I was arrested in Entebbe, Uganda, for taking pictures of the airport.

'You're a spy!' shouted an irate official.

'What's secret here?' I queried.

'I saw you photographing our Air Force,' he went on belligerently.

I looked around and saw some old twin-engined Oxfords. 'My God!' I exclaimed, 'I was trained on those planes 25 years ago.' After much arguing with the Chief of Security I was released minutes before my V.C. 10 jet took off.

Landing at Jan Smuts airport in South Africa with five cameras, ten lenses and 250 rolls of film hardly made me look like a tourist, so I expected trouble at customs. My nervous system was not eased as I entered immigration to hear over the Tannoy system, 'Mr. Spencer, please make yourself known.' A gruff official glared at me and said, 'Your vaccination has expired.'

I hired a well-known African photographer, Peter Magubane, to 'shoot' scenes in the townships, as my white face would have been picked up almost immediately. With a colleague driving and using long lenses through the window, I photographed the 'WHITES ONLY' signs, segregated beaches in Durban and the 101 small facets of life that made a mockery of human dignity in that part of the world.

Photographing prisons and prisoners risked a jail sentence and called for particular care. We needed pictures of the infamous Robben Island, a penal settlement for black political prisoners. It was South Africa's 'Devil's Island'. I chartered a small plane from Cape Town, ostensibly to take aerial pictures of Table Mountain. I made the pilot circle further and further out to sea and while his head was turned towards Table Mountain I was able to get a shot of Robben Island. While looking down I thought of Nelson Mandela incarcerated there for so many years, and remembered the afternoon in Johannesburg when I met Nelson in Ernie Shirley's house. At that time he was 'on the run' and the South African police force were looking for him. He was a quiet and gentle man and showed no signs then of becoming the figurehead he is today.

I moved quickly about South Africa, making hotel and air reservations in different names to keep one jump ahead of the Special Branch. I kept the really controversial pictures until near the end of my visit having shipped out of the country the film already 'shot' and my note books. Lifting a camera in South Africa was rather like lifting a gun in any other country, especially at the targets I had in my sights. Finally, I tackled the outspoken opponents of apartheid: brave liberals like politician Helen Suzman, writers Nadine Gordimer and my old friend, Alan Paton. Lastly, *Rand Daily Mail* editor, Laurie Gandar.

Dodging the Special Branch for four weeks was beginning to play on my nerves so it was with a sense of relief that I felt the wheels of the Central African Airways Viscount retract into position and clear South African soil.

I returned to London in mid-September in time for a party Larry Burrows gave at the Wig and Pen in Fleet Street. This was the last time I saw Larry alive as he was killed later in a helicopter crash in Laos.

I was soon back in Africa again. Hugh Moffet was on the line: 'It looks like things are blowing up in Rhodesia. I want you and Jim Hicks to pull every possible string to hop the next flight to Salisbury.' We knew many of our colleagues would be scrambling for tickets so immediately phoned British United Airways' press officer who got us the last two seats.

At Lusaka Airport we followed Hugh Beadle, the Rhodesian Attorney General, into the control tower where we heard Ian Smith declare U.D.I. (the country's Unilateral Independence from Britain). Beadle looked shattered.

Rhodesia was the old African pattern all over again: riots, riots and more riots. Ian Berry of Magnum and I were photographing police raiding a township near Bulawayo when a Landrover drew across the front of our car and four armed cops ran towards us. I hastily taped the three rolls of film I had just taken under the dashboard when a burly sergeant pushed me into the passenger seat and drove us to police headquarters under arrest. They tried to confiscate our equipment but we refused to hand it over. 'You take our equipment, you take us with it,' I told a tall, lean, red-headed police Inspector. 'You are not allowed to enter black townships without a permit nor are you allowed to photograph police erections,' he snarled at us.

'Police erections!' I gasped. 'You cannot believe we've travelled 5,000 miles for that sort of picture.' He was not amused.

After three hours of hassle and numerous telephone calls to Salisbury, we were released. Although thoroughly searching our car they did not find the three rolls of film. Thereafter, we were followed by Special Branch men, often clumsily. At 4 a.m. the following morning police entered Jim's bedroom and took away his American passport. This was their method of intimidation – and let's face it, it was scary. Jim and I were then kicked out of the country.

In the New Year I was in Morocco investigating the death of Ben Barka, an anti-government activist who had been shot mysteriously in Paris. The man suspected of his murder was King Hassan II's sinister Minister of the Interior, General Mohamad Oufkir who, in turn, was shot during an attempt on the King's life. With the help of our Rabat stringer I met the King who invited me to photograph a 'Thousand and one Arabian Nights' spectacle in the palace when hundreds of his mounted Moorish Guards paraded before us. I never solved the mystery of Ben Barka's death but I did get the vital pictures of General Oufkir with the King.

It is said that a photographer cannot be any good until he has made every mistake in the book. On that premise, I must be good. Indeed, it was impossible to believe there was another mistake I could make but I found one on my next story. I was late for an interview with Ronan O'Rahilly, boss of the first North Sea pirate radio station. I hastily parked my car outside his Mayfair office, slung my large camera bag on to the pavement and dashed up to his expensively furnished office. Throughout the interview I was plagued by a foul smell. I checked my shoes but it was not that. Only when leaving and lifting the camera bag off the delicately shaded carpet did I realize there were soft dog's droppings squelched into every crevice of the bag, leaving a revolting mess on the carpet.

Early in February 1966 Liz Taylor and Richard Burton played in a production of *Dr. Faustus* at the Playhouse in Oxford. It was Elizabeth Taylor's first ever appearance on a stage and the reason for our story. My visit coincided with a critical notice in LIFE of Richard's performance in *The Spy Who Came In From The Cold*. Rather an unkind one, I thought. Burton had seen it and when I introduced myself from LIFE, he was blatantly rude and refused to have anything to do with me. The fact that it was really Liz I wanted and not him did not placate his ego either.

Though the media was banned from the dress rehearsal, I managed to get in and photograph it. I also had a long talk with Liz. It was a Saturday and Liz said, 'Richard is mad keen on rugby football and there is an international match this afternoon he wants to watch on T.V. Come round to the Randolph Hotel and watch it with us. I'll try to pacify him.'

With a certain amount of trepidation I arrived at their room and Liz let me in. Richard continued to be unfriendly during the one and a half hours I remained in their room but I took pictures nevertheless and he did not object.

A day or so later Burton's manager phoned me saying, 'Richard has changed his mind and will cooperate with you. They have a photo session with Angus McBean and you are invited.' Quite rightly, McBean was not happy at my presence, especially as I used his lighting set-ups. Two more photogenic subjects it would be impossible to find so I was not surprised when one of these shots ran as a full colour page. I found Liz quite delightful and, while I had not expected to find her so plump, nor did I expect to see a face quite so exquisite.

It was obviously vital to get THE picture as Liz made her entry on to the stage for the first time on the opening night. Photography was prohibited in the theatre, so I wrapped a small S.P. Nikon in chamois leather to deaden the shutter sound and sat beside Lesley in the fourth row of the stalls. As Liz stepped on to the stage you could have heard a pin drop. I carefully composed the picture and gingerly squeezed the shutter release. It sounded like a stick of dynamite exploding. Lesley nearly died of shame as every face in the theatre seemed to turn our way. Further embarrassment was only averted by Burton's stirring lines, 'Is this the face that launched a thousand ships?'

An irate gentleman sitting next to Lesley announced that he was the theatre manager. I unloaded the film out of the camera and Lesley slipped it into her handbag. We left during the first curtain call and drove to London Airport to ship the film in time for New York's morning deadline.

Two days later I met Rudy Chelminski in the luxurious Marski Hotel in Helsinki for a story on the great freeze-up. Stories with the tall, fair-haired Rudy were always fun and usually ended in adventure. This apparently placid assignment was to be no exception.

We heard that the Baltic was frozen over and that we could drive across the ice to Mariehamn Island in the Aland archipelago. We managed to persuade two of the world's top rally drivers, Timo Makkinen and Rauno Aaltonnen, to drive us there in their hotted up Mini Coopers.

We left the Finnish coast at Kustavi in a winter so severe that even the old timers could not remember anything to match it. The Finns had graded a road system for the 47 miles across the ice and even erected road signs and speed limits. It twisted through hundreds of small islands. It was exhilarating driving with these masters. Sometimes they took bends on the ice at 80 m.p.h., always under perfect control, helped by large studs set into the tyres. Normally, we would have had to make this trip by boat.

From Mariehamn we chartered a Cessna aircraft fitted with skis and landed on the ice beside nine ocean-going freighters trapped in the ice south of Turku. We taxied up alongside one of them, parked the plane, climbed up a companion ladder and had lunch with the Captain. He had been there a week.

At Mariehamn we heard that a crazy Finn had crossed the next stretch of open sea to the Swedish coast in a snowcat. We found the 32-year-old Sven Lemberg and asked him the possibility of taking a car over the ice and so have a story on being the first car ever to drive across the Baltic from Finland to Sweden. 'Wait a moment,' said this cheerful man, 'The road you have just crossed is over shallow water and hundreds of islands help consolidate the ice, but it is 65 kilometres (40 miles) the way we would have to go, across open sea some 200 metres (650 feet) deep. The temperature is -25°C. In places the ice is not too thick and if it broke and we went into the water we would soon die.'

Rudy and I looked at each other and I noticed a corner of his mouth drop a little.

Sven went on, 'But if you are 'game' I am happy to go with you.'

What could we say?

With Sven's help we found an ancient four wheel drive Mercedes Benz Unimog which had been laid up for a year. We told its 70 year old owner of our plan and that we would pay for the vehicle if we lost it. We gave him a written undertaking to this effect on behalf of LIFE magazine, unbeknown to LIFE. Rudy and I figured that if LIFE had to pay out, there would be no come-back on us. The old man also bet us a bottle of Swedish schnapps that we would not make it.

We hired a mechanic to work all night and service the Unimog. Sven gathered together a few supplies, including a large drum of diesel oil, two planks and a length of rope. He borrowed a large skin for the unfortunate who had to ride in the open back of the truck and brought an auger and drill to check the thickness of the ice.

Rudy and I did not have time to get any special winter clothing other than the hats, sweaters, anoraks and thick fur gloves that we possessed. I had a couple of silk inner gloves I always carried to allow me to manipulate cameras and change film in cold climates.

We left the Aland Archipelago as dawn was breaking. It was bitterly cold. Rudy volunteered to ride in the back as we knew my cameras and hands would freeze up. As it was, I had to keep the cameras inside my anorak as they had not been treated with anti-freeze

Living Dangerously

oil. Within half an hour we were out of sight of land. The Unimog laboured as it forced its way through the snow covering the ice. The snow also made the driving difficult for Sven as he could not see the condition of the ice. We crossed a fantastic desert of ice and were blinded by the nothingness ahead. Behind, our tracks disappeared into a white mass of infinity. Sometimes we passed beautiful mounds of ice that the wind had carved into weird sculptures. It was impossible to believe that there was 600 feet of troubled waters beneath us as we ground along at 10 m.p.h. We soon had a terrifying reminder.

We were almost in the middle of the channel when the Unimog suddenly lurched and almost threw Rudy out of the back. 'Jesus!' I heard him scream, 'We've broken through the ice.' A geyser of water flew up beneath the rear wheels and the ice started to sag under the 6,000 lbs. weight of the vehicle. Through the windscreen I witnessed a nightmare vision. The ice flow started heaving and undulating like a bed sheet blown in a soft breeze. Up it went in a ponderous slow-motion swell.

'It must break.' I thought. We all baled out fast. It was the moment the three of us had been silently dreading for the last two and a half hours since leaving land. The undulations subsided and there was an ugly crack behind us. We found ourselves on an ice floe about 50 feet across.

'I think, maybe, this is the end of our trip,' Lemberg remarked laconically. We left the Unimog and made our way back, crossing a one foot gap of open sea on to solid ice. I wondered how we were going to explain the loss of our Unimog to New York.

'Stay here,' Lemberg ordered.

He cautiously made his way back to the Unimog and collected the two planks of wood and placed them across the gap. He augered the mushy ice floe that was only 8" thick. Sven stood on the running board as he started the engine, then entered the cabin long enough to engage the gear as he reversed slowly on to the planks and the safety of solid ice.

Sven was worried about the ice breaking up still further and decided to steer north before turning west again towards the Swedish coast. The manoeuvre added to the sea crossing but ensured an uneventful journey except that the ice surface became rough and made life uncomfortable, especially for Rudy in the back.

It was an unusual experience 'sailing' into the picturesque little harbour of Grisselehamn in Sweden, having driven over 38 miles of open ocean in four and a half hours. Stolid fishermen looked up in astonishment from the decks of their icebound boats as we drove up alongside the quay. We were welcomed by a charming old man of 72, Axel Gottold, who was a retired customs official. The vital proof of the crossing was a bottle of Swedish schnapps but it was Sunday and the shops were closed. Axel kindly sold us one.

The return journey was easy. The Unimog ran much faster retracing its own tracks and we knew the hazards to avoid. In two and a half hours we were back in Finland. It was my turn in the back and I nearly froze stiff. This was the first crossing ever made across the Baltic ice.

Early in March 1966 the London office was contacted clandestinely by the IRA (Irish Republican Army) who suggested we do a story showing their side of the question for the reunification of Ireland with the six counties of the North.

Lee Hall joined me and we flew over to Dublin. Lee phoned our contact number and a short, stocky Irishman with greeny blue eyes soon introduced himself to us in the Gresham Hotel bar. We went up to Lee's room and he examined our passports. He was not too happy with my British one. He then looked at our LIFE passes and some by-lined stories from the magazine that we had brought along. Eventually he was satisfied. Stepping out through the glass swing doors on to St. Stephens Green we noticed two characters standing idly on the other side of the road. 'Your boys?' I enquired.

'No. They are Special Branch officers.' At least we knew that we were being followed.

That evening, after three previously organized and well timed car changes, we were taken out to meet some of the IRA. top brass in Dublin. Hiding their faces in shade they allowed me to photograph an operation being planned against Northern Ireland, though they were careful not to divulge the actual details.

Someone had recently blown up the famous Nelson pillar in O'Connell Street, which had stood proudly for more than a century overlooking Dublin. The IRA denied that they had done it though one of their splinter groups probably had. The Irish army was going to blow up the remains the following night. The IRA had a sympathiser with an office overlooking the pillar and less than 30 yards from it. Since the area was to be cleared before the explosion, they arranged for us to use the building. Frank Allen flew over from London with the Ascor 600 strobes. We mounted them, as we did for Churchill's funeral, on the shutters which we then kept closed until the area had been cleared. We connected a motor-driven camera on a tripod to the lights and retired to the rear room with a remote control lead.

We lay all night on the floor, not daring to make a sound. At 3.30 in the morning a resounding explosion made me subconsciously fire the strobes. Shattering glass and falling debris brought us to the window. Most important, we found the equipment was undamaged. We had a unique colour picture of the explosion but, like so many others that needed this sort of organisation to achieve, it never ran.

Lee and I worked with the IRA and the Republican movement throughout the months of March and early April, returning three times to Dublin before we had completed the story. We accompanied Rory O'Brady on one of his campaign tours to the beautiful north of County Donegal where he spoke to Republican sympathisers. Another night we were picked up in the early hours of the morning from our hotel and taken by the routine three car switch out to a lonely farm where Richard Behal was hiding. He had shot up a visiting British gun boat and was jailed for the offence, but the IRA had organized his escape. He was currently the most wanted man in Ireland and here we were drinking coffee with him and eating sandwiches while I photographed him and Lee took down his story.

We finally persuaded the top IRA brass to take us up into the hills to visit one of their secret training units. This time we rendezvoused in a well known pro-Republican pub in Dublin. Lee Hall's vast consumption of the delectable foaming Guinness impressed our tough escorts who, at closing time, whisked us away through deserted back streets to another waiting car. We made two more car changes before the road narrowed as it climbed into a rough track hemmed in on both side by high hedges. Our bearded driver turned off the lights and we crawled to an isolated farmhouse. It was raining.

The car was hidden in a barn and we were ushered into a small, dimly lit corrugated iron roofed shed. For a moment it seemed that the room was full of men, though in fact, there were only eight. They wore black berets and were dressed in crumpled variations of British army uniforms. On one wall a mini-arsenal of weaponry glistened, ranging from automatic Bren guns to Thompson sub-machine guns and Sten guns. As we entered, an officer was instructing them how to make booby traps while on a blackboard were details of bomb making. The officer called his men to attention. He saluted our contact, whom we later discovered was a senior member of the IRA. He told them to carry on with what they were doing and to take no notice of us. They viewed my small cameras with suspicion. There were two bare light bulbs in the shed and I had to make careful use of shade to avoid identifying faces. Being caught in possession of arms was a serious offence, even in the Republic of Ireland.

A tough-looking officer briefed us as to what to do if the regular Irish army or police arrived. He had told his men which local farmhouses were friendly and which were not. 'Disperse in every direction and run like hell. Take cover where possible as they are sure to open fire on you. Get out of your uniforms and hide your weapons. Remember, they are hard to come by.'

As dawn started to break the patrol left the farm. The mist was low on the hills and, coupled with the ragged barbed wire fence, made exciting, spooky pictures. We returned to the farm where the lady gave us steaming hot cups of coffee with bacon and eggs. Weapons were wrapped in sacks and put in the boots of our cars, together with boxes of explosives and hand grenades.

On our way out to Dublin airport we were tailed by a police car. Our driver immediately swung off the main road and screeched around small streets back into Dublin where he dropped us at a taxi rank and told us to make our own way to the airport. He took the incriminating film, promising to have it delivered to the London office in the morning, which he did. I hopped the next flight to Paris and supervised the prints being made in the office dark room. Despite my original precautions, considerable shading had to be done to the prints to avoid recognition of any of those involved.

Much later, when the story was published, the London office was approached by Special Branch police who wanted to interview me. Fortunately, I was out of the country at the time but made it clear I would go to jail rather than disclose details.

There is a lot of controversy on this aspect of journalism, but to me it is vital that journalists maintain this principle of impartiality and independence if they are to infiltrate guerrilla operations and be trusted. It does not matter whether or not you agree with their aspirations; they have an argument which ought to be heard in a democracy. Equally, when we work with intelligence organisations to our mutual benefit, we never disclose secret information unless it is material to be filed for publication.

Over the next six years Northern Ireland was to become a regular beat. During the Queen's visit to Belfast on 4 July 1966 Hugh Moffet and I were following the Royal procession down Queen Victoria Street when an IRA supporter hurled a 12 lbs block of concrete from a fourth story building under construction. The Queen's driver saw it falling; braked so hard that he threw the Queen and Prince Philip out of their seats before accelerating and escaping. We followed and just managed to get into Government house before the police closed the gates. I leapt out and took a picture of the dent in the armour plated bonnet of the Rolls Royce. What had undoubtedly been an assassination attempt on the life of the Queen was hushed up by the Palace at the time.

*Athens, Greece. The mother of our boy as she hears of his death
(July 1963) Chapter XXIV*

Northern Ireland troubles. Fires are lit in the streets (August 1971)
Chapter XXX

The IRA tried to assassinate the Queen by dropping a concrete block from a building site, denting the bonnet of the Royal Rolls Royce (November 1971) Chapter XXIV

An aerial of the Aberfan disaster (October 1966) Chapter XXV

The film Chitty Chitty Bang Bang. Dick van Dyke takes off. (August 1967) Chapter XXVI

Over the bonnet of the airborne car with the Neuschwanstein Castle in Bavaria (August 1967) Chapter XXVI

Actress Goldie Hawn on a Sheperton film set (April 1970)

Below: Actress Carrol Baker with Masai warriors in Kenya for film 'Mr. Moses', LIFE magazine cover (February 1964)

Right: Elton John in London for PEOPLE Magazine cover (December 1977) Chapter XXXIII

*Richard Burton and Elisabeth
Taylor (first time on stage) in
Dr. Faustus at Oxford
(February 1966)*

*Nureyev at
Covent Garden
(November 1976)*

*The 'Nutcracker' ballet
at Covent Garden
(February 1968)*

Sting of the Police rock group (July 1983) Chapter XXXII

Aerial of Me109s 'being attacked' during the making of the 'Battle of Britain' film in Seville, Spain (April 1967) Chapter XXVI

The 1967 Israeli/Arab war. The Dolphin at Sharm el Sheik. The first Israeli ship to sail up the Gulf of Aqueba after the war. Cutting off entry to Aqueba by Egypt was the reason for the war (June 1967) Chapter XXVI

Arafat and members of the patrol Bill Wise and I accompanied on a patrol into Israel (December 1968) Chapter XXVIII

CHAPTER XXV

Gun running, Verwoerd's assassination in South Africa, Aberfan

The year 1966 was the peak of the 'Swinging London' era when males started exhibiting plume feathers and girls challenged them with their mini skirts ever shorter. The Kings Road was at its trendiest. Nadine Liber, LIFE's ebullient and attractive fashion editor, came to London to work with me on the new fashions. She organised the elegant Duke of Bedford wearing a frilly 'Mr. Fish' shirt to appear in the drawing room of Woburn Abbey surrounded by priceless Canaletto paintings and the man who started it all, John Stevens, in Carnaby Street.

In May, Jim Hicks and I worked on a gun-running story which brought James Bond to life for us. It also opened our eyes to the big business in selling arms.

Major Bob Turpe, stocky and dark complexioned, looked every bit the part. As he stood surrounded by thousands of guns in his London depot, he told us, 'The first request after a new state gets its independence is for guns, guns and more guns. I can supply anything from a miniature pistol to tanks and jet aircraft.'

We went with Bob to the Carthage Club in Brussels on the narrow Rue Chain et Pain, the 'bourse' (or 'stock exchange') for the world's arms dealers and gun runners. Waiters wore red fezzes and served furtive-looking people who examined pistols at their tables as if they were studying dirty postcards.

From Brussels I flew south to Tunis, chartered a plane aptly registered TS FAB (my initials) which took me into the heart of the Sahara Desert where I joined a Mehari camel patrol equipped mainly by Bob Turpe. On a patrol past 'Beau Geste' castles I had to ride a camel and made a bad start by falling over the top of the animal's head when it suddenly stood up. Once safely in the saddle again I enjoyed the lolloping stride as we rode for mile after mile over endless sand dunes. Here one needs a strong stomach to avoid sea-sickness.

Antonioni was directing the film *Blow Up* on location in England. He seldom allowed visiting photographers on his set but allowed me there since I was working on his personal profile. I noticed a foreign photographer sneak in on the set. His unscrupulous behaviour was well known. During a lunch break he switched the shutter speeds on all five of my cameras, hoping to get his pictures exclusively. Fortunately, I heard the change of 'note' from the shutter, and Antonioni had him chased off the set.

At this point I was working on five stories in addition to Antonioni: one on actress Vanessa Redgrave in *The Prime of Miss Jean Brodie;* gun running; pirate radio in the North Sea; the Northern Ireland troubles, and our NATO jet fighters in Germany. Working on so many stories at a time causes logistical problems: flying from one country to another and back again sometimes in the same day, juggling with the European weather and temperamental people, and keeping six sets of captions and unprocessed film separately.

LIFE wanted a stunning cover for the NATO essay. Rudy Chelminski had an idea for an aerial picture comprising a close formation flight of the latest jet fighters belonging to the seven NATO nations. Setting this up had taken months of wading through bureaucracy, but by June he had gathered all the fighters and their back-up crews together at Chaumont in France for what must rank as one of the most expensive set-up pictures ever taken.

Once again I found myself high up in the deep blue sky pushing an F102 delta wing jet through the sound barrier. My American pilot was on hand to do the vital actions but allowed me to fly the fighter. It was a thrill to feel that kick in the back as the after burner cut in on take off and almost exploded us into the air. It was over 20 years since I had last flown a jet and yet I felt as though I had never left the cockpit.

But our luck was not to hold. Literally hours before the weather cleared and we were about to take off there was a disastrous air crash in the United States when a giant General Electric B.70 experimental plane engaged in aerial photography collided with another jet. The Pentagon in Washington immediately signalled that their Phantom could not now take part. A LIFE cover without the U.S. jet prominently featured in the foreground seemed pointless but we went ahead nevertheless with the remaining six fighters.

A pleasant brief interlude for me was to photograph the Bunny croupiers at the London Playboy Club. Then a story on Jonathan Miller on the television version of *Alice in Wonderland*. The great British satirist and brain surgeon forced me on one occasion to remark, 'Jonathan, I have not the vaguest idea what you are talking about half the time. I am only an instant intellectual.'

'What is an instant intellectual?' he queried.

'Someone who only reads the literary pages of the Sunday papers.'

Jonathan had an ideal face to be caricatured by distorting his already exaggerated features with an extreme wide angle lens. No one enjoyed the results more than he did.

He attracted some top names for his film on Alice. On a bleak, windy day we went down to Fairlight Beach at Hastings for the famous dance of the mock turtle, played by Sir John Gielgud and the Gryphon, Malcolm Muggeridge. Vanessa's father, Sir Michael Redgrave, played the Caterpillar and Peter Sellers was the King of Hearts. The setting made for lovely colour pictures as the waning sun back-lit the shimmering pools of water left in the rippled sand. Ominous clouds enhanced the backdrop.

The summer was on us when the Associated Press tapes tickered the news that prime minister Johannes Verwoerd of South Africa had been assassinated. There was a rush to Heathrow where correspondents again scrambled to get aboard the first flight to that unhappy country.

At the press conference in Pretoria for the funeral arrangements I was pointedly refused all press facilities and permits. Since I had already hired two teams to work with me, I borrowed a set of press passes and car stickers from Sandy Gall and commissioned a commercial artist I knew in Johannesburg to reproduce three sets. With these we had no difficulty in getting a team into Union Buildings for the main ceremony and on the vantage points along the funeral route. There had been a gentleman's agreement at the press conference not to photograph the graveside scenes, but I had been kicked out and knew nothing of this, so was surprised to find myself alone as the coffin was being lowered into the ground. Relations and the cabinet no doubt thought that I was the official photographer.

A few months later I received a letter from the South African Ministry of the Interior saying that in future I would have to apply for a visa (not required by the British) before I could re-enter their country. This was their way of saying, 'You are banned.' I was not altogether happy about this as I believe a journalist's job is to be able to get into countries and not be banned. The authorities would not give a reason but I presume it was for this act as I had never been involved in political or underground operations outside my job as a journalist. I had earlier been banned from Ghana as a 'fascist' and now from South Africa as a 'communist'. Can't win!

I am sure countries are wiser not to ban pressmen other than in exceptional circumstances, as correspondents will get their story regardless and, because they are human, a lot less favourably.

By the end of October I was to cover two very different tragedies. The first was in Lisbon after two men had tried to row across the Atlantic. Their boat, the Puffin, had been discovered adrift without signs of its two occupants. Heart-rending drawings on the walls of the small cabin gave indications of the hell they had suffered before they died.

The second tragedy was back in the United Kingdom and was one I will never forget. I was at home trying to catch up on months of expense accounts when Jim Hicks phoned: 'There has been a dreadful mine disaster in South Wales. I am trying to arrange a charter plane to get us there right away. Frank Allen will pick you up.'

I dropped everything. My mind flashed back over six years to the last mine disaster I had covered in South Africa, so I had an idea how to tackle this one. Over the years we had to cover so many horrors and tragedies that we could virtually write the shooting script before even getting to the scene.

In the small Cessna aircraft Jim explained that this was no ordinary coal mining disaster but that a 600 foot high coal slag had collapsed in the heavy rain and descended like a black avalanche over the small mining village of Aberfan. First reports on the tape suggested that nearly 200 children lay entombed in their school beneath the grimy mess.

The road up to Aberfan from Cardiff where we had landed was jammed with cars, forcing us to crawl along at 15 m.p.h. Then we heard the sirens. A large rescue crane was following a police car on the wrong side of the road. We pulled over and our driver tucked his car behind the crane which we then followed into Aberfan.

We worked throughout the night. Temporary lights cast eerie shadows through the coal dust and smoke as tough miners dug feverishly into the slime, in many cases searching for their own children. A shovel touched something soft and a small, blackened corpse was lifted tenderly out of the mud, swathed in a blanket and, with another small bundle, placed on a stretcher and carried to the nearby church.

As dawn broke over this dreadful sight, allowing us to get a better idea of what had happened, it was obvious that our lead picture had to be an aerial photograph. Jim and I hastened back to Cardiff. We were now on the last few hours of our colour deadline in New York. There were no charter planes to be had but, by joining the Cardiff Flying Club and persuading a local Cambrian Airways pilot to fly us over Aberfan, it looked as if we might just make it.

The weather was low and overcast. I badly needed sunshine to get the black contrasting with the green around the slide. Over Aberfan small shafts of sunlight were trying to break through the murk. Each time we circled, endeavouring to catch a shaft of sun on the disaster, I looked at my watch. Jim had previously checked the flights out of Cardiff and our only hope lay in getting our film on to a Cambrian Airways flight to Dublin where there was less than half an hour to make the connecting flight to New York. We circled until the very last minute and, as though the heavens were opening up, a beam of sunlight suddenly floodlit the ghastly scene below.

My pilot knew the Captain on the Dublin flight and called him up on the radio. We landed as he was taxying out. My pilot leapt out, ran over and handed his friend the film packet, complete with the captions I had written on the return flight. Jim telephoned the airfreight department in Dublin and persuaded one of the men to complete the documents, meet the Cambrian pilot and get our packet on to the New York jet. That picture made one of the rare upright 'double trucks' in the magazine.

Journalists work best when under pressure and fighting the clock. Most of our assignments were rush jobs.

We found the situation very changed when we returned to Aberfan. Black-faced, exhausted and weeping fathers had time to assess the full horror of what had happened. They were to discover that 144 people, mostly their own children, had perished. We were threatened with shovels as we photographed their measureless grief made even worse by the steady downpour of rain. Only yesterday the valley had echoed to the laughter of these children, so we fully understood their hostility to our intrusion. We tried to explain, as we have had to do before, that only by showing this tragedy to the world, and particularly in pictures, could the full horror be brought home to people and so help avert a similar disaster. We did not tell them at the time that the publicity would also bring them immense material help and force the lethargic bureaucracy into the kind of instant action they would need when the pain and sadness eased.

We had problems both from the miners and the police in getting inside the elementary school, but once inside we saw the pathetic sight of school books, toys and personal belongings which had floated up on the black slime to half the height of the simple school room.

The worst was still to come for us when we had to visit bereaved mothers in their homes .This invasion of privacy at such times is something that every journalist loathes. It is arguable whether we should do it but I still believe it has to be done. Who can enjoy listening to a mother trying to tell us through her tears that she has just lost her only two children as she hands us copies of their photographs, or one old grandmother who, almost in a coma, told us she had lost eleven grand children? One sobbing miner told us he had lost his wife and both his children. She had just taken them to the school when it happened. It was only on the train back to London that the kaleidoscope of the last few days unfolded itself in my mind.

Having lost my own son in tragic circumstances, it was all the more poignant for me.

In February 1967 Henry Luce, the cofounder of Time Inc. with Briton Hadden, died at the age of 68. He once said, 'Producing every issue of LIFE is like producing a new show on Broadway every week.' He had an audience of some 30 million at that time. We all felt a great figure had left us. Nothing would be quite the same again.

In the meanwhile I joined Jane Howard in Dublin. She had flown over from New York to do a story on a great American poet, John Berryman. John had a marvellous craggy face covered with a wild grey beard and a mop of dishevelled dark hair. He wore glasses which often slipped down his nose when he described something in a loud booming voice well laced with four letter vernacular. We talked to his attractive young wife, Kate, about what we could do on the story and she said, 'It will be easy because he only moves from this funny little house a few yards down the road to the pub and then back here again. That's all.'

Kate was right. John started the day with several treble Martinis before breakfast He then shuffled down the road to a typical Irish pub filled with men whose faces might have been chosen from Central Casting. He knew them all well. He sat there for several hours drinking large Irish whiskies, talking and writing some of his beautiful poetry. Mostly, though, he wrote during the night, the strain and pain eased by yet another bottle of whiskey. One evening Jane and I took John and Kate to dinner at the Gresham Hotel in Dublin. After John had bombarded the elegant Catholic guests with four letter words, we were asked to leave.

On 27 May 1967 Loudon Wainright, another colleague, flew in from New York and together we chartered a Cessna to fly out beyond the Lizard to meet Gypsy Moth IV at the end of the first round the world solo sail. We made low sweeps to get close-up aerial pictures which were not appreciated by Francis Chichester. The next morning I met Sheila Chichester and her son Giles at the Royal Western Yacht Club in Plymouth and she invited me to accompany her on the Admiral's barge the following morning to meet her husband. LIFE, after all, was a foreign publication as far as the British were concerned and with all the world's press in Plymouth for the great arrival, I saw problems. We tried to charter our own boat but this proved impossible. I was having dinner that night with the rest of our team when the Admiral's ADC entered and said, 'I'm awfully sorry, old boy, but I am afraid we cannot take you on the barge as it is creating too many problems with the rest of the media.'

'That's quite alright,' I answered, 'I thought this might be the case, so Sheila, Giles and I will go out in our own charter boat.' I lied. I knew the embarrassment this would cause the Admiral.

Sure enough, the next day I was greeted aboard the Admiral's barge. The Admiral, who knew nothing of the press controversy, could not have been more pleasant. He allowed me to manoeuvre his barge through the armada of boats to get the pictures I needed. Within minutes of Francis Chichester crossing the finishing line, the Admiral took us alongside Gypsy Moth IV and I jumped aboard, giving Sheila a helping hand. Francis took us in slowly under motor as we wormed our way through the hundreds of small craft that had come out to welcome him home. We dropped anchor off the jetty while the sun went down, giving us a dramatic sunset to add to the already colourful scene.

Thirty thousand people turned out for the welcome. Francis Chichester was back 226 days after leaving Plymouth. His final leg from Sydney had lasted four months so he was ready for some of the bottles of champagne we had brought aboard. For the next 50 minutes he remained below deck as we drank champagne out of plastic glasses and he talked to his family. Eventually, Sheila said to her husband, 'The Lord Mayor of Plymouth is waiting on the jetty. We must go.'

'Oh, I had not planned to go ashore until tomorrow.'

Contrary to press reports at the time, and despite the amount of champagne he had drunk, he stepped ashore quite steadily. Chichester was knighted by the Queen for his exploits. We remained good friends until his death. Sheila invited me to his memorial service in Westminster Abbey.

Bunny Croupiers at the London Hilton, July 1966.

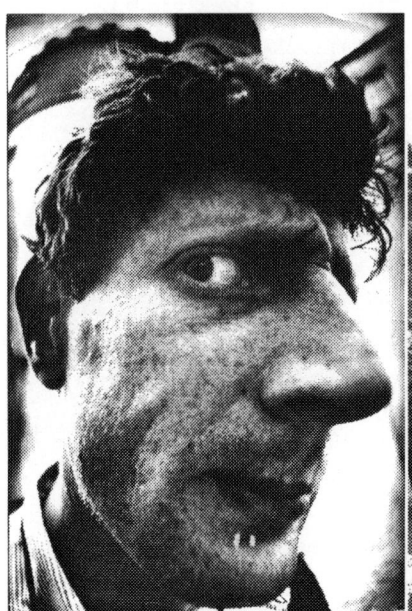

Jonathan Miller, July 1966. He was then directing the TV film of Alice in Wonderland

John Berryman in Dublin.

CHAPTER XXVI

Arab/Israeli war. Working on films and rioting in Paris

Three days after Chichester's arrival I was called from the dinner table in Plymouth to speak to Dick Pollard on the telephone from New York. Dick was the LIFE Director of Photography. 'Hi Terry. You guys did a great job with the 'Ole Man and the Sea.' We are making a big layout but that's not why I'm calling. We hear that units of the Russian fleet are leaving the Black Sea and heading for the Mediterranean. Can you get to Istanbul tomorrow?'

'Jesus, Dick! Plymouth is a long way from London but I'll try.'

Dick gave me contact numbers in Turkey and the date he wanted the colour film in New York.

One of the locals told me there was a milk train to London, leaving Plymouth at 1.15am and arriving London 6am. I threw my gear together, checked out of the hotel and made the train. Fortunately I kept a float of $2,000 in traveller's cheques but had to collect film from the bureau before returning home. It was a quick 'hello and goodbye' to Lesley and somehow I caught the 1155am BEA flight to Athens which was running 40 minutes late. I had a tight connection to make for Istanbul so persuaded our Captain, an ex R.A.F. pilot, to radio ahead and ask Pan American Airways to help me make the vital connection. A car met me as I left the Comet and whisked me over to the Istanbul flight while another car collected my luggage out of the freight hold and dumped it in the First Class compartment with me.

Charlie Lanius of Pan Am escorted me through Istanbul customs and immigration and drove me to the Hilton Hotel. We had a few scotches in my room overlooking the Bosphorus before we left for the British and American embassies to seek information on the Russian warships. The British embassy either did not know or refused to give me any information but my contact in the American embassy told me that the ships were due to pass through the Bosphorus at 4.30 the following morning.

Charlie helped me find a suitable location from which I could photograph the ships and we settled for the roof of the Turkish Airlines building which had a commanding view of the water on either side of Istanbul. A good tip persuaded the night porter to let me get up there in the early hours of the morning.

I left my comfortable bed at the Hilton at 2.15am but could not get a taxi. Half running, half walking, I lugged a heavy tripod and cameras with long lenses to the Turkish Airlines building, arriving at 3.15am. I rang the door bell but could not rouse the night porter. I rang incessantly to no avail. My adrenalin rose to bursting point. I saw myself having come all this way in the nick of time only to fail because a lousy little man had gone to sleep on the job with a pocketful of my money. Using two fingers I gave a powerful whistle. I stood there in the darkness of the street blowing my eardrums inside out with shrill whistles. I expected any moment to be arrested for creating a public nuisance at this hour of the morning.

At 4am a sleepy figure appeared at the door and led me up to the roof, expounding apologies. I need not have panicked. The first Russian ships did not pass my vantage point until 6am.

These sort of jobs in strange countries are worrying. It is easy to be picked up as a spy and explanations to the contrary can be exhausting.

I had a problem getting this film out of Turkey to meet our tight deadline as it could not go through normal channels. Passengers would sometimes carry it for you in those days but in the Middle East they were scared of carrying drugs. Aircrews are unreliable because they 'slip' several times and forget to hand on your packet. In this instance I gave it to an air hostess, telexed New York to have the flight met and it arrived on time.

I was lazing by the Hilton pool the next day when my small transistor radio galvanised me into action. The sombre voice of the announcer said that war had broken out all over the Middle East. Cairo and Tel Aviv had been bombed and Jerusalem was being shelled. I slipped a towel around my waist and rushed, still dripping, into the telex room and asked New York which way I should head. I hopped a taxi to the British embassy and persuaded them to renew a second passport I carried for Israel. Later that afternoon an A.P. report said that a colleague on LIFE, Paul Schutzer, had been killed in Israel minutes after the war broke out but that Mike Mok, his reporter riding in a separate armoured personnel carrier, had survived.

At 6pm I received my cable, 'GO TO BEIRUT URGENTEST.' A call to the American embassy confirmed what I expected, that all airports throughout the Middle East were closed to civilian traffic. My contact, however, told me that they were organizing a military air evacuation of civilians out of Beirut. He would be at the airport at dawn and would help me stow away on one of the empty transport planes.

I was worried about carrying one and a half hundredweight of equipment into a war zone, but I had no alternative. I packed it up to make it as manageable as possible and went down to dinner. I checked the telex office after dinner to be handed another cable from Milt Orshefsky on the New York news desk: 'PAUL SHUTZER KILLED IN ISRAEL CANCEL BEIRUT AND PROCEED TEL AVIV URGENTLY STOP GOOD LUCK.'

The American embassy advised me to get to Rome where Israeli El Al planes were landing to refuel. There was a connection to Rome that night. I telexed our bureau there to pull out all the stops with the Israeli embassy to get me on one of these flights.

We were delayed in Milan. When I reached the Rome bureau in mid morning I was given another cable from Milt: DO NOTNOT GO TEL AVIV BUT TRY AND GET IN ON ARAB SIDE.' I made a telephone call to Hugh Moffet in Paris; He said 'To hell with that. Go to Tel Aviv now that you are in Rome.'

I managed three hours sleep in my suite at the Excelsior before I was awakened and driven out to the Leonardo da Vinci airport. My surplus gear was safe in the office. I hung around the airport for the rest of the night and most of the next day. My only excitement was a glimpse of the gorgeous Gina Lollobrigida as she swept past me en route for some exotic part of the world to which I would also rather be heading instead of to Israel as things were.

At 4.15 in the afternoon I was aboard an El Al plane already crowded to capacity. We had to make the flight in the dark because of Arab fighters, though with modern means of detection I feared them as much at night. The cabin was blacked out, as was Tel Aviv when we arrived. When our wheels touched the ground the Israeli passengers cheered and sang patriotic national songs.

LIFE had a huge involvement in the Mid East-war. They had seventeen men covering both sides, including Theodore White, Tommy Thompson and photographers Cornel Capa, Bill Ray and several of my buddies, including Rudy Chelminski. I teamed up with Bill Wise who helped me obtain the necessary press credentials and accreditation without which one cannot operate in war zones.

By the next morning, what must surely rate as the greatest military operation of all time was virtually over bar the shouting. There were still isolated pockets of fighting up in the Golan Heights, and in Sinai where Bill and I headed.

It was Egypt's act in preventing Israeli ships passing through the Straits of Tiran that sparked off the war. Bill and I decided to check out Sinai and head for Sharm el Sheikh with the hope of riding back into the Gulf of Aqaba on the first Israeli ship to return.

Most of the Israeli army were civilians hastily turned soldiers. This applied particularly to the press information office. One can reasonably understand that they had little time to make plans for press coverage, nor did they have the resources to help the media. So battling through the bureaucracy was an exhausting and frustrating job. Bill and I decided to take off on our own and managed to hitch a lift aboard an air force DC3 transport plane going south into Sinai. This was a break for us. As always, when you get out into the field amongst the men doing the fighting, bureaucracy, regulations and restrictions disappear like a cloud of smoke.

Our DC3 took us across Gaza and along the main road to Suez. The pilot allowed me to sit by the open door and get photographs of the aftermath of the desert war waged a mere 500 feet below. We flew over miles of twisted, burned-out wrecks and saw literally thousands of rotting bodies strewn across the sand. They looked like toy soldiers knocked over by a careless child. We landed at numerous

Living Dangerously

outposts in the desert where local commanders welcomed us and showed us gruesome sights in their areas. We saw formations of Russian T.38 tanks stopped in their tracks by Israeli anti-tank weapons. They were still in battle groups. Many of the tanks were garlanded with bodies in grotesque positions due to rigor mortis. Some of the bodies were welded to the steel of their tanks by the intense heat. The putrid smell of death turned the strongest stomachs.

One of my strangest memories was of thousands of pairs of Arab boots that lay scattered about the sand as though they had been abandoned by their owners in the terror of the moment. The other memory was of the fervour, enthusiasm and determination of the Israeli soldiers to make this 'the war to end all wars in the Middle East'. I had not seen this sort of spirit in any other army.

Yet another unforgettable sight was flying over the Mitla Pass, a few miles inland from the Red Sea, where the greatest tank battle in history had just been fought. It surpassed El Alamein in North Africa or anything I saw in the Falaise Gap in Northern France during World War II. For fourteen miles we saw an almost continuous snake of burned out tanks, vehicles and the mass of equipment carried by a modern army on the offensive. Bodies covered the sides of the hills like ants as terrified men had tried to escape the massacre.

When we reached Sharm el Sheikh we were introduced to Captain Menachem Cohen and at noon on a clear sunny Sunday (11 June 1967) we boarded his black-hulled ship and passed through the Straits. The limp Israeli flag on the stern of the ship suddenly caught a gust of wind and flew out proudly as though to honour this great day. I needed aerial pictures as the Dolphin sailed up the Gulf of Aqaba, so the naval commander at Sharm arranged for a small aircraft to rendezvous with us on a desert strip near the water some fifteen miles up the Straits. Captain Cohen put us ashore in a cutter and a few minutes later Bill and I were flying over his ship in the magnificent setting of the multi-coloured sea caused by the reflection of the underwater coral. Our pilot dropped us at Eilat where an Air Force pilot flew us over the Negev Desert back to Tel Aviv. Here we found that the bureaucracy had tightened up even more. All copy and film had to be censored before leaving Israel. We had already arranged for one of the team to fly out of the country, hand-carrying material to avoid censorship.

The reporter has to rely on local news briefing and hand-outs. These are obviously biased in favour of the side he is covering. Often, they tell you direct lies so that the correspondent who reports these wars from the comfort and safety of headquarters – and some do – gets a distorted idea of what is really happening. Also people doing the fighting will talk whereas those back at base tend not to. Those reporters who venture into the field often go with organised tours set up by Press Information Officers and are shown only what governments want them to see. On their return their files will be censored and a clever censor can re-slant copy simply by astute cuts. The reporter who files an antagonistic report, which in his view is honest, can expect hostility and even have his press facilities removed. In extreme cases he can be kicked out of the country. A less apparent government 'weapon' is to delay transmission at the cable office until the story is 'dead', or delay airfreighting film until the 'peg' is lost. I have seen all this happen, not necessarily in Israel but in Vietnam, the Congo, South Africa and elsewhere. The experienced journalist knows how to avoid these hurdles.

The culmination of this historic Six Days War was the ecstatic scene at the Wailing Wall as many Jews returned to kiss the Wall for the first time in nearly 2,000 years.

By the end of June the LIFE team had left Israel, but not before a farewell party at Mandy's Club. Mandy Rice-Davies, along with Christine Keeler, was the girl involved in the Profumo case in England where reported orgies nearly brought down the Conservative government. Mandy was the perfect hostess. She had that peaches and cream complexion suggesting that butter would not melt in her mouth. Donald Wise and I had been remarking that some of the most beautiful girls in the world seemed to be in Tel Aviv. Mandy chirped up, 'They are lovely, aren't they? But I am told they are very promiscuous!'

Sean Flynn was at the party. He had the swashbuckling character and semblance of his famous father, Errol. Sean later went missing in Cambodia on a photo assignment and has not been heard of since.

Living Dangerously

The party lasted all night. As dawn broke Robin Stafford of the *Express* took us out to Lod Airport to board an El Al plane for Rome. The aircraft was filled with pressmen and the result was a hectic breakfast party over the Mediterranean.

Mike Mok was still badly shaken after his experience with Paul Schutzer so Hugh Moffet thought it a good idea if I took him to Ireland on a peaceful smuggling story. The British paid farmers in the North a subsidy on the butter they produced. By smuggling this butter across the border into the Irish Republic it could be sold at the full price and make £125 per ton for the smuggler. Hugh reckoned it would take us a week to find a smuggler and give Mike a good rest. In fact, the day after we arrived in Dublin we went to see Tony O'Reilly who was then working for the Irish Milk Marketing Board but who many years later became head of Heinz and a multi-millionaire tycoon. O'Reilly gave us the name of a high-ranking customs officer who, in turn, gave us the names and addresses of the three top butter smugglers in Ireland.

The first name we visited was suspicious of us but after a cup of tea and plenty of chat we showed him our LIFE credentials and copies of the magazine on the Middle East war which bore not only our names but our pictures in the Editor's note.

'How did you track me down?' Paddy asked (not his correct name).

'We can't tell you that but anyone in our business has good contacts.'

'Fair enough. You look too intelligent to be customs men!' he joked. 'As it happens, I am doing a trip tonight with a seven ton lorry. Be here at 2.30am but don't raise any suspicion leaving your hotel at that hour of the morning.'

We parked our car well away from the hotel and climbed out through an open window so as not to disturb anyone. Paddy was on the telephone when we arrived talking to one of his contacts on the northern side of the border. He was enquiring the whereabouts of police patrol cars and local customs officers. It seemed impossible that his line was not being tapped. Anyway, the coast was clear. I sat with Mike in the front while Paddy drove the lorry. An escort car followed us.

'The border is interlaced with hundreds of miles of small unapproved roads, crossing and re-crossing the border,' Paddy told us in his broad Irish brogue. 'Also there are many farms in this area straddling the border so you will see, we have few problems.'

It made us realise how easy it was for the IRA to move arms and explosives into Northern Ireland.

Paddy told us that our route had taken us into Northern Ireland three times before we arrived at a lonely farm. A figure came out to greet us. Paddy backed his lorry into a barn laden with boxes of butter. It took two hours to load and was getting light when we started our return journey. It was on this journey that the escort car was busy. It raced ahead to check for road blocks and then returned back down the road to ensure that we were not being followed. A soft, watery sun loomed on the horizon as we pulled into another barn back in the Republic of Ireland. The butter we had unloaded was being repacked into cartons marked 'Irish creamery butter'.

We did another trip with Paddy the following night to the north and at dawn left for Dublin with the re-packed butter on Paddy's large truck.

'We would have to be unlucky to be caught now,' Paddy smiled and pulled into a roadside café for breakfast. The girl brought us steak and two eggs but nothing to put on our bread.

'Do I have to go outside and fetch me own butter?' Paddy smirked.

We planned another trip two nights later but a cable from New York advised that Jackie Kennedy was due in Dublin and we were to cover her visit. We attended her meeting with President de Valera and then covered the glittering reception given by Jack Lynch, the prime minister. The following day we accompanied her to the Curragh for the Irish Derby. She certainly looked glamorous.

I flew back to Paris with Mike to supervise the prints for our butter smuggling story. As with the IRA it was essential that the pictures gave no details which could put Paddy and his associates behind bars.

Living Dangerously

I was away most of the month of August with Jane Howard, first in Tangier working with a best selling author, Paul Bowles and his wife, also an author, on the subject of cannabis, Then it was off to the Mediterranean island of Mallorca for a story on Temple Fielding, the man who wrote travel guides to Europe.

It was while on Mallorca that I received a cable from Lesley: 'HOUSE SOLD STOP HAVE TO MOVE IN TWO WEEKS STOP WHERE TO?'

Funny joke. I thought. I was home four days later. Lesley met me at Heathrow; 'Isn't it good news about the house? He paid the full price,' she said.

'What is all this about "house sold"?' I enquired.

'Surely you have not forgotten that nice all-in wrestler called Spencer Churchill coming to see you about buying our house? It was the morning you returned from Israel. You and he polished off a couple of bottles of wine to celebrate the sale.'

I finished the month of August starting to work on the movie of *Chitty Chitty Bang Bang* at Pinewood studios. Since a scene suitable for the Panavision motion picture camera seldom worked for my still cameras, Cubby Broccoli, the producer, agreed that I could ask for half a minute at the end of each scene I needed to photograph. This resulted in endless arguments with the first assistant director, Gus Agosti, and did not make my job an easy one. In any event, it is frustrating for a photographer working on a film set, as you hang around all day drinking countless cups of tea and talking to people who seem to have nothing else to do. At the end of the day, if you are lucky, you may have one picture in the can.

Other problems for visiting photographers on a big movie set include having to cope with professional jealousy and temperament. This requires extreme tact at times.

The pleasant side of being on *Chitty* was to work with the charming Dick van Dyke. It was difficult to take a bad picture of him. Playing opposite Dick was the equally delightful Sally Ann Howes, daughter of Bobby Howes. Then there was Roland Emmett and his ingenious fantasy machines that became such a feature of the film.

One of the two aerial cameramen on *Chitty* was Johnny Jordan who had recently had a leg severed by a helicopter blade while working on a James Bond film in Japan. He was soon to fall thousands of feet to his death out of a camera plane in South America. Johnny helped me mount a remote controlled Nikon on top of his aerial Panavision camera to record some beautiful pictures of the mythical car flying over the fairytale Neuschwanstein Castle in Bavaria.

Lesley was able to accompany me on the film, and while the unit moved from Bavaria to the south of France she and I crossed the Brenner Pass into Italy to the fabled city of Venice. It was exciting waking up in the morning. A weak sun shone into our room and the waters of the Grand Canal lapped the wall below our window. Gondolas glided past under the expert control of their colourful masters. In the evening we visited Harry's Bar, made famous by Ernest Hemingway.

The film unit moved to St. Tropez for the water scenes and being late October, it was quiet. Lesley and I decided to find a hotel away from the one reserved for the film unit. We hired a penthouse on the top floor of the little Hotel de la Tour overlooking the lively little harbour. The unit visited us most nights as the LIFE magazine hospitality knew no bounds.

Katharine Hepburn was in London rehearsing for the film *The Lion in Winter*. LIFE wanted a cover story on this fine actress. I knew that Miss Hepburn did not like photographers. Few actresses over 50 do. I also knew that she could be pretty brusque with them. So it was with some trepidation that I went with Jim Hicks to the Connaught Hotel to collect her. She was wearing trousers as she walked down the stairs, crossed the lobby and greeted us. She was still very much the Katharine Hepburn I remembered and admired as a kid. Together with her companion, Miss Willborn, we drove off in a Rolls Royce provided by the film company. Her folding bicycle was in the boot. She rode around Hyde Park while I photographed her, before going to a small studio I had prepared in Soho.

By now she had discovered my name. No doubt because of her love for Spencer Tracy, she kept calling me 'Spencer Terry'. Maybe the name endeared me more to her than might otherwise have been the case. In the Rolls she turned round and said, 'I really hate LIFE photographers. They try to make me stand on my head or do something equally crazy.' I thought I detected a glint in her eyes.

'My God,' I answered, 'That's a great idea, Miss Hepburn. I have never seen an upside down LIFE cover yet.'

After we had completed our picture session with the marvellous Miss Hepburn, I said to her, 'Now let's do those shots of you standing on your head!'

'You think I can't do it, don't you? Bring me a cushion.'

'No. A cushion would ruin the clean lines of the yellow backdrop.'

I was using the Ascor 600 strobes which take nine seconds to build up between flashes, Katie stood on her head for 36 seconds on the concrete studio floor while I exposed five sheets of large format colour film as she moved her legs in five separate poses.

I should mention here that you often have to exercise considerable sensitivity in dealing with creative people. One wrong word can ruin your relationship. It is another reason why I do not believe the photographer should himself be a show piece. Eccentrics are often second rate photographers. Beards and 'way out' clothes make him conspicuous. Someone once knocked at the front door of our house in Windsor, looked me up and down and asked, 'Are you the owner?' Far from being annoyed, I was flattered.

Katharine Hepburn was another great star whose every picture was a winner. She insisted on vetting the colour before it went to New York, a habit we tried to avoid except for a select few. Jim Hicks later phoned to say she liked the whole take. LIFE editors thought hard about using an upside down cover but settled on a more conventional one in the studio, using Katie on her head as a full page picture inside the magazine.

I only mention my visit to Copenhagen in February 1968 to illustrate the dangers sometimes experienced by magazine photographers. I was with Temple Fielding in the Valencia night club, watching a tall, lithe girl dance in the nude. Suddenly, she stopped her crazy gyrations. A light must have reflected from my camera lens. She glared across in my direction, then rushed towards me, her breasts quivering with rage, her long red talons poised for attack as she tried to grab my camera. I was saved by the manager who assured her I had permission. 'He hasn't got my bloody permission,' she screamed out for all the guests to hear. The manager escorted her off the floor. I felt the colour slowly deserting the nape of my neck as I joined Temp at his table for a much needed scotch.

In March Jim Hicks and I flew to Seville in Spain to work on Harry Saltzman's film, *The Battle of Britain*. I was soon strapped into the rear cockpit of a converted Messerschmitt 109 fighter weaving in and out of large formations of Heinkel 111 bombers. I was nauseated by the familiar smell I had always associated with German World War II planes. On each of our small wings were the dreaded swastikas I had learned to fear all those years ago.

Some of the London blitz scenes were filmed in the Old Kent Road in London where disused warehouses were set alight under wavering searchlights. One of the first people I saw on the set was Lord Snowdon who greeted me with his usual cheerfulness, 'I haven't seen you for some time. Where are you living these days?'

'Just down the Long Walk from your sister-in-law,' I smiled, tongue in cheek. For a moment he was not sure which sister-in-law I was referring to until I mentioned Windsor: in those days he was married to Princess Margaret.

Supper was being served in a nearby pub which had quietly kept open until midnight for the unit. The bar was packed. Tony and I edged towards the counter. As I ordered two large scotches I noticed several uniformed police officers enter the back of the bar and order everyone out.

'God, can you imagine the London newspapers in the morning?' exclaimed Tony. 'Police eject Lord Snowdon for drinking after hours in an East End pub. At least, YOU can witness that I was not drinking.'

'But for the grace of God,' I added.

People criticise some photographers for using their titles or their sex to further their reputations. Why not? Tony Snowdon is a fine photographer by any standards, and his royal duties did not make his job any easier.

Living Dangerously

I had just two hours in bed that night before flying to Paris in the morning. It was nearly mid May. I checked in to the Crillon and went down to the bar. Jack Starr, veteran Paris correspondent for the London *Daily Mail,* was talking to George Gale of the *Express* and another old colleague, Adrian Porter of the A.P. They filled me in on what was happening in Paris, particularly with the student situation that was beginning to look ugly. Dick Stolley, the new LIFE bureau chief in Paris, joined me for dinner at the Crillon and I heard the Vietnam peace talks side of the story. This was what I had come to help cover.

After being up most of the previous night I was in a dead sleep when the phone beside my bed rang at 2.30 am. It was Dick Stolley: 'There's trouble around the Sorbonne. Can you get down there right away?' I must have grunted an affirmative though I hardly knew what city I was in at that moment.

I persuaded a taxi driver to take me along the Rue de Rivoli as far as the Place de la Bastille, but he would go no further. I prepared my four cameras and strobe light as I hastened across the Pont Sully where flames and the bursts of tear gas canisters directed me to the Sorbonne University on the Left Bank. I dislike walking into riots on my own, especially in a strange city at night.

From what I saw that night in the Boulevard St. Germain, I knew I could expect little mercy from the CRS, the ferocious French riot police. They acted like chained dogs suddenly released as they bashed students with their long batons. One American youth had an eye kicked out by the CRS as he lay on the ground after being brutally clubbed. As it happened he was only a bystander. Police fired tear gas into students who were pulling up stone blocks from the road and hurling them at their attackers. Large shop windows collapsed in heaps of shattering glass as they were hit by stones. The left-wing students had made barricades across the road, using gleaming new cars which were then set alight. Kids rushed around with scarves over their mouths against the tear gas, coughing and spluttering as tears ran down their cheeks.

I was trying to get past a barricade when a 'flic' came at me with his truncheon. He carried a shield which failed to conceal the goggles and gas mask covering his face. He wore a small round steel helmet and a black shiny mac over his dark blue battle dress. It was an awesome sight that galvanised me into action. I leapt through the burning barricades and was grabbed by students eager to help anyone fleeing from the CRS.

My peace of mind did not last long. There were TIME-LIFE labels on my cameras in case they were lost. If I had been prepared for these troubles, they would have been removed. As it was, left-wing students took me for an American and tried to rip the cameras off my neck. This time I was inadvertently saved by the police. Tear gas canisters rained in on us and the police made a diversionary raid on our barricade. I think I ran even faster than the students and found myself in the beleagured Sorbonne. An Egyptian student befriended me and took me out by a back door into the Boulevard St. Michel.

The back had been ripped off my camera and the film fogged. I cannot admit to having lost a great set of pictures because when the trouble started the situation was too dangerous to let go flashes at the CRS or at the students. I had risked it in Athens but then I had the company of Jim Hicks and was not alone.

In July Dick Stolley asked me if I would like to do an underwater story off Antibes in the Mediterranean. Dick thought I was an experienced underwater cameraman whereas previously I had only dived to 30 feet in the clear waters of the Caribbean and Indian Ocean. However, the opportunity was too good to miss.

I checked into the Hotel Provençal in Juan les Pins and contacted Louis le Houx, an old Cousteau diver and principal of the Club de la Mer. Le Houx had persuaded Joan Miro to create a permanent statue to the 'Goddess of the Sea' to be cemented into a grotto 65 feet below the sea, four kilometres out from Juan.

July 27 was a day of clear blue skies, but a breeze made the sea a little choppier than I would have liked. André, a professional diver, took me out to La Fournique. I felt quite sick with fear as I donned a full wet suit and shouldered the heavy compressed air bottle. We rolled over backwards off the gunwale of the boat into the sea. This knocked the mouthpiece out of my mouth and I swallowed a bellyful of salt water. I also had a slight cold, making it difficult for me to clear my ears to compensate for the rapid change of pressure while descending. My ears seemed to be exploding and a taste of blood told me my nose was bleeding. I followed André closely as he dived effortlessly down to the grotto and showed me the pedestal on which the statue was to be mounted. Beams of light shone into the grotto from three tunnels and lit the scene with exquisite beauty.

My confidence increased as I began to enjoy the experience. One of my worries had been that I would feel claustrophobic at this depth, but this was not so. The thrill of being in a third dimensional world was such that I lost André and this worried me as I did not know where I was. Soon a tap on my back and André was behind, signalling me to follow him and for the next 30 minutes we explored the depths. It was exhausting work. My leg muscles were not in training for this sort of exercise. André showed me his depth gauge which registered 25 metres (over 80 feet). We surfaced slowly to avoid the 'bends' and I was elated to break the surface into brilliant sunshine.

After lunch André took me down on a second dive. We were exploring the sea bed when he swam alongside and again showed me his depth guage. It registered 35 metres which I calculated to be 115 feet. I felt fine and gave him the thumbs up so on down we went to 40 metres (130 feet) before slowly surfacing. I now felt confident for the big ceremony in the morning.

Captain Cousteau's Calypso took us out to La Fournique beacon where we rolled into the sea and swam down to the grotto alongside Miro's statue which was lowered by the ship's derrick. Trying to shoot pictures in the cramped grotto with 20 other divers jockeying for position was reminiscent of the scrambles on the Pope's tour. At one moment I was jammed against the stony ceiling of the grotto when someone's flipper kicked me in the face and dislodged my mask but, thank God, not my mouthpiece as I was so tightly wedged and could not even replace my goggles. After a few minutes the jam eased as bodies drifted slowly out of the grotto and I was able to get my pictures of the statue being fastened in position. When the water became too murky I surfaced to reload my Nikonos underwater camera and rest. With a new compressed air bottle I descended again to get beautiful pictures of the Goddess in her final watery resting place.

Israeli/Arab War, June 1967: Israeli soldiers interrogate an Arab civilian in the Gaza strip. "No, no. Not me!"

Tangiers, Morocco, Aug 1967. Paul Bowles and Jane Howard watch me smoke pot mixed up by Paul's friend.

CHAPTER XXVII

The Biafran war

I returned to London to find little work to do. Boredom set in. The war in Biafra was hotting up and I suggested to Jack Newcombe, the new London LIFE bureau chief, that we should cover that conflict. I must have been mad. Back came the reply from New York: 'YOUR BIAFRAN SUGGESTION A GOOD ONE. WANT YOU RENDEZVOUS WITH MIKE MOK AT THE TIVOLI IN LISBON STOP GOOD LUCK - MORSE.'

Strings had been pulled in Geneva to get Mike and me aboard one of Hank Wharton's aircraft flying relief supplies into Biafra. We tracked down Wharton in Lisbon but he was not helpful and said that he had nothing going down there in the near future. This was bad news.

The 21-month-old tribal civil war of Ibos fighting to secede from the Nigerian Federal government was causing a desperate situation. Biafra was now completely cut off and the only way in for men and supplies was by air from the Portuguese island of St. Tomé to the south of Nigeria.

However at 5am the next morning Mike stumbled into my room, 'Hurry, we've got to get out to the airport fast.' At the airport we were met; put into the back of a closed van and smuggled out to a deserted corner of the airfield.

No time was lost in getting us into an old Super Constellation as the dawn was breaking. We were roughly treated by a Biafran security guard armed with a rifle. 'No photographs on this trip,' he yelled at us.

I was delighted to recognise our captain as the pilot who had flown Jm Howard and me out of Kindu in the Congo after we were arrested by the UN in 1961. Frank McAllister had been one of the Flying Tigers crossing the 'Hump' into China during World War II and was not the man to stand any rot. So while Mike engaged our guard in conversation I sneaked a set of pictures of the other shady aircraft on the tarmac. Once airborne we realised the reason for the guard's hostility. Far from carrying relief supplies to the beleagured Ibos, we had ten tons of ammunition and explosives on board. It was a monotonous 12 hour non-stop flight to Bissau in Portuguese West Africa, so I waited until our guard was asleep before I risked photographing our deadly cargo.

At Bissau, a refuelling stop, there was a nasty black mess on the tarmac where one of Wharton's planes had been blown up by a saboteur a few weeks earlier. The Portuguese here were involved in their own guerila war, so security was tight. I had to use a sub-miniature camera held in the palm of the hand to get pictures of the airport. These sort of pictures seldom add up to much as it is impossible to compose them properly.

It was a further ten hour flight to Sao Tomé so we stretched out and slept across ammunition boxes. At Sao Tomé other Wharton pilots were glum over our prospects of getting into Biafra. Three planes had tried the previous night and had been forced back by 90mm anti-aircraft guns mounted on barges on the Cross River. Also, the latest news was that the 'Feds' (the Nigerian forces) were only 18 miles from Uli airstrip where we had to land.

It was obvious that our story was running out fast. I asked if anyone had been hit by flak, 'Mercifully no,' answered one of the pilots. I turned to Frank. 'You and I have flown through a hell of a lot of flak and survived...'

'Sure. Let's go,' he cracked back.

It was a 250 mile flight to Uli and it had to be done at night without any navigational aids. Fortunately for us it was dark and cloudy, though we had a glimpse of the silvery, snaking Cross River 15,000 feet below, giving our co-pilot and navigator, George Robertson, a good pin point. Objects looking like myriads of white tennis balls came floating up towards us but were not close enough to our 'Flying Bomb' to worry us.

Uli air strip, code named 'Annabelle', was an ordinary straight piece of road that had been widened to allow a mere 12 feet of clearance on either side of our wheels. This allowed no margin for even a slight swing on landing or take off. The 'runway' was marked by 60 watt globes painted red and there were standby paraffin 'goosenecks' if the power failed, which was often.

I stood in the cockpit of our Super Connie behind the two pilots ready to photograph our night landing and watched our altimeter getting lower and lower and still we did not break cloud. Although we knew the area was flat, we became increasingly anxious once the needle dropped below 1,000 feet.

Suddenly George shouted. 'There she is!'

The altimeter registered 400 feet. I could just discern a crazily narrow strip of dim lights through the mist ahead. We were too close for Frank to lower his landing gear so he did a tight turn to port as the wheels locked into position and the flaps began to lower. It seemed quite impossible to me that this overladen monster could be brought down on that narrow strip in daylight, let alone at night in these weather conditions.

Right down to the moment of impact I still could not believe there was room for our wheels between those dim lights. Frank jammed on the brakes and we came to a halt – still in one piece.

'You've got it made, Mac, Beee-yooo-teee-ful!' George shouted.

I have never seen such brilliant flying. Wrecks scattered around the airstrip bore macabre evidence, if any was needed, of Frank's skill.

Shortly after we landed, tragedy struck. The second plane followed us in. Piloted by a young American black called Augie Koming (the black child in the *Our Gang* series), it failed to clear the trees at the end of the strip and crashed. Augie joined several of his colleagues in the mission cemetery at Uli.

After my famine experience in the Congo we were more or less able to plan our shooting script even before we reached Biafra. I was determined to illustrate the horror, fear and despondency of the situation through the expressions on people's faces. I felt those pictures would be more poignant and leave a deeper effect on the minds of our millions of readers than the blood and gore they might not want to see at their breakfast tables. Though Mike and I saw countless dead bodies during the following week, I only photographed one. That was of a child on the back of its mother. At that moment I did not even know it was dead.

The pathetic but determined half-starved Ibo soldiers under the leadership of Rolf Steiner, a German mercenary, were in a country that was fast crumbling. Biafra, originally the size of Ireland, was now decimated. What was left of its 13 million Ibos were slowly starving to death.

After what I had seen in Vietnam, I was again surprised at the rare use of land mines both here and in the Congo. Most of the roads were made of gravel and ideal for this devastating weapon. Moreover, mines can be laid in reasonable safety and detonated either on impact or fired selectively by remote control.

Our host in Biafra was a tall, slim and tough Irish priest. Father Joe Prendergast wore a long white soutane and possessed one of the few remaining Jeeps that worked. He showed us something of the starvation. As in the Kasai, it was mostly the young and the old who suffered. There is not much 'give' where starvation is concerned. We saw this in a mission station at Okpala where guards had to use sticks to beat back hungry, emaciated people at a food distribution centre.

Emekuku was a mission hospital six miles from Owerri and only 20 miles ahead of the advancing 'Feds'. Seven out of 20 children died after admission. The hospital, like most others, was splitting at the seams with humanity.

We saw swollen bellied-kids with advanced kwashiorkor resulting from starvation, staggering around on spindly legs and arms looking like match sticks. Their normally black hair had turned a reddish brown. In one of the wards were two badly deformed children whose rib cages protruded through their parchment-like ebony skins. They sat on the edge of the bed they shared, staring across at a small lump under the sheet in the next bed. The staff were too busy to bury the pretty little girl who lay dead beneath. The scene so moved Mike Mok that he gave a pint of his blood, 'liberally laced with alcohol' said Mike confessing his strong propensity for scotch whisky. The Ibo mission nurse answered pertly, 'Never mind. It will help some poor child to laugh.'

The end was near for Biafra. The airlifts were scarce. The airstrip had already been bombed four times that week. Mike and I thought we should make plans to get out and I did not want to miss our Mallorcan holiday. Bureaucracy told us that we could not leave without exit visas and the immigration man at Uli had no idea who could issue them in the present chaos.

Aba was the administrative capital and was being abandoned in the wake of the advancing 'Feds'. Mig fighters and Ilyushin bombers had created havoc in the town. The road out of Aba was an almost continuous stream of exhausted, bedraggled and ravenously hungry refugees carrying their worldly belongings with them. One man was well prepared. He carried everything packed into his coffin, strapped horizontally on to the carrier of his bicycle. Another had a live goat and some chickens tied to his bicycle. I was surprised the latter had not yet been killed for food. Girls in colourful saris glided along with large white bowls balanced on their heads.

In Aba we rooted out a fat, pot-bellied bureaucrat whom we were told could authorise our exit visas. As we entered his cool, well equipped office and he realized we were journalists, he leaned across his wide desk and shouted, 'It's guns we want – not food'. It was obvious he did not need food nor did he have any personal intention of using a gun. He was typical of the fat, opulent politician sitting back comfortably flicking the ash of his cigar as he ordered another batch of young men 'to die for the cause'.

I have never known a dead man benefit from any cause. For leaders, their first thought is often to surrender on terms guaranteeing their own safety. I have watched the slow insidious build-up of myths designed to arouse a spirit of patriotism in adventurous youth and convert decent, honest boys into cold-blooded murderers, myths convincing the kids that the cause is just and in the name of God. Does this not sometimes make the perpetrators of these myths themselves common murderers? I have also seen the indecent haste at which such propaganda is dropped when the need for young lives no longer exists and how quickly a 'grateful' government forgets and lets them melt into obscurity.

Anyway, our slob promised he would look into the matter of our exit visas but we left empty handed and returned to Uli.

Father Prendergast woke Mike and me around midnight, 'We must get you to the airstrip right away. A DC7 has just landed and will be the last plane out of Biafra. I am trying to find Lloyd Garrison *(New York Times)*. Do you know where he is?' We did not.

Mike and I hung around 'Annabelle' until the early hours of the morning while the aircraft was being unloaded. We were concerned that the officious immigration officials would not let us leave without exit visas. We looked enviously as passengers boarded the D.C.7. As the last passenger was mounting the steps and in the middle of an argument with a nasty little immigration official, a man from the Information Department came up. 'Are you Mok and Spencer?' he asked, 'I have been looking for you. I have your exit visas.'

I must admit that Mike and I displayed a little indecent relief and shook each other's hands.

Our problem did not end at Sao Tomé. The airlift had been suspended and there were no planes flying in or out of the island. We 'appointed' one of the nuns working at the airfield to be our honorary stringer and asked her to phone us if anything landed, irrespective of its next destination. Mike and I then toured the idyllic island. We bought boxes of avocado pears and mangoes for a few cents and took them to a white beach fringed with palm trees where we swam in the warm water.

Our spirits were low. Mike and I drank scotch late into the night. After what seemed only a few hours in bed I was woken by a small hotel page who summoned me to the telephone. I was surprised to see the sun was up already. It was our nun. 'I have good news for you,' she said. 'A Dutch Boeing 707 has landed with the first consignment of US supplies for Biafra but we cannot get them in to Uli. Your happiness is our sorrow. People are literally dying for this food.'

Captain Jan van der Erde joined us for breakfast and willingly offered us a nonstop lift to London. Unbelievable. Our luck had held. 'What's more, you can take 40 tons of excess baggage as we will be empty,' Jan added with a laugh.

We covered the 4,300 miles in eight hours, most of it sleeping comfortably on air mattresses. It was the longest free hitchhike of my life.

Incidentally, the Biafran pictures won second prize in the World Press Photo competition, proving that there is another way to portray such suffering.

London was steeling itself for October 27 when the biggest ever left-wing anti-Vietnam demonstration was planned. Judy Fayard was in London from New York. She must have been a top candidate for the most attractive LIFE reporter but Judy was not just a pretty face. She was tough. She could break through the tightest, milling mob faster than anyone I knew. She never left my side during the five mile gruelling march when we had to run from one disturbance to another. Many LIFE reporters at times like this helped the photographers with their heavy camera bags and Judy was no exception.

The more I travelled around the world, the more I marvelled and respected the British 'bobby'. Nowhere did he surpass himself more than during the unpleasant and often vicious riots occurring in Grosvenor Square as anarchists and others tried to get into the American embassy. Despite extreme provocation and abuse the police kept smiling back at their attackers, lessening their will to strike. There was one great picture which I did not get, of a man's heavy boot connecting with a policeman's face as his helmet shot into the air. Tear gas was not used to dispel the mob that had grown to tens of thousands, nor did I see a baton strike a head. Anywhere else in the world we would have witnessed a bloodbath.

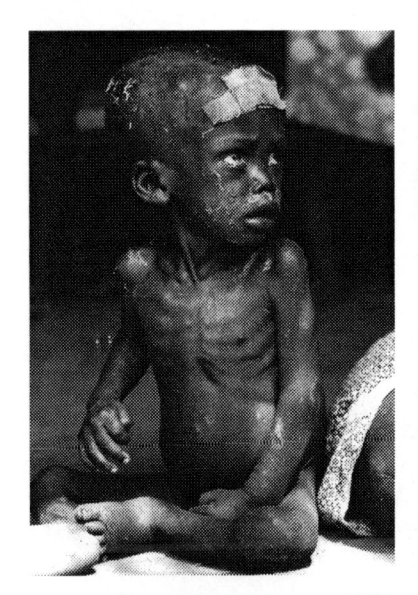

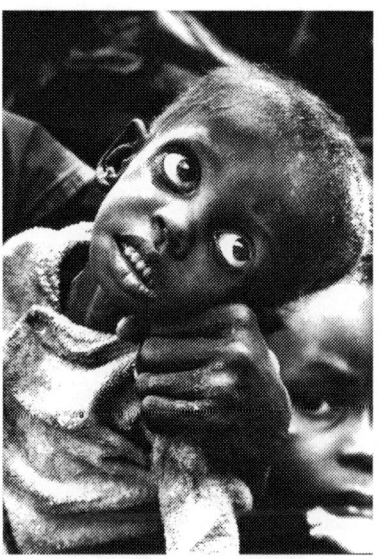

Biafra, post-war, January 1970. Left: a small casualty of the war, right: agony shown in the eyes of this half-starved child.

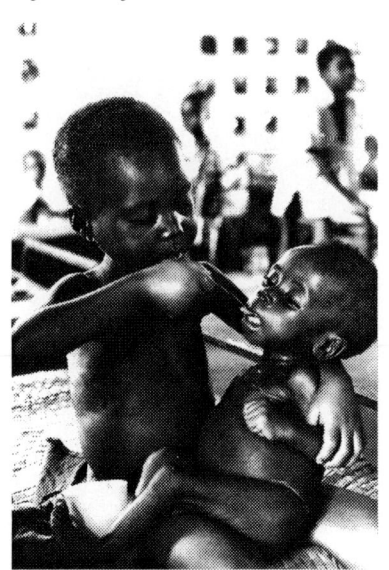

Biafra, post-war, January 1970. Left: woman and child on back, right: one small child feeds another in a hospital.

Living Dangerously 271

CHAPTER XXVIII

Back into Israel with Al Fatah guerrillas

On the 5th November 1968 Dick Stolley phoned: 'Can you go to Jordan in the morning?'

'Yes,' I answered, 'What's doing?'

'We want to try for a story on Al Fatah.'

'Who's he?' I enquired hesitatingly.

'Bill Wise will be working with you and will fill you in. Good luck.'

I met Bill in Amman. He explained that Al Fatah was the fighting wing of the Palestine Liberation Organisation (PLO), operating guerrilla groups into Israel. It was little known outside the Middle East in those days. Bill also told me that he had no good contacts in Amman. We were up against a daunting situation, trying to infiltrate this secret organisation.

We stayed in the ostensibly luxurious Intercontinental Hotel. My third floor balcony looked out across a city built on many small hills. Beneath my window I spotted Don Wise and Dick Beeston sunning themselves beside the pool. Don knew the Middle East well and Dick was based in Beirut. I knew they would give me any lead they might have, but they were unable to help.

Bill and I had worked as a team during the recent Arab-Israeli war and realised this would add to the suspicion that we were CIA agents rather than journalists. Nevertheless, we decided it better not to hide the reality. Bill composed letters to Al Fatah telling them that we were with LIFE magazine, offering them space to put their point of view before our millions of readers throughout the world and promising that what they had to say would be printed whether or not we agreed with it. We handed out copies of this letter to waiters, taxi drivers and to anyone whom we thought could vaguely have contacts with Al Fatah. Thereafter, we made ourselves 'prisoners' in the hotel, not daring to leave in case someone contacted us.

We met a Palestinian, Dr. Kimhawe, who seemed to know about Al Fatah operations in the refugee camps, youth military training and the medical organisation. He joined us for dinner in the hotel and later that night we received a mysterious telephone call to go to a street corner in one of the less populated quarters of Amman. A taxi took us there. It was a spooky, lonely back street. Bill and I hung around under the only dimly lit lamp post. Willowy figures walked past and two cars slowed up to look at us but drove on. We waited two hours then made our way back to the centre of the city where we hopped a cab back to the hotel.

We were down in the dumps. We had been in Amman for five days and seemed to be back where we started.

The following evening Bill received another call apologising for the slip-up and making another rendezvous later that evening. The same thing happened. We waited two hours and no one turned up, but somehow, we felt we were getting places and were being kept under surveillance. The third night the telephone rang yet again. 'I'm sorry for what happened last night. Our leaders have had to leave Amman and will not be back until Saturday. You must be patient.' He refused to engage Bill in conversation.

Ours is a business of perseverance and persistence. This was a good test case. Then one evening Dr. Kimhawe phoned: 'Would you care to join us in a fundraising get together for Al Fatah this evening?'

At the meeting we felt the strong anti-Americanism over their support of Israel. We were questioned throughout the evening when we told them that we had both covered the last war from the Israeli side. We emphasised that one of the reasons the Arabs were getting such a bad press in the outside world was because they either tried to arrest or limit the activities of correspondents operating with them during the war. On the other hand, the Israelis laid out the red carpet for us.

For four days nothing happened while we remained continuously in the hotel. Our patience was rewarded when a man turned up in a new Landrover and told us to accompany him. He took us out to Baq'as, a large sprawling tented refugee camp. It had been raining and the place was a quagmire of slushy clay. Our guide explained, 'There are 540,000 refugees here of whom 350,000 fled from Israeli occupied territory during and after the last war. They now lead miserable, pointless lives in camps seething with hatred and frustration but they provide ideal material for our recruitment.'

He turned to me. 'Terry, what would you do if you were suddenly kicked out of your house in Windsor simply because someone wanted it?'

My immediate reaction was, 'Windsor! My God!' He has been certainly checking up on me…

He took us to a nearby training camp where kids of between six and sixteen were being put through a tough military course including weapon handling. As we parted he said, 'Tomorrow I will show you the real thing.'

He was at the hotel at 5am and took us out on a long, dusty drive to an established Al Fatah training camp up in the hills. The recruits were undergoing a formidable commando training course in which live ammunition was fired perilously close to them at times. We photographed the camp commandant who had a perfect Castro-type bearded face but, except for him, we could not show faces. Otherwise, we photographed what we liked.

At dinner that night a man came to the hotel and told us to follow him immediately. We had an impressive meeting with a senior Al Fatah officer who had been educated at a German university. His left leg was in plaster after a recent raid into Israel. He looked more like a young academic professor than a deadly killer. He talked a little English but spoke mostly in Arabic through an interpreter, outlining many of the guerrilla plans we saw carried out in later years. He mentioned aircraft hi-jacking, assassinating top Jewish leaders in various capitals of the world, booby trapping and putting bombs into Jewish businesses, airline offices and shops. He discussed operations inside Israel and added, 'The more people who know about our plans the better. There is nothing they can do to stop us.' He was erudite and not the terrorist leader we had expected to meet. We stressed the urgency of our story, and our wish to spend some time attached to a guerrilla unit. He would not commit himself but we felt we were now on the right trail.

Returning to the hotel we bumped into Ed Hughes who was a good friend of mine but the last man we wanted to see in Amman at that moment. Ed was the *Time* bureau chief in Beirut and had good Palestinian contacts through Abu Said who ran the bureau. Ed wasted no time in breaking into the contacts we had so assiduously made.

Ironically, it was Ed who achieved for us what we had been unable to arrange for ourselves – a visit to the secret headquarters of Mohammed Yasser Arafat, the 39-year-old boss of the PLO – but at a cost. I had to agree to shoot a roll of film for *Time* knowing this very exclusive picture would beat our LIFE story by several weeks, but there was no alternative.

Ed joined us for lunch on the Monday and whispered, 'Get your gear together. We are off at 3pm.' A Palestinian, wearing the familiar kaffiyeh head-dress favoured by the Fedayeen guerrillas, drove us down a winding mountain road through deserted villages to the Dead Sea. We left the road and climbed a hilly track to a banana plantation guarded by well-armed Fedayeen who ordered us to dismount. I felt uneasy, not helped when Ed cracked, 'Hope we are not being taken to our execution!'

'A bit late to worry now,' I added with a sickly smile.

Yasser Arafat, then code-named Abu Omar, emerged from what looked like a deserted farm building. He was short and stocky with a dark moustache and wore dark glasses. Slung over his left shoulder was a Russian Kalishnikov automatic rifle. He came straight over and shook us by the hand. 'Welcome to my headquarters.' After the interview and pictures Bill and I urged him to let us join one of his operational units but he, too, would not commit himself.

We returned in the pouring rain. On the way up a narrow road in the dark our Landrover was nearly overwhelmed by a massive landslide. We saw it coming down in time to brake. It hurtled across the road in front us and made the road impassable. We backed down in even worse blinding rain to find another landslide had blocked the road behind us. We were marooned and in danger of more landslides down the steep banks below which we were trapped. We listened intently for an hour then heard a truck grinding up the hill. It was laden with Jordanian soldiers who, to our relief, had shovels.

On another occasion we were taken to a hospital at Salt where we visited a ward of wounded Al Fatah Fedayeen. Several men had legs blown off by peanut mines after crossing the Jordan River into Israel on night raids.

Several nights later a phone call beckoned us to a street corner rendezvous in Amman followed by a change of cars bringing Bill and me face to face with two of the four top men in Al Fatah. They were both university graduates from the USA and questioned us in detail. After a long meeting we were returned to our hotel. At last, we felt we were IN and celebrated at the Ali Baba.

In the early hours of the following morning there was banging on my door. It was Bill. 'Terry: get your gear together. We are off. It's for real!' Could it be true?

We were collected before dawn and driven by Landrover north to Irbid. Bill and I did not say much. We were about to penetrate the formidable forces of General Dayan with a band of guerrillas. No one had greater respect for the Israeli forces than we had after what we had seen so recently.

At Irbid we were transferred to a more operational-looking Landrover and descended to North Shuneh near the Jordan River. We were assigned to a patrol and allowed to photograph what we wanted but again – no faces. In fact, several Fedayeen had no objections as they were well known to the Israelis. Our patrol wanted Bill and me to carry weapons but this we refused to do. It is something I have never done. We try to report without bias but it is often difficult when you have been in tight corners with men who might have saved your life and whom you like. It is tough to write against them or to photograph them in a slanted fashion. This could be the reason why journalists sometimes give glowing reports about the side they are on. Freedom fighters to them are terrorists to their colleagues on the other side. I have found it impossible when working with guerrillas not to admire their bravery and determination, often against fearsome odds.

The old adage that the camera never lies is a myth. It can distort by omission or by emphasis or by slant. The camera can be infinitely more misleading than the written word.

Bill and I were not only impressed by the calibre of the Al Fatah leadership but with their modern equipment, evidence of which we saw everywhere along the Jordan River. Most of our patrol carried new Kalashnikovs and wore good quality American combat uniforms.

We travelled north to our jumping off spot south of Lake Galilee. Our two Landrovers were parked in a cutting and we stealthily made our way down to the Jordan River with our patrol. It was only 30 yards wide at that point. Across the other side was Israeli-occupied territory. Our leader had just stepped into the water when shadowy figures jumped up and grabbed him. They were Jordanian soldiers who escorted us back to our Landrovers and we returned to North Shuneh.

We were more successful the next night when Bill and I crossed the Jordan River with our patrol. I kept thinking of those little peanut mines scattered around the front line. We crept into a concealed position where our patrol fired eight 130mm Katushka rockets into what we were told was an Israeli army camp. Bill and I were in Israel with an Al Fatah patrol! We were elated after the frustrations of the last month and New York's pessimism. As we retreated back across the river we saw flames billowing into the air about six kilometres distant.

We reached Esh Shuna just in time. The Israelis started shelling and their jets rocketed our position in full moonlight. We huddled in a concrete bunker.

We covered another raid into Israel but this time from the relative safety of a hill position in Jordan. It was another bright moonlit night and three patrols attacked a kibbutz – or so we were told. With a long telephoto lens mounted on a tripod and the lens kept open for five minutes, I recorded the flashes and explosions that ensued. I am sure that not since Matthew Brady photographed the American Civil War have action war pictures been taken off a tripod Soon there was the high pitch whine of Israeli jets approaching We dived for cover in a shallow slit-trench hewn out of the rock and prayed that none of their rockets would make a direct hit on our position.

We were glad to get back to Irbid for a break but had hardly entered the town when jets flew over and bombed us. It was almost as if they were following our patrol. We spent the night with an Al Fatah doctor and drove back to North Shuneh at dawn.

We liked the leader of our new patrol who spoke good English and seemed well educated. He had undergone extensive guerrilla training in China and in Cuba. He told us something of the sophisticated weapons they were using, ingenious booby traps, suitcase bombs fitted with chemical fuses which could be accurately timed and were silent, and also land mines. He also quoted General Nguyen Giap, the brilliant North Vietnamese leader. When fighting a guerrilla war you never attack strength but seek out your enemy s weaknesses and then attack with superior forces. You must fight a guerrilla war on your own terms.

Our leader added that operating inside Israel is a different situation. 'We can only work in areas where we have friends and contacts with good hide-outs. Here we maintain large supplies of explosives ready for instant action. Forged passes, identity cards and documents pose no problems for our experts. Disguise is another important feature in a small country where faces are known to the enemy. We dye our hair or wear wigs. We grow moustaches or even glue on false ones that can hastily be removed. Grease can lighten or darken our complexions and a wad in a cheek can alter a whole face. Add to this a slight limp and you can saunter through any check point.'

Just like any army, once away from headquarters we found the men doing the job easy to get on with and prepared to bend the rules to help us. Our leader agreed to my taking pictures by infra-red once we crossed into Israel that night but only after he had seen the effect of the dim flash.

There was little cover when we made our way down to the river once again. The full moon made me feel exposed as I waited for that first burst of Israeli machine gun fire but it did not come. We crossed the river at a shallow point and half way over our leader let me go ahead. With my back to the Israelis, I let go the first infra red flash of the men in the water. Although the flash was no greater than the glow from a cigar, it scared the hell out of the men at that tense moment. We scrambled out of the water to the comparative safety of some bushes.

As we crept stealthily up the bank with our patrol now spread out in line, I once again had visions of those men at Salt with their legs blown off by the peanut mines we knew were scattered around this area. We had also been warned that the Israelis were erecting electronic barriers along 40 miles of the Jordan River. Ours was a probing patrol whose job was to reconnoitre for Israeli patrols and give the all clear to the fighting patrols following us in, together with supplies being ferried to underground agents operating within Israel.

As we penetrated away from the river our leader stopped, listened and then moved forward quietly. I had to be careful not to let my cameras clink together. After a while. when all seemed safe, he allowed me to go ahead, face the patrol and let off two more infrared flashes.

In less that three hours we had recrossed the river and were climbing up the exposed bank under a bright moonlit sky. We were wet and exhausted when reaching the safety of the Landrovers without having heard a shot fired.

In North Shuneh shortly before dawn, an ambulance was loading two bodies carried back from another raid into Israel. We were surprised at the reverence of these men for their dead but when told that every dead Fedayeen was a martyr whose soul went straight to Paradise, we understood.

Bill and I were given a lift in a truck to Irbid. During the night the Israelis bombed a nearby village we visited. Twenty-four people had been killed and many others wounded. In a small house we found an entire family: father, mother and three children strewn across the living room floor in grotesque positions of death.

With heavy hearts but considerable relief, Bill and I flew back to Beirut.

Our story closed as a lead but LIFE never used the revelations Bill disclosed of Al Fatah tactics subsequently deployed throughout the Western World with such devastating results. Maybe they thought them too scary at the time, or more likely, did not believe Bill's files.

Al Fatah at war, November 1968. LIFE correspondent Bill Wise takes shelter in a crevice in the rocks during an Israeli air attack on our patrol.

A patrol crosses the almost dried-up river Jordan into Israel. This is probably the first war picture using infra red inside enemy territory.

CHAPTER XXIX

LIFE magazine began to fade away

Dick Francis was small, as one might imagine, and dapper as befits the Queen Mother s ex-jockey. His most infamous act was to ride Devon Lock, coming to grief within seconds of the winning post in the Grand National, an incident that transformed him in to becoming a best selling writer of thrillers connected with the race track. I photographed him at the Windsor races alongside the Queen Mother, with whom he was on the friendliest of terms but no story on him would be complete without getting him back into the saddle at his training stables. He charged my motor-driven camera so closely that I leapt aside in terror making a picture that looked as if the horse had galloped right over the camera.

Enoch Powell was my next target. I never realised that one had to pay British politicians £50 for an interview. With this money safely in his pocket he saw us in Wolverhampton. I had previously covered two of his anti-black meetings in other parts of the country and was not particularly relishing this one. His meetings brought me back to the Afrikaaners in South Africa except that here he had a large number of hostile blacks.

I was not sorry to leave Wolverhampton for the pleasant atmosphere of France in the village of Mégève where I had spent much of my early childhood and knew the area well, but it had changed a lot since those days when my sister and I used to ski down to the village school from our Châlet St. Christophe to be towed up again behind a horse-drawn sledge with the horse making loud and rude noises as it laboured up the hill. Teedee and I could never restrain our giggles.

LIFE magazine virtually took over the elite Mont d'Arbois hotel to entertain some of their more important top advertisers. Lane Fortinberry, a senior editor, was our host. He hired ex-Olympic skier, Jean-Claude Killy, to join the party and ski with some of the better skiers. My only job was to meet the guests over lunch at a mountain châlet and take pictures of them with the great man. These were then made into a presentation cover of LIFE as a souvenir for them. On one such trip I took a bad fall when my ski hit an icy rut. One of my three cameras hit my left ear causing it to bleed profusely. I arrived at the lunch looking as if I had escaped from a slaughter house. For the rest of the week I skied, swam in the warm hotel pool, wined and dined and night-clubbed until the early hours of the morning with LIFE picking up the tab for me and all the guests.

On returning to England LIFE wanted pictures of Jimmy Hendrix but neither he nor his manager seemed able or willing to cooperate. I stood by night after night getting nowhere. I cabled New York and we agreed to abort the story. Then at one o clock the next morning the telephone beside our bed woke me up. It was the Speakeasy Club: Jimmy is here. Can you come up right away? I threw on some clothes and rushed in to London. I drank with Sandy Blake and Hendrix in a dark corner of the club until five in the morning but Hendrix did not feel like performing so I returned home with a terrible head and no pictures.

My other highlight was to go over to Ireland for a story on writer Robert Bolt and director, David Lean. Lean became so involved in filming *Ryan's Daughter* that great tact was needed to get any pictures at all and then mostly through long lenses.

I fell in love with the Dingle Peninsula and was determined to bring my girls out to see this beautiful part of the world. I did this a year later and then built our dream cottage in the south west.

Another assignment seemed to be one of those plums which was the envy of everyone but I had learned that the exciting, fun stories are often the hardest to do. When people around you are having fun, you have to work and cannot join in. Alcohol slows one up too much so I seldom touch a drop when working.

Jack Newcombe and I were assigned to cover the maiden voyage of the Queen Elizabeth II to New York. Boarding the ship at Southampton was an anticlimax. Far from my imagination of a trans-Atlantic liner, we were cooped up in a floating Hilton hotel that sped across the Atlantic at 28 knots. There were lifts to all floors – or did they call them decks? Fortunately for us, the bars were no Utopia of cheap liquor. I imagined I would find pictures everywhere – I did not. The veteran photographer, Alfred Eisenstaed was aboard shooting for *Time*.

Eisie summed it up: 'At my age I cannot afford to waste five precious days of my life.'

We phoned New York from half-way across the Atlantic to say that we had no story but that the arrival should be memorable and ought to be covered from a helicopter. We were greeted on the Hudson River by fireboats with their hoses gushing ever changing sparkling fountains into the air; sirens blasted from hundreds of boats and two R.A.F. Harrier fighters formatted close to our top decks before darting up into the blue sky and returning a few feet off the water at near supersonic speed. Finally, Mayor Lindsay of New York came aboard to welcome the ship to his city.

The news in the New York office was depressing. Most people sensed that the magazine was in its death throes. Economy cuts were being severely imposed, something we had never experienced. Only a short time back we heard that the *Saturday Evening Post* had ceased publication and that LIFE had taken over one and half million of their subscribers, pushing the advertising rates to $64,000 a colour page. The $64,000 question!

Back to London to face seven depressingly slack months.

In June I descended 4,000 feet into the claustrophobic bowels of the earth to photograph a FORTUNE story on a new method of cutting coal. A German mine south of Essen in the Ruhr had developed a nozzle that forced out ultra powerful jets of water, cutting the coal as though it were butter. The job required considerable preparations in that I had to install powerful underwater flood lights. George Karas, who ran the LIFE lab, air-freighted a set over from New York to Cologne. For all the years I worked for LIFE I was never short of equipment, film or money. If necessary they would fly in someone to bring you urgent necessities.

At 3.54 British summer time on the morning of 21 July 1969, Neil Armstrong put a foot on the moon, closely followed by Buzz Aldrin, while Mike Collins circled in the space craft, Columbia. We had organised an all-night party at our house in Windsor, most of which I missed as I had to cover the celebrations in Trafalgar Square. However, I was home at dawn in time to watch the historic pictures live on television. We could also see the moon low on the horizon

Living Dangerously

through the drawing room windows. It was a memorable experience to look at the moon all those thousands of miles away and to know that at that exact moment men were actually walking on its surface. Glancing back at the television screen gave one the impression of seeing it all through a super powerful telescope. Nevertheless, the detailed colour pictures NASA later passed on to the magazine to publish made me realise that television missed the perspective and detail of the still picture. With the exception of the live drama on the moon itself, the still picture lingered long after the image of the small screen had disappeared.

Some years later I was to meet the first man on the moon when he was given the freedom of the town of Langholm in Scotland, as a member of the Scottish Armstrong clan. I asked Neil Armstrong, 'Every time you look up at the moon, do you always think, "I was there?"'

'Always,' he answered, 'and moreover, I know exactly where I was on the moon at that precise moment.'

Our next story involved trouble where it was least expected. Towards the end of October there was a rumour rife in the U.S that Paul McCartney was dead and that an impostor was deputising for the departed Beatle. I knew Paul better than anyone on the magazine and LIFE wanted to refute the myth.

Dorothy Bacon, through her numerous contacts, discovered his hideout in the remote hills of Western Scotland. We were determined to locate him. We flew to Glasgow, drove north-westwards past graceful lochs and magnificent mountain scenery to Castleton. We found out where the McCartneys lived and drove up to investigate. They were well protected. There were farmers on each of the two roads leading up to the McCartneys and neither had any intention of letting us pass without the McCartney's permission.

We discovered in the pub that both farmers would go to church the following morning, a Sunday. So Dorothy and I returned to the more remote farm at eleven o clock and found it deserted. Only his barking dog disturbed the peace of the hills. Parking our hired car on the small road we started walking. We trekked over the hills, through bogs and waded across fast-flowing streams, arriving at the lonely farmhouse as the unshaven Paul walked out of the front door carrying a slop pail. He took a startled look in our direction and the angel face distorted in creases of rage as he slung abuse at us. I had preset my camera and, when he turned to re-enter the house, I took a quick shot, knowing it would be my last. He heard the click, turned, and threw the slop pail at me. I took another shot of it in mid-air or rather tried to, since at that moment he charged me with flailing fists and I was hit for the first time in nearly twenty years of covering trouble around the world – by a Beatle! I was wearing a heavy coat and felt nothing. Far from feeling bitter, I fully sympathised with him. Anyway, we had discovered that Paul McCartney was very much alive...

In June 1969 there was the inauguration in Caernarvon Castle for Charles as Prince of Wales. A few days before he had decided to climb the 3,600 foot Mount Snowdon. Jack Newcombe, Curt Prendergast and I were the only three journalists to make the climb. Prince Charles was not happy to have us with him. He and a handful of his aides strode off at a fast pace. At one point near the summit I somehow managed to get ahead but when he saw me, he purposely took another route, ruining my background of the lakes and the mountain. As he finally had to come level with me he put out his tongue.

It was only after our arduous struggle to the summit that we realised why we were the only journalists on the climb. There was a mountain railway to the top by another route and that is how the rest of the press corps were comfortably able to cover our arrival.

I had Prince Charles on the cover until the last minute when it was pulled off for a Vietnam story, but LIFE did however use a full page of him with his tongue out at the camera.

Rudy Chelminski came over from Paris to join me on a story about skinheads. They were the prelude to soccer violence as we know it today. The skinheads were gangs of youths with closely cropped hair whose uniforms were tight jeans trailing half way up their shins and held up with garish braces. Heavy bovver boots adorned their feet. The boots were studded with nails and sported metal toe caps, Useful for kicking hostile football supporters and policemen, one of their leaders told us.

Most of the stories Rudy and I worked on seemed to include trouble and this one looked no exception. Also, infiltrating a gang without contacts posed problems. On a Saturday afternoon Rudy and I went to the Arsenal football stadium and bought tickets in the cheap standing-only portion of the ground. Though our presence in that part of the stadium raised a few eyebrows, we had no difficulty in recognising the skinheads who were already creating trouble and being arrested.

We sidled up to one tough-looking boy of about fourteen who seemed to be a leader and told him we would like to do a story on his gang. To our surprise he beamed with enthusiasm and said, 'When do we start?' Right now seems a good moment, we thought.

We trailed this gang into dingy bars on the outskirts of North London where they were chucked out for drinking under age. We were followed by police cars to football matches where they all carried weapons of some sort. One boy had an ugly-looking bicycle chain nailed to a wooden handle. We rode with them on trains to away matches and saw some them being arrested. We took four of them into Piccadilly Circus where groups of hippies lounged around Eros. We wanted to photograph the reactions of the hippies to the skinheads. 'Don't under any circumstances get involved in a fight,' we urged them.

'That's going to be tough,' said the leader, 'hippies are our No. 1 target.' The hippies' reaction was electric, but nothing happened.

Ironically, like the tough Rockers back in 1964 whom I so feared before meeting them, we found the skins to be decent kids beneath the tough extravert veneer and their natural lust for action and excitement. Most of them were training to be artisans. They drank all the beer they could afford but despised drugs and long-haired layabouts.

From skinheads we went to pop stars and to the Isle of Wight to cover the Bob Dylan concert. Dylan stayed in a house with Beatle George Harrison and burly bodyguards ensured no one even had a glimpse of the man before the concert. That included us. Over 150,000 fans camped in a field at Wooton Bridge. The smell of pot drifted over the camp but the fans were well behaved except when Dylan was an hour late coming on stage. After the concert hordes of photographers shot a young couple fornicating openly in a foam bath before a large audience. I missed the event but anyway it was hardly an apt subject for my family magazine.

The last few months of 1969 had been depressing. There were few good stories being done outside of the USA. In December Ralph Graves, our new Managing Editor, summoned all the European bureaux to lunch at the famous Laserre restaurant in Paris. We talked a lot at these luncheons and discussed frankly our personal problems, frustrations and what we thought was wrong with the magazine. Ralph was the only optimistic person at that lunch. Satellites were now producing almost instantaneous colour television pictures of events. We could not compete. Television was also taking millions of dollars of advertising revenue away from us. The camaraderie existing among LIFE magazine people was unequalled, so it was a depressing thought that this great club looked like folding.

Between Christmas and New Year Dick Stolley and I stayed with the glamorous Antonia Fraser at her Scottish estate for a profile on this industrious writer. On the Sunday we drove for hours up on the glens of the 185,000 acres of the Lovat estate and never saw any land not belonging to Hugh Fraser.

Antonia first became famous by mistake. She was a secretary at Weidenfelds when they brought out a book, *The Hundred Most Beautiful Women*. As the book was going to press, someone discovered that there were only 99 beautiful women so Antonia was hastily photographed and included in the book.

Antonia had her six children with her and a house full of guests. She also had a crate of 30 books to be reviewed and was busy writing *Cromwell*, yet she found time for us, entertained us and showed us over their vast estates with husband, Hugh. 'Let's have a wee dram,' was the phrase that seemed to punctuate many moments of the day. There were miniature bottles of whisky in our bedrooms, bathrooms and in the cars. This helped the fun of the story.

Antonia is now the wife of playwright Harold Pinter.

Left: Viscount Bath of Longleat, March 1967, in his elegant library at Longleat, with his pet lion.

Above: Bob Dylan

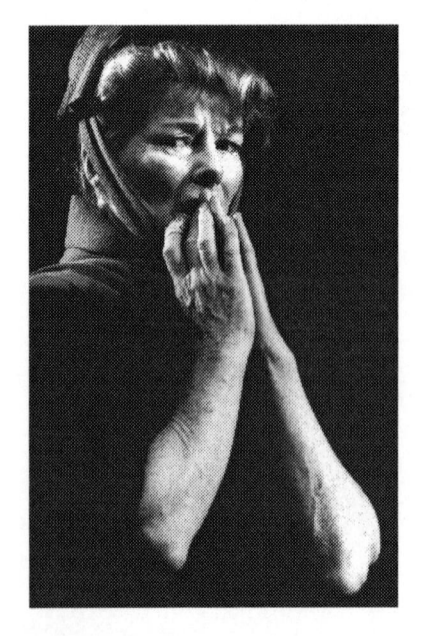

Left: Audrey Hepburn, November 1967 in A Lion in Winter *in London.*

CHAPTER XXX

End of Biafran war, Nassau and Egypt

At the beginning of 1970 news came that Biafra was about to fall to the Nigerians and end the civil war. Once again there was a scramble by newsmen to get aboard the BOAC VC10 jet to Lagos. Few of us had time to get visas. Immigration at Lagos airport proved no problem as in the melée caused by journalists arguing to be allowed entry without visas, I slipped through the barrier without showing my passport. I foresaw trouble on the way out but I would face that when the time came.

The arrogant, goatee-bearded customs officer glared at my equipment. 'I can see you have plenty,' he growled.

'Yes,' I answered, slipping him a pound note and two rolls of film. Even if he had opened my large camera box containing lenses, remote control equipment, spare and specialised cameras, it is unlikely that he would have discovered the 100 rolls of film I kept in a secret compartment beneath this paraphernalia. Film was often a touchy commodity in developing countries and trouble spots so I took no chances.

The foreign press corps had virtually taken over the Federal Palace Hotel. It was in a hostile mood because the Nigerian government was preventing correspondents getting up to the front. Indeed, it had just arrested an NBC team who tried it by road. For a week we tried every ruse, pulled every string with our respective embassies, but to no avail.

I was delighted when Rudy Chelminski arrived to work with me. Two days later the Nigerian Information Department told me I was on the list of a few journalists to be flown to Port Harcourt in the morning. Rudy's name was not on the list and all the argument in the world could not persuade them that we were as much a team as any television unit.

Because of our tight deadline, Rudy and I made reservations on a London flight the following Wednesday. We also checked all possible flights out for our film package. There were 100 pressmen in Lagos, all trying to get to Port Harcourt. In the meanwhile, they had to endure the bureaucracy of the cable office staff who would only transmit copy if they agreed with the contents or liked the paper. If not, 'Sorry, the transmission has broken down,' and there was nothing one could do about it. We met the same problems trying to telephone London or New York. West Africa Wins Again (WAWA) was one of our popular phrases but this time they really were winning.

We decided to play WAWA at its own game. As expected, there was chaos at the airport the next morning. I was armed with my RED pass. Rudy had nothing. By 7.30am the entire press corps was there trying to get passes. We hung around in the humid heat until 3.30pm. No Information Department representative turned up and there was no sign of our aircraft. We heard that the UN Secretary General U Thant was arriving to be met by President General Gowon. We decided on a mass press protest march to the reception area, much to the consternation of the young President. Gowon took immediate action and detailed his Information Minister to handle our grievances. He promised that the RED pass holders could leave later that afternoon if we would return peacefully to the transit lounge. In the stampede to get these extra passes I removed the official's own RED pass from his pocket for Rudy. We flew in to Port Harcourt that evening and were met by some open trucks bumping our way along the corrugated and cratered road to Aba in the south of Biafra where we lay down on the cold concrete floor of an abandoned house for the night without food.

The Information Department put us in a convoy the following morning for a carefully selected Cook's Tour of Biafra. Several of my old buddies including John Bierman of BBC TV and Tony Carthew of the *Daily Mail* were on our truck. Since I knew the area well after our last trip, we decided to hijack the vehicle and see the country for ourselves. There were several photographers in the group including Terry Fincher and Harry Dempster of the *Express*, plus Dennis Royle of the A.P. Dennis was later killed in a helicopter crash. These men were not on our truck as I could not afford their competition, especially the agency men who radio their pictures to any publication taking their service. This would kill anything I was able to get. Thus, alas, I was seldom able to work with any of these fine people. Most of us had seen these horrors before: the long lines of hungry refugees wandering aimlessly down pot-holed roads pushing bicycles loaded with their worldly goods, some with sheets of corrugated iron balanced precariously on their heads to form some protection against the torrential rain. Bodies lay beside the road belonging to those who could go no further. The putrefying smell in the African heat was sickening. The roads were littered with the skeletons of burnt-out vehicles. We saw Nigerian soldiers looting homes and loading beds and furniture on to their trucks while the owners cried and pleaded. This was the consequence of all wars.

Our deadline was running tight and all the correspondents were desperate to file, so we headed back to the airfield at Port Harcourt, arriving at midnight. Someone had organised field rations which we ate ravenously, forgetting for a moment the thousands of faces we had seen who pleaded for just one mouthful of food.

WAWA again reigned supreme. There were no planes to take us back to Lagos. The only one to arrive was the President's own private jet bringing guests for a VIP wedding feast. It was loaded with champagne and every delicacy imaginable. This was the final straw for the enraged press corps after the starvation we had just witnessed.

The Nigerians became frightened at our hostile attitude. They mounted an armed guard and put us under virtual arrest. Rudy and I were able to climb out of a back window and contact the pilot of the jet. He was a Pole called Roman Hrycak and had been an R.A.F. fighter pilot. We had many friends in common. Then Roman discovered that Rudy was an American of Polish descent. He readily agreed to take our packet to Lagos and even volunteered to take Rudy with him if there was a spare seat.

There is a common understanding that you do not welch on your colleagues in this sort of situation. But first, realising that in West Africa the left hand seldom knew what the right was doing, we went to see Colonel Tuon, the airfield commander, telling him that we were guests of the government and requested a written permit allowing Rudy to travel on the jet. Tuon did not know that we were prisoners! With the permit safely in Rudy's pocket we re-entered the

Living Dangerously

terminal building by the same window and told our colleagues what had been achieved. Rudy would take all their film and copy out IF he got on the jet. Violent arguments ensued as to how and in what priority their files and film would be sent out of Lagos. Men from some European TV companies who were not our regular colleagues behaved like wild animals. After hours of this behaviour they decided nothing would go out. They were not too worried about ours, knowing it could not be published for several days.

Rudy and I hung around anxiously until the late evening when Roman appeared with the wedding guests. 'It is okay,' he whispered to Rudy, 'I do have a spare seat.'

There was another mad scramble by a section of the press corps to get on the jet. They were held back at gun point by soldiers. Rudy had his permit and, not knowing he was a journalist, they allowed him aboard. Right up to the moment of take off I was worried that someone would discover what we had done and pull him off the plane.

We were taken to a hotel in Port Harcourt for the night and the following morning a missionary led me to the Niger Maternity Hospital where I saw one of the most horrific sights of my life. As we entered the courtyard there was a buzzing noise from 500 tiny tots that sounded like a swarm of locusts. We were confronted by hundreds of skeleton rib cages contoured through parched skins covered in sores above bloated bellies. It was all I could do not to vomit as we entered the various wards. There was excreta everywhere: on the beds, on the floors, often mingled with blood. I knew that the pictures I took would be too late to make the magazine but I shot some of the horror nevertheless. One picture I took showed a tiny child on the bare concrete floor who had slumped forward and drowned in his own excreta. Another skeleton of a child with his spindly legs dangling over the side of an equally filthy bed looked forlornly at the dreadful scene.

We were flown to Lagos that afternoon and Rudy met me at the airport. He was smiling and the full weight of his 6'2" frame slapped me on the back. 'I have good news for you, you son of a bitch, the magazine closed four pages. Other than radio pix, they will be the first pictures published of Biafra. Not a bad scoop for a weekly magazine.'

It was good to see Rudy. He was always enthusiastic. That evening over large scotches on the cool terrace overlooking the sea at the Federal Palace Hotel, he told me his story,

'Roman radioed ahead soon after take off and arranged for the Swiss Air manager to meet the presidential jet. They had a cargo service going to Accra in Ghana, minutes after landing. Arriving on the presidential jet our packet became top priority and in Accra it was handed personally to the Captain of a Lufthansa DC8. He had radioed ahead to ask Frankfurt to have it taken across to a transAtlantic plane due out only minutes after his arrival. I eventually managed to get a call through to London to have the flight met but by the time the Bonn bureau in Germany acted, our packet was already over the Atlantic.

What a celebration we had that night with Roman at Antoines.

It was the turn of the Nigerian authorities to become hostile when they felt the impact of the stories published about Biafra. Rudy and I knew it was time to escape. There was a traffic snarlup on our way out to the airport, making us arrive only minutes before takeoff. In the hurry to rush us on to the flight, immigration failed to notice that I did not have a visa.

Photographers knew that LIFE was famous for pictures rather than words, though it was run entirely by men who wrote words. So the photographer had to walk a tightrope when working with some reporters but not with Rudy. There were three other notable exceptions – Jordan Bonfante, Bob Morse and Tim Green. We worked together as a close-knit unit, each knowing what the other was thinking and in a crisis anticipating what the other would do and where he would be. Hardships and danger, frustration and privation breed a lasting and deep friendship so that most of my best friends today were working colleagues. Journalism must be the last of the great comradeships. As I've said earlier in the book, few people work harder and play harder than foreign correspondents.

Living Dangerously

It was the end of January 1970 with the temperature around −25°C when I accompanied rally driver Timmo Makinen in his Mini Cooper in a one mile standing start race on the Tapiola circuit near Helsinki in Finland. There was a difference between this and most car races in that this one was on ice. Timmo won the race at an average speed of 50 m.p.h. round the small circuit. He took the bends in one long skid, sometimes within inches of other cars trying to overtake us. I had to hang on strenuously from being forced against the side door as I tried to photograph the action.

That evening Rudy and I wallowed in a sauna in the Helsinki Hotel before plunging into ice cold water. A dear old lady then loofahed both of us down while we were starkers. I asked her if she ever got embarrassed doing this to men. 'Embarrassed?' she answered, 'Only once and then I said "thank you, Sir, for the compliment".'

Work was slack at the office so I did a story for *Cosmopolitan* magazine. It was the ideal dirty weekend from the girl's point of view. We used a professional male model and a very pretty young university girl. We had them together in a large double bath in one of London's swishiest hotels. They shared a bottle of champagne with caviar before piling into a luxurious double poster bed. After breakfast a real life, good-looking masseur oiled the girl's nude body all over and gave her a massage with her skin glistening under my powerful lights. We took them to the Casino de Paris Club to watch a striptease show; then in a vintage Rolls Royce for a sumptuous picnic in Hyde Park. Afterwards there were moonlight love scenes and a night club before they returned to bed once again. It was the first story I photographed working to a script, rather like a movie, where everything was contrived to the last detail. The only unscripted part was that the couple continued their relationship well after the end of our story.

My next job was different. An American offshore real estate company had bought $600,000 worth of advertising in LIFE International and I was assigned to take the photographs. Gramco was run by two young multi-millionaires, Raphael Navarro and Keith Barish, the latter only 25. Our first trip was to Spain in their private executive jet. The cigar-toting Pierre Salinger, President Kennedy's express secretary, was closely associated with the company and came along with us.

Madrid was one long round of receptions. I could only stay for two days as Lane Fortinberry had organised another junket in Mégève with Jean Claud Killy for his top advertisers and this was a party I did not want to miss.

Towards the end of March 1970 I was on my way across the Atlantic for Gramco. First to Bermuda, then to Nassau where Raphael had his luxurious home and head office. For a week I again lived the life of a millionaire. We visited outlying islands in lavish motor cruisers; we fished; we skin dived and we water skied. I then flew across to Miami to photograph Keith Barish and his family. Keith took me to Crystal House on Miami Beach for Maine lobsters, and when told they did not have any, he threatened to buy the joint! I enjoyed getting well paid for this sort of work.

There was utter chaos at the airport on my return to Nassau that evening when I arrived for my flight to London. It was like being back in West Africa. Despite having a confirmed booking and being checked through with my baggage, I could not find my name on the seating list. There was a Spicer, however, and I took his boarding pass. The air hostess showed me to my seat and then the confusion started. The airport manager came aboard and ordered me out of my seat but I refused to budge until he showed me another which he was unable to do. So I stayed, and took off with the flight an hour delayed.

In London I took Raphael and Keith to our old LIFE bistro in Soho, the Toscana. We were discussing millionaires when Raphael remarked, 'You know, Terry, the life you lead makes you the millionaire, not us. Money can't buy your life style.'

There was a large party in London to celebrate the 20 page advertisement in LIFE International at which Navarro announced that they would take out a similar advertisement in *Time*. Soon after, Gramco folded; I hope not as a result of my photographs.

In June 1970 Jordan Bonfante arrived to take over the London bureau for LIFE. He had hardly settled in when 50 years of bottled

Living Dangerously 295

up religious and political frustration exploded with unusual fury in Northern Ireland. We caught a flight to Belfast, the first of many in the years to come. During 15 hours of gun battles in the streets, six people were shot dead and many others wounded both from bullets and rocks. Petrol bombers had set light to buses and shops. The British army had already moved in numbers of troops for the impending Orange Day marches when predictions of violence seemed certain to come true.

We teamed up with Vic Patterson, a local photographer who had a radio in his car which could pick up the police wavelength. This kept us informed and enabled us to reach riot areas minutes after the trouble started.

It was vital in those early days to learn the boundaries of the Catholic and Protestant areas as those were the trouble spots. You had to know the area you were in when trouble started, though the graffiti on the walls left you in no doubt. Vic explained that the Lower Falls and Andersontown were Catholic, the Shankhill Road was Protestant and there was a mixed and dangerous area in East Belfast. In the west of Ulster was Londonderry of which one side was Protestant and the other, referred to as 'Derry', was the Bogside and entirely Catholic. Vic went on to explain that most of the villages on the Irish border were pro-Republican, particularly such towns as Newry and Crossmaglen.

Few independent observers would disagree that over the years the Catholic minority in Northern Ireland was exploited and prevented from gaining a political foothold or from getting top jobs. The Protestants argued that they could not trust the Catholics in responsible positions as their goal was to incorporate Ulster into a united Ireland. As we have seen in similar situations around the world, an explosion was inevitable.

Jordan and I agreed that Belfast was quite the dreariest city either of us had ever seen. There were rows and rows of small red brick houses in dingy, narrow streets. Occasionally the houses were painted a kaleidoscope of clashing colours, hardly improving the depressing scene. If there was any sign of green vegetation in central Belfast we never saw it. It was hardly surprising therefore that young Catholic kids brought up in these surroundings could be enticed into joining the IRA and others into joining the various Protestant paramilitary forces. Mostly, they were unemployed and bored. Excitement was their driving force.

Jordan and I had to go down to Armagh where there was more trouble during a demonstration to have the fiery Republican girl, Bernadette Devlin, released from jail. The police and army outnumbered the demonstrators by four to one so that there were only minor skirmishes in the town.

July 12th 1970, the usual day for the Orange Day marches, was a Sunday, so the marches were planned for the following day. The Reverend Ian Paisley, however, held a large meeting in a meadow at Knockagoney outside Belfast. Knowing the way Paisley whipped up antagonism against pressmen and seeing no signs of any media at the meeting, I was loathe to go down to his Union Jack bedecked platform. Jordan was already on his way, however so I had no alternative but to follow. Jordan was amazed that the British stood by and allowed this man to scream out the most abusive anti-catholic rhetoric in such a tense situation. There was no doubt we were in a land of hate.

We noticed at Paisley's church service that Sunday morning that most of his church wardens had pronounced bulges under their left armpits. They were taking no chances. That night Jordan and I patrolled the Protestant and Catholic areas. The Catholic areas seemed ominously quiet, whereas bonfires raged in the streets of the Protestant areas. Around them kids shouted and danced like small demons.

The next day was Monday and the day for the big marches. We braced ourselves for trouble – so did 18,000 British soldiers.

Fifty thousand Protestant Orangemen were celebrating King William III's (William of Orange) victory over the Catholics at the Battle of the Boyne in 1690. This was the start of the rift between the religious denominations.

Men in bowler hats carrying large Orange banners and Union Jacks marched behind brass bands from the city centre out to Finaghy Park. Barbecue fires burned and beer flowed as people listened to more fiery, racial speeches.

The army road-blocked every street leading out of Catholic areas and managed to avert trouble.

It did not take long for Jordan and me to make up our minds that, after the Congo, Northern Ireland was our most unfavourite trouble spot. Paradoxically, the press corps suffered fewer casualties in these countries than in any other parallel situation. Northern Ireland was a paradise for the journalist who covered the troubles from his hotel bedroom. Every organisation employed numbers of people to woo him. The army had some 40 press officers plus back-up staff, the Royal Ulster Constabulary had 12 press officers and the local government had 20. There was equal competition from the paramilitary groups, all of whom had front men who got in touch with correspondents to put over their propaganda.

President Nasser of Egypt died on September 28 and that meant catching the next morning's flight to Cairo. At Cairo airport we had trouble getting our visas. 'No money, no visas.' said a fat, pot-bellied immigration officer.

'May I change a traveller's cheque?' I pleaded.

'You cannot go to the bank without a visa,' he added with a twisted smile. I have long since learned not to argue with such people despite what every nerve in my body is suggesting. Someone did get some money and we checked in to a large suite at the Sheraton Hotel overlooking Gezira Island on the Nile, where Rudy Chelminski had booked earlier.

We spent the next day reconnoitring the funeral procession route and planning camera positions. October 1 was the day of the funeral. Being a Thursday made it tight for our Saturday night closing. We arranged for a girl to fly our film to New York and so avoid delay by Cairo and Kennedy airport customs. We also made arrangements with the A.P. Cairo office to process some of the film and radio pictures to the office. LIFE did not like radio pix as the quality was not up to their reproduction standard but it would be a back-up.

After dinner that night Rudy and I rode thoroughbred Arab horses into the Sahara desert in the pitch black darkness of the night. Led by an Arab horseman we rode at full gallop for mile after mile up the side of sand dunes and down the other side as the horses literally dropped away beneath us. It was like driving a fast car over a humpback bridge. I had to grip like hell to prevent myself being catapulted out of the saddle. The Arab would suddenly swerve as it followed the horse a few feet ahead. I could just make out the fluffs of soft sand thrown up by their hooves, otherwise everything around was black. We stopped at one of King Farouk's old desert retreats for much needed cool beers while little boys kept our horses on the move. Our guide took us back to Cairo on a less undulating route past the floodlit Pyramids.

We took up our positions early on the morning of the funeral before the mobs started swirling into the city. My set-up was the most comfortable I had experienced on such occasions. We had hired a room with a balcony from where I was able to photograph the procession crossing the Nile, while room service plied us with cold drinks to help ward off the oppressive heat. The procession crossed the river with dignity but when it tried to get through the main crowd, the Arabs went berserk: they cried; they tried to leap on to the gun carriage carrying Nasser's coffin but were beaten back by soldiers. At one point hundreds of people were forced back off the main road and tumbled down on to an underpass like a monstrous flood flowing over a waterfall. We saw our colleagues fighting this mob to get their pictures and felt a little smug at our own comfort. Though several people were reported killed, it was surprising that many more did not die that afternoon.

Bad news greeted our return to London. The special International edition of LIFE was folding. This meant even less work for those of us on the foreign bureaux. We also heard that LIFE was further reducing its circulation from 8.5 to 5.5 million copies a week.

Biafra, Jan 1970. The appalling conditions in the children's hospital. Child on the floor lies dead in its own excrement while another lies dead on the bed with the crying baby.

Mods ...... and Rockers, July 1964.

300 Living Dangerously

CHAPTER XXXI

The glorious islands of the Seychelles contrasting with the grimness of Northern Ireland and the even sadder end of LIFE magazine.

One sunny morning in April Kenny Goff phoned from our London cable room: 'I have a message from Mary Leatherbee which will make you happy. It reads, 'RALPH (Graves) HAS GIVEN THE GO-AHEAD FOR YOUR FORGOTTEN ISLES STORY. WANT YOU JOIN ME NAIROBI APRIL 12 - LEATHERBEE.' Suddenly, all the gloom and depression of months without a good story disappeared. This was a dream assignment.

There was a time on LIFE magazine when you could suggest anything you wanted to do, providing it would make a good story, and then they would send you to the other end of the world to do it. I had suggested the Seychelles, far out in the Indian Ocean, way back in 1960 when they really were remote islands, but the Congo had intervened.

I met Mary Leatherbee in Nairobi, and took her into the Nairobi National Park adjoining the airport. Within minutes of entering the main gate I spotted a crowd of cars on an open plain. This generally signalled the presence of lions, not always easy to see in the park. What we saw surprised even me. A male lion was engaged in ardent love-making with a beautiful sleek lioness. We were able to approach to within ten yards and photograph them in full sunshine. A lion can make love every 20 to 30 minutes for up to 60 hours, so I had plenty of time to record every possible facial expression, which made me realize that the enjoyment of sex is not the prerogative of man alone. Mary was a middle aged lady and rather formidable at first so I was relieved to see her take out her movie camera and film the event.

Mary and I flew down to humid and sultry Mombasa where we joined the luxurious 2,500 ton Lindblad Explorer for the 1,000 miles cruise to Mahé, the capital of the 92 smaller islands forming the Seychelles group. En route we called in at 'Africa Bank' and went ashore in the rubber Zodiac dingies. The island consisted of just three palm trees on a silvery beach a few feet above the Indian Ocean. Rod Salm, the marine biologist on the Explorer, and I dived 60 feet below the ship to revel in the beauty of the coral formations. I had light at that depth to photograph without flash. Rod had a fright when a shark made a dart at him as he surfaced but it veered off at the last moment.

The Seychelles were still remote in that only two ships called there a month besides the Explorer, catering exclusively for the wealthy. There was still nearly a year to go before the new airport would be ready.

The Seychelleois, whose skins went through all colours of the spectrum from white to black, were friendly and supplied us with exotic Creole food accompanied by heady, locally brewed hootch.

During my month on the island I photographed six out of the ten rarest birds in the world. Moreover, being generally undisturbed by humans, they were tame enough to let one approach to within 15 feet of them. Mostly they sheltered from the sweltering sun in dark undergrowth, forcing me to use two powerful strobe lights to get good technical detail. We found the colourful magpie robins of which there were then only 20 left on Fregate Island. I tripped backwards over a big boulder when photographing one and received a shock when it starting moving with me straddling it. It was a giant tortoise weighing nearly 700 lbs.

Quite the most beautiful and idyllic island of the Seychelles was La Digue, only three miles long and two across. There I met a fascinating bearded man in his sixties whose hair was tied up at the back with a black pirate's bow. He was building his own schooner with the help of two locals, using primitive tools. Rupert Kellway-Bamber told me, and his eyes sparkled as he spoke, 'I had a lucrative engineering job in England that I gave up, sold everything and my wife and I came out to this Paradise where I have been for the last ten years.' Rupert built his own house among the palm trees. His land stretched down to a white beach and coral rocks bounded by a reef. He had gone native and was almost self-sufficient. He grew a variety of tropical fruits; brewed his own palm wine; grew corn and fished. He planned to make some money by chartering his schooner, 'although money is the last thing I want,' he added quite seriously. I envied Rupert's life – at least for a short while.

On Mahé I looked for Cruze Wilkins who, I was told, had spent the last 20 years of his life digging for treasure. He was painstakingly decoding clues left by pirates who were supposed to have hidden booty in the area of his diggings. The clues were from mythology and used the signs of the Zodiac. Far from the crank I expected to see, Cruze had both feet firmly on the ground and believed he was nearing the end of his search. I do not think he ever found anything.

I rose at dawn as the Explorer slipped out of Port Victoria on Mahé heading eastwards past St. Ann's Island into a dramatic sunrise. We called in again at La Digue and Praslin for the benefit of our passengers before setting course south for a day's cruise to the coral atoll of Desroches where a handful of people lived producing copra. Rod and I dived to photograph the brightly coloured tropical fish and caught a fat, bloated porcupine fish.

We left the Seychelles and cruised southwest for two days to Aldabra, arriving at dawn. A soft green light shimmered off low overhanging clouds as though a beacon was guiding us to this unique atoll. It was the reflection from the large lagoon that formed almost the entire centre of the island. The island itself rose no more than 20 feet above sea level at any point.

The Zodiacs took the party on to the reef where they had to wade ashore. I had seen a giant ray and knew the waters abounded with sharks. There are about 100,000 giant tortoises on the atoll and they appeared quite unperturbed by humans. We wanted to see the champignons, comprising eroded coral with dense thickets on top looking like mushrooms, as their French name implies.

The lagoon was shallow and there were sharks about when horror struck. I had a sudden and desperate attack of runny tummy. We were with five crowded Zodiacs and sharks or no sharks, I had no alternative but to dive overboard and relieve myself with a split second to spare. At first the passengers thought I was mad until they realised my predicament!

The next day we were at Glorieuse, an island only a mile in diameter. We walked around its sparkling white beaches or forced our way through the dense palm plantations. There were three inhabitants on the island manning the government weather station. A typhoon had uprooted some giant casuarina trees and tossed them out on to the sand where they had become petrified resembling sculptures. They were my setting for some glamour girl pictures.

The next morning saw us off the Comoro Islands and we went ashore in one of the ship's lifeboats. It was off the Comoros that the first coelacanth was caught and identified. Moroni, the capital, was a mini Zanzibar, very Arab, with its mosques and narrow cobbled streets. The market was packed with pink and gold, green and scarlet fruit and vegetables sold by vendors just as colourfully dressed. Picturesque dhows lay at anchor, leisurely loading spices and vanilla beans for Madagascar.

It was depressing for me to return to Zanzibar after the fascinating island I once knew. Paint was crumbling off the walls of the houses; the beautifully carved Arab doors needed attention; the streets were dirty and there was a general air of depression over the town. Before leaving in the morning Captain Aas asked Rod and me to dive along the hull of the Explorer and check for any possible damage after the ship ran aground on entering the harbour. Diving in a harbour where sharks are scavenging for food is not sensible, but Rod had to go so I went with him. The water was murky. We saw no sharks nor any damage to the ship, so the Explorer returned to Mombasa.

In London it took me two weeks to edit the 5,000 colour tranparencies and write captions. I had long since learned that the greatest picture was useless without an accurate caption.

It was late October 1971 before I received a cable from Mary Leatherbee saying our Seychelles story had closed for eight colour pages. A year later Mary was drowned in a rapids accident. A sad loss.

In mid-June Jordan and I flew to Copenhagen on a story about the US student invasion of Europe. The story was of no particular interest, but a strip show we visited on the west side of the Istergade certainly was. The 'theatre' resembled a mini boxing stadium if you substituted a large double bed for the boxing ring. Seats were tiered around, filled mostly by middle aged men, though I saw a few women in the audience. The first act lasted an hour, featuring various forms of sex acts. The second act featured an attractive couple in their early twenties who came on stage and seductively undressed each other. They made love in every conceivable position. At the end of 40 minutes the boy withdrew as ardent as when he started. When I asked him afterward in his dressing room how he managed to perform this incredible feat, he replied, 'I have to do this show four times a day and if I let myself go each time, I couldn't possibly make love to the girl when we go home at night. You see, she really is my girlfriend.'

Just about the most difficult sporting event to get press tickets for is the Wimbledon centre court on finals day. LIFE wanted Stan Smith and Yvonne Goolagong covered. We applied for tickets but were brusquely turned down. Harry Dempster was a colleague of mine on the London *Daily Express* in the pressroom. 'Harry,' I pleaded, 'I've got to get on to the centre court. How do I do it?'

'Load yourself with equipment and follow me. Keep talking and stay on the inside as we pass the steward at the gate so that he cannot see that you do not have a press pass.' I had no seat but Harry gave me his cushion and I kneeled on the grass in line with the net. It was uncomfortable but a good position as I could cover both sides of the net. Yvonne won and made our story for the women's final but when I repeated the effort the next day for the men's, Stan Smith lost to John Newcombe and we had no story.

Twice during that August of 1971 I had to cancel our holiday to Ireland. The morning we were due to leave for the third time, Jordan phoned to say that the worst ever-rioting was engulfing Belfast and we had to get over there right away. Lesley and the girls were not happy.

Travelling over on the plane we planned what we could do that had not been done before. We had seen mobs throwing stones. We had seen soldiers wearing face visors and bullet proof vests charging into crowds as they swung long batons and carried shields against

Living Dangerously

stones. We had seen them firing rubber bullets and watched tear gas canisters exploding as people ran and women screamed. We had witnessed the tit-for-tat killings and seen first a Catholic pub blown up followed by a Protestant one. We had seen shops after they had been split apart as bombs exploded, killing shoppers and causing terrible mutilation. The international press corps had grown to such mammoth proportions that often the scene looked like a movie set. We had seen rioters stepping up their activities on the arrival of film cameramen, especially when they switched on their powerful lights. We had also seen some of them whip up a section of the crowd to perform for their cameras.

'So what new angle can we take?'

'No one has yet photographed the IRA in action,' Jordan volunteered.

'For good reason,' I added.

After my earlier contacts I had concentrated on covering the Republican groups while other teams worked with the British army. In most of the other guerrilla operations I had covered like Cyprus, Al Fatah, Angola and the Congo, one could work on both sides of the fence but this was inadvisable in Northern Ireland if you wanted anything other than superficial coverage.

The rioting was in full force when we drove into the beleaguered city. Bulldozers and double decker buses had been set on fire and used as road blocks. In the Catholic Ardoyne area we saw buildings that had been gutted and were still smouldering. Once again, we teamed up with Vic Patterson and his car radio which directed us towards trouble as it broke out.

When night fell it looked as if the whole city was alight. Then at two o'clock in the morning we saw a chance to get the story we had hoped for. The army was trying to surround the Inglis Bakery in Eliza Street, only a few hundred yards from the City Hall but in a strong Republican area. Three IRA gunmen were holding out there. We left Vic Patterson while Jordan and I found out which side the army were on and then made our way down dark, narrow streets to the other side. We were stopped and held by Catholic vigilantes well before we got anywhere near the bakery. They suspected we were

Special Branch men – God help us if we had been. Fortunately, a contact I knew appeared and relieved the tension. We told him we were trying to get into the bakery. 'Be very careful,' he warned us. 'The army are in buildings all around and have night scopes on their rifles.' We knew.

Glued to the walls, we edged past burning bakery vans and were greeted in the bakery by a tall, thin man carrying an American automatic rifle. He was introduced to us as Joe. We subsequently learned he was the great IRA hero, Joe McCann, who was later killed in a gun battle with the army. There were two other armed men lurking in the shadows. Joe had boot-black covering his face and wore a woollen balaclava over his head and most of his face. He crawled out to a position where he was silhouetted against a burning bakery van and under a large Irish Republican flag. I shot a roll of film while sporadic sniper fire rang out into the night.

Jordan and I were glad to get out of the bakery as we knew it was only a matter of time before the army would occupy it and we did not want to be there at that moment. In fact, it happened two hours later. One of the gunmen was killed, though Joe and his colleague survived to fight another day.

We patrolled the streets of Belfast for the rest of the night. Two men in a car at that hour of the morning aroused suspicion and we were continually stopped by both Republicans and army patrols. Next morning Father Hugh Mullin was killed by a bullet as he administered the last rites to a man lying in the street after a gun battle. Ironically, the man subsequently survived.

We covered the priest's funeral at Portaferry, southwest of Belfast. The scene could not have been surpassed by any film director. The long funeral cortege wound its way through the picturesque village at dusk as a soft, gentle drizzle fell. They passed the single-story cottages on the waterfront, facing fishing boats, before climbing the hill above Strangford Lough. Father Mullin was laid to rest in the small country churchyard under the shadow of an ancient stone tower on a hill behind the church. Solemn men and weeping women completed my picture – summing up the tragedy of Northern Ireland.

Ciaran Donnelly, a local photographer and I drove up to Londonderry after Rudy arrived from Paris with Hubert le Campion. They brought a morale-boosting cable from New York saying our Northern Ireland story had closed as a six page lead and that Managing Editor, Ralph Graves, so liked the Father Mullin graveside picture that he ran it across a double truck (two pages) in Gallery, a section reserved for artistic pictures.

Ciaran and I headed out for Magilligan Fort where a large Republican meeting was being held in protest against internment without trial. This was the most contentious single factor in Ireland at that moment. Dark, dramatic clouds hung over the stark, partially crumbling fort on which the protesters scrambled. The sea reflected a steel grey in the background. The police wisely decided not to attend so there was no trouble.

The boredom of the next three months was broken somewhat by a story in Tripoli, North Africa. Bill McQuirter had organised the first interview by a foreign correspondent with Libya's fiery leader, Colonel Ghadafi. Once again, this story meant long hours in the hotel waiting to be summoned before the President. It came after three days. At 6.30 in the evening a car collected us and took us to Ghadafi's 'tent' within the confines of the military barracks. His room was simple and sparsely furnished. The colonel wore clean fatigues and had a copy of the Koran beside him. I was able to take 150 pictures of him during the two hour interview. As with Al Fatah, he let Bill into many of his controversial plans for the future. He then invited us to accompany him the next Thursday to his rally at Sabratha, some 70 kilometres from Tripoli where we were the only non-Arabs present. Bill had pulled off quite a scoop. We celebrated with a bottle of scotch he had managed to acquire from the embassy in this otherwise 'dry' country.

I was back in Northern Ireland in November to photograph the militant Republican women who backed the IRA . It is impossible for guerrilla groups to operate in urban areas unless they have massive support from the locals. We saw the times when this support cooled for various reasons and the British army received numerous tip-offs as to where arms and explosives were hidden.

A contact introduced us to the women's leader who took us to the Clonard Road area of Belfast to see a short, plump, blond-haired woman called Flo O'Regan. Her son had just been shot. His body lay in an open coffin in her little sitting room. These women acted as vigilantes for the IRA. Whenever an army patrol came into the area they blew whistles, let off hooters or banged the pavements with dustbin lids. This gave the IRA time to escape and accounted for the few arrests.

One morning I was photographing Flo while other women were warning the IRA of an army patrol, when around another corner suddenly appeared British soldiers. I was arrested. Flo and other women tried to wrench me from the powerful grips of two hefty paratroopers. What they failed to do in strength, they made up for in abuse and jeers.

Another evening I was photographing a young girl complete with her large sinister-looking dark glasses and black beret, when an army patrol came up the small passage we were in. We both scaled a wall and hid in an outdoor lavatory until the patrol passed by, and then completed our pictures.

Violence was still rife in the city. A bomb exploded in a restaurant and blew both legs off a young girl. While we were having lunch in the Hamil which had become the Press Bar, a bomb blew up a garage around the corner. For a moment I thought our building was going to collapse.

I drove to Londonderry to photograph a woman who visited the notorious Bogside to deliver 'meals on wheels' to old people. As we were about to enter this Republican section of the city, I was roughed up by some youths belonging to a loyalist tartan gang and narrowly avoided losing my camera bag.

The smell of tear gas always seemed to hang over Freedom Corner as one passed beneath a large sign reading, 'YOU ARE NOW ENTERING FREE DERRY'. I was photographing my lady when across the road some 40 men hi-jacked two large trucks. I tried not to see them and hid my cameras. I would have been shot instantly had I pointed a camera in their direction. They took no notice of me and I beat a hasty retreat. It was galling, though, to think of the unique pictures I had missed.

We had the feeling that interest in our stories no longer existed in New York, for many of the better pictures were being overlooked. This never used to happen. Over the years I rarely disagreed with the editing. Jordan joked that everyone was too busy looking for jobs to bother. It was depressing. A more or less routine life did not suit me after years of adventure, travel and glamour. I was going through an unsettling period of my life. It was terrible to witness the slow, agonising death of the greatest magazine on earth. Jordan was equally frustrated. He could hardly get New York to answer his cables. We used to retreat to an Italian bistro in Bond Street and vent our feelings on each other. There was not much else to do. Once the morale goes on a magazine, the creativity has gone. Despite new talk about increasing the editorial budget, we felt that the end was near.

I was surprised to receive a cable to go to Hillevaag in Norway to photograph a colossal concrete tower to be sunk in the North Sea as an oil rig. It involved hiring a sea plane for aerial pictures and spending money – something I had almost forgotten about. The picture ran as a double truck in 'BEAT OF LIFE' and was to be my last picture in the magazine.

On 8 December 1972 Dorothy Bacon telephoned me at home. She was obviously distressed. 'Terry, I have a bombshell for you. LIFE is folding at the end of the year!'

It came as no surprise, but I suddenly felt terribly sad over the fate of so many friends. In a way I was glad it was all over, although it was rather like going to one's own execution.

The death of LIFE magazine was the end of a publishing era never to be repeated. It was the death of one of the world's most elite clubs and 'good-bye' to many of the world's lovely people. We were not just colleagues but friends.

It was the end of the big spending. LIFE had paid its staff of over 600 more than any other publication and yet the cost of the ink was supposed to be even higher than their combined salaries! One writer remarked that like the dinosaur, LIFE died of gigantism. Paradoxically, it was science and the advent of satellites that could transmit pictures across the world, not in ten hours but in ten nonoseconds, that helped kill the magazine.

LIFE had a powerful influence on millions of people. I hope I contributed in a small way.

Lesley used to say that I was more married to LIFE magazine than I was to her. She may have had a point. I hope not.

Joe McCann, IRA Belfast divisional commander, in action in the bakery in the centre of Belfast, July 1971.

An IRA patrol.

An IRA training camp in the Republic of Ireland, March 1966.

Double Bath, January 1970, in a shop in London's Mayfair.

Northern Ireland troubles, Feb 1972. I am saved by Corporal Bell from being beaten up by a Royal Marine Captain during rioting in Newry.

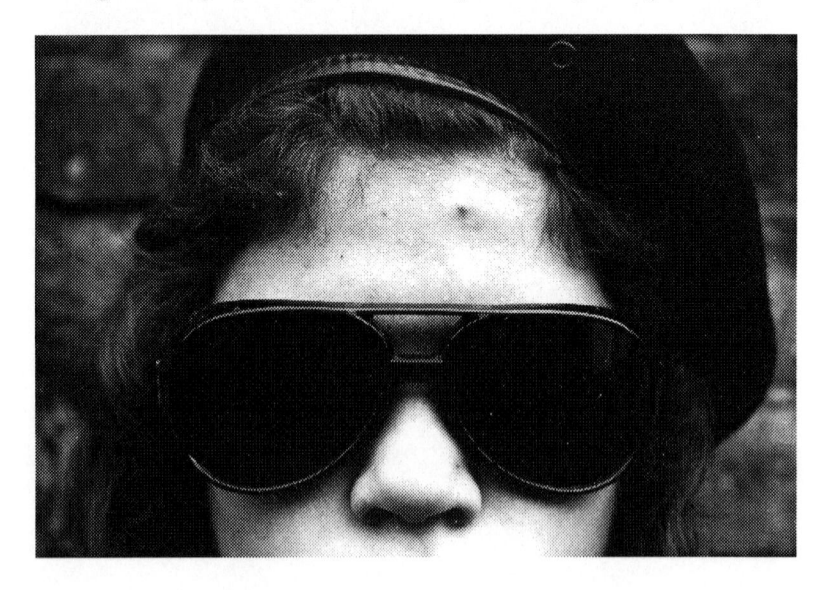

Northern Ireland troubles, November 1971. Militant Republican woman sympathetic to the IRA.

Demoliton of remaining part of Nelson's Column, Dublin, 1966.

CHAPTER XXXII

On to an easier life

After the demise of LIFE Magazine, it was farewell to news and I concentrated instead on feature stories. I felt no nostalgia seeing colleagues going off to Cambodia, Bosnia, Yugoslavia and other wars, but enjoyed freelancing and the degree of freedom it gave me.

Over the next few years I was involved in some 600 stories before I gave up active photojournalism. I plan to mention just vignettes on some of the more interesting people and events I encountered.

In early 1974 I started working on the 'dummy' for what was to become the most successful American weekly - PEOPLE Magazine. The first actual story was on James Alfred White, alias James Herriot. He had just written *All Creatures Great and Small* but otherwise was little known. With Jerene, a tall Texan lady, we trudged up to the hill farms around Thirsk in Yorkshire with soft-spoken James, dressed in tweeds and wellies. He was essentially a cattle vet and rather scathing about pet vets whom he thought were sometimes more interested in the owners than in the animals. James only started writing at 50, whilst usually in his sitting room watching T.V. with his wife, Joan and his two dogs. It was only after *All Things Bright and Beautiful* was published in America that his books really took off into many millions of sales. 'I regard myself as essentially a veterinarian who scribbles in his spare time' said Herriot, who at the peak of his fame still used to be called out at 3 a.m. to remote farms on the moors.

Then there were the pop groups. By far the most fun individual of the twelve pop groups I photographed had to be Boy George with the made-up face of a glamorous girl. He wore outlandish sort of male clothes and could out-talk anyone and certainly out-shock all. I first met Boy George in June 1983 in his minute attic flat in St. John's Wood in North London. His bed was crammed with dolls and furry animals, mostly presents from his fans.

George's real name is O'Dowd and he comes from a large family of six children. His father was an army boxer and another brother planned to box professionally. His father told me he was 15 when he started dressing outrageously at school, and despite getting ragged unmercifully, he refused to give in. His band, Culture Club, reached great heights in the United States, in Britain and on the Continent. George did not play any instrument but wrote songs for his group by singing into a tape recorder and getting guitarist, Roy Hay, to write them down.

Freddie Mercury of Queen in 1977 lived with a girl called Mary Austin in a posh Kensington maisonette with their two cats, and parked outside was their Rolls Royce. Freddie was 31 then and Mary 26. Mary once said, 'I am a bit puzzled about my relationship with a simulated bisexual. But he is mentally all over the place anyway'. Freddie sadly died of AIDS a few years later.

Ian Anderson of Jethro Tull was a very different character. He was 29 in 1977, could go quite beserk on stage, smashing his flutes (he carried 16 on tour) and returning to his XVI century farm house on 74 acres in Buckinghamshire to become the perfect English gentleman. Shona, his attractive wife, tended to drive the Bentley while the bearded Ian enjoyed riding one of his four trial motor bikes. He chain smoked ('tobacco only'), rode horses and went out shooting on his estate.

Led Zeppelin in those days had the reputation of laying waste all in their path, but how different were their home lives. Robert Plant was the leader with his long, thick, curly hair. There was nothing more he enjoyed than trekking over the Welsh hills where he lived with his Eurasian wife, Maureen and their two young children. The other three members of the band were all multi-millionaires and lived the life of country squires and family men. The Heavy Metal age was from 1969 to 1971, catering mostly for the under eighteens when Led Zeppelin emerged. Very sadly the Plants lost their small son soon after I was with them and asked for the recent pictures I had just taken.

I was at dinner in our Highgate house when the telephone rang. It was Brenda Draper, the London picture editor of *Time* & LIFE, 'Terry, can you get down to Shepperton right away? I have just had a tip-off that the Police rock group are in the studio making a promotion film.'

Living Dangerously

With my daughter, Raina, we left the table right away and drove furiously down to Shepperton. where Raina immediately recognised Sting, their leader. She spoke to him and. despite hostility from the hangers on, he invited us to stay. The members of his band could not have been nicer or more cooperative. It was a great night. We arrived home and piled into bed at 2 a.m.

Showbiz – the generic name used to cover films, the theatre, musicals, television, the stars and more humble people – played a big part in the life of Time Inc. magazines, and I spent a lot of time in this field, not that I particularly enjoyed it. I sometimes joke with Lesley that showbiz people tend to think of themselves while journalists think about other people . She does not agree – perhaps with good reason!

One thing I learned from showbiz people is that temperament is only thrown by those who can afford to throw it. It dissolves proportionately as they lose popularity. You can work wonders with actors by boosting their ego. Dealing with stars is like dealing with a beautiful girl: be a little hard to get but not so hard that you never get got. Just let them see you are concentrating on the lesser stars and they soon react. No better example of this was Robert Mitchum. He was the great star and 'Baby Doll' Carrol Baker was merely an up-comer but because I had been sent out to Kenya to do a story on Carrol he would barely talk to me, far less pose with Carrol. The shots I made of them together had to be grabbed.

I really do not have the patience to work on films though I have had to do quite a few. One has to contend with bitchiness and professional jealousy and have the tact needed to deal with artists; hanging around at their beck and call; having your plans changed at will and without being consulted and having to force that sickly smile when you next meet them – all the time wanting to slit their throats. Almost worse is having to hang around while the Director of Photography lights the set in a manner that makes you think he never wants to end his contract. You end up the day with a few frames in the can.

Nevertheless, I met some lovely as well as not so lovely showbiz people. A lovely one was Princess Grace of Monaco (Grace Kelly). I flew south to Monaco in July 1975, staying at the famous Hotel de Paris. I went with her and Caroline to a large banquet in the hotel that night and lounged around the following day by the pool waiting to be summoned to the palace. It was late by the time I received the call and the light was failing badly. I had no time to set up a battery of lights. Princess Grace was charming and so beautiful, with fabulous hair hidden in a turban! However, since this was a great break I had to make the best of it. A picture of the set up made the PEOPLE Magazine cover along with others of the Rainiers whom I shot later in the palace after a glamorous musical concert in the Palace courtyard.

Not so lovely was my visit with Margot Fonteyn a few months later. I was so looking forward to meeting her as I had been one of her great fans for years. I arrived at her house overlooking Hyde Park on the dot of 4 p.m. and was made to sit in a semi-darkened drawing room for over an hour. Not even a cup of tea was offered despite a maid drifting around the house. Margot had just written her book and to every question the reporter asked her she answered, 'You'll find it in the book'. Of course, the sort of questions asked were not in the book.

Trying to photograph her at Covent Garden was not easy either. She wanted the story but did not want to cooperate. I like to put this down to the fact that she was having a lot of worry with her husband, Dr. Robert Arias, who had been almost fatally shot in Mexico and was confined to a wheelchair.

The stage doorman at Covent Garden thought 'Rudolph Nureyev is the rudest man I know' but that was not how I found him. I photographed him on several occasions and always found him most helpful. On one occasion in Blackpool, the theatre manager refused my permission to photograph Nureyev in the theatre and despite the rain, he came down on to the sea front for pictures.

I spent a lot of time with the Redgrave family in the 1970s. Vanessa was a revolutionary from the age of 14 and campaigned for her Trotskyite brother, Corin, for the Workers Revolutionary Party in Brixton. She also sold her house to finance a documentary on behalf of the Palestine Liberation Organisation. She comes from a

Terry Waite in London a week or so before he left for his fatal trip to the Lebanon, Nov 1986

Actor John Cleese in the City of London, September 1983

Rex Harrison dressed as King George III, June 1976.

Ripper prostitute - the girl in the car when the 'Ripper' was arrested, Jan 1981.

320   *Living Dangerously*

Above: Robert Plant of Led Zeppelin with a down-and-out in London, October 1976; Below: Freddie Mercury & Queen, September 1977

Living Dangerously

left-leaning family as her father, Sir Michael, many years earlier had been banned from the BBC for supporting the People's Convention. Even her mother, actress Rachel Kempson was slightly involved.

Vanessa was married to Tony Richardson at one time, producing two daughters and a son. Natasha Richardson is doing well in showbiz today. Vanessa is terribly short-sighted. I watched her making-up for *The Prime of Miss Jean Brodie* when, with her eyes an inch or so from the mirror, she transformed herself from someone I failed to recognise at the stage door into a glamorous actress.

An unpleasant job I had to do was a film for CBS Television on location 240 miles north of the Arctic Circle in Finland, in temperatures of -20°C. It was not the cold but the behaviour of an actor called John Savage. He put every possible difficulty in my way, insisting on 'kill rights' (i.e. the chance to veto any pictures taken of him) which he could not have, then he sulked and refused to cooperate, despite Willie Nelson going out of his way to be helpful. Finally, Executive Producer Frank Konigsberg took Savage aside for a quiet talk. After that I had no further problems with him.

It is sad for me to think back to that day in March 1979 when I photographed Superman (Christopher Reeve) at the peak of his career and then to see him today, devastatingly paralysed after his dreadful riding accident but his spirit undaunted – thanks to his attractive wife, Dana.

John Cleese was as amusing off screen as he was on and took any antic in his stride. In the early 1980s I took him down to the City of London and had him standing precariously on high railings wearing a bowler hat, umbrella and enacting hilariously funny routines for the camera.

In March 1975 I visited Francis Bacon in his dingy little studio in South Kensington. I was met by a wild-looking character in a black polo sweater and trousers that might have been slept in the previous night. His untidy hair was parted on the right.

'I'm in a foul mood', was his greeting as he showed me into his kitchen, piled high with dirty cups and half empty bottles. 'Scotch or coffee?' I opted for coffee.

With cups in hand he showed me his studio which might have been out of Dante's Inferno. There was barely a space not littered with old papers, tin cans, hundreds of paint brushes in tins, smashed up old frames. A rickety table was piled high with utter junk in what only can be described as total chaos. He used the walls to try out a multitude of colours. Canvases were strewn around the floor, many just daubed as he experimented. I am sure he would have given me one had I asked but I did not like them particularly. I wish I had just one now as he was to become one of the greatest living painters. Bacon was born in 1909 and died in 1992 but was only to become famous in his late 30s.

A really memorable character was Henry Moore as he strolled round his large garden in Perry Green near Much Hadham, dwarfed by marvellous pieces of sculpture carefully sited for maximum effect. He said he could spare only two hours for pictures and interview but a month later, after working with Princess Grace in Monaco, a reporter and I drove along the holiday-jammed Mediterranean coastal road to Vingtimillia, south of Pisa in Italy, to spring a surprise on his 77th birthday. He was not expecting us but nevertheless could not have been nicer or more cooperative. He showed us around the marble quarry where Michaelangelo chose his material; took us down to the beach at Herreux; and we visited his local market before returning to his small villa for lunch. I photographed the great man peeling onions and potatoes for his Kiev-born wife, Irina, whom he had met at the Royal College of Art 46 years earlier. 'Irina is my best critic', he said. Henry Moore was becoming a multi multi millionaire. He turned down a knighthood but accepted the Order of Merit.

Maggie Thatcher had won an overwhelming victory for the Conservatives in 1975 when I covered her shopping and in her little Chelsea house. She was timid, unused to the mob of cameramen surrounding her. Very different from the 'Iron Lady' she was to become.

Colonel Ghadafi, Oct 71, in his 'tent' in the army barracks in Tripoli.

Princess Grace in her Drawing Room, The Palace, Monte Carlo. July 1975

Ava Gardner at home in London, Nov 1981.

Margot Fonteyn, in her dressing room at Covent Garden, Jan 1976.

Francis Bacon, painter, in his studio in South Kensington, March 75.

Boy George in London at the start of his fame, June 1983.

Roger 'James Bond' Moore opens a bottle and enjoys the good life, Sept 1977

Henry Moore with one of his sculptures at his home in Buckinghamshire, June 1975.

Living Dangerously

CHAPTER XXXIII

Odds and Sods

I thought I had put riots behind me when I gave up covering news, but that was not to be. I went to Ireland to cover the funeral of Frank Stagg, an IRA man, in the Leigue cemetery in County Mayo. It was a bleak morning with the rain pouring down when along with 7000 mourners and 1000 blue helmeted policemen armed with clubs, rubber bullets and plastic shields, I made my way to the cemetery. Stagg had hardly been buried when the crowd surged through the police cordon from all sides surrounding the grave where I was standing. Men started slinging stones and girls screamed. The mob squeezed in so tight that I was wedged against a tombstone with a leg caught under a policeman. Girls reached a high pitch of screaming now in terror of their lives as they fought for breath. Cries of, 'Get that bloody photographer' did not help, though they could not reach me and I could not escape. I was reminded of this incident many years later after the terrible Hillsborough disaster at a football stadium when so many people were killed during a similar crush.

Working for *Time* and LIFE gave one an entrée to busy lives not accorded to many other photographers. Roger Moore allowed me to photograph in his house: he had never allowed journalists to visit him at home before. At that time Roger Moore was said to be the most handsome man in Britain. He epitomised charm, sophistication and modesty. To women the perilous glint in his eye and his easy-going candour could be quite devastating. Jerene Jones, who reported our story, certainly found this to be true.

Moore lived a real love-life story in his gracious, ivy-covered house near Denham film studios with his beautiful Italian wife, Luisa Mattioli, and their three children. The cigar-smoking Moore would answer the phone or the doorbell himself. Luisa helped him in his study, the walls of which were covered in Bond posters.

The Saint and James Bond created a dashing image that Roger Moore appeared to live up to. He was the quintessential Londoner, aged 50, dressed in a smart blazer and light trousers. He collected

Jerene and me from our Bond Street office in his brown Rolls Royce and drove us to the Victorian Embankment for pictures.

The year ended with my having to shoot a cover of Elton John for PEOPLE magazine. I set up a studio in the Time Life Building in London. Elton John arrived with a large entourage of hangers-on and I could not recognise my victim as they all mounted the stairs! Fortunately the swarm around the Queen Bee gave me the clue. He turned out to be most cooperative and pleasant. Seeing a Henry Moore sculpture of a nude female outside the window, Elton moved out and feigned rather suggestive poses on her body. Knighted by the Queen in 1997, Elton composed and sang at Princess Diana's funeral service. He donated all the proceeds, amounting to millions, to the fund in her honour. They were good friends.

A little later in the month I drove north to St. Albans on a nudist camp story. Coming in from the cold, so to speak, it was weird to be sitting up at the bar with people drinking and behaving quite normally though all stark naked. The only oddity seemed to be me. Near the bar men and women were playing snooker, again quite naked. Outside I watched a game unique to the naturist movement called Miniten. It is played with a tennis ball and curved wooden bats with the rules somewhat following badminton. The game must have been a little uncomfortable for the more well-endowed women. Nearby, a man was driving a tractor in the nude. Naked men and women were riding motor cycles while others were casually idling about their tents. How normal it all was.

Lesley and I were in Ireland on the 27th August 1979 and had just set sail from Cork aboard the Innisfallen bound for England when my small radio blared out the news that Lord Mountbatten had been murdered in his boat off Sligo by the IRA. It was unbelievably frustrating to be so near a really major news story and not able to get off the boat.

Sir Alec Douglas-Home as Prime Minister and Lord Carrington as Foreign Secretary were two of the only politicians I covered that I felt were just too honest to be in those jobs. I drove up to Bradlow, near Aylesbury, to be greeted by the bespectacled Lord Carrington and his charming wife at the door of their manor house and 900-acre cattle farm. Lord Carrington is the epitome of a perfect English gentleman. Debonair, immaculately dressed by Savile Row, he had done all the right things: gone to Eton, Sandhurst, joined the Grenadier Guards during the war and won a Military Cross. He belonged to the Carlton and all the right clubs.

The best way to find out about people is to talk to their employees. One of his farm workers said, 'He's a proper gentleman in every way'. He was friendly and jovial with his workers.

Lord Carrington was 60 at the height of the Rhodesian (now Zimbabwe) crisis and must be given the credit for solving the problems of handing over the country to black majority rule against the antagonism of Prime Minister, Ian Smith.

Quite one of the most horrific stories I have worked on for sheer self-inflicted torture was with an American, Jim 'Doc' Counsilman who at the age of almost 59 was the oldest person ever to swim the English Channel.

Captain Matthew Webb was the first to make the crossing in 1875. He was in the water for 21 hours. In 1979 there were over 2100 attempts and only 214 people succeeded. 'Doc' was determined to be one of them.

Despite high blood pressure Counsilman increased his weight from 188 to 214 pounds to cope with the cold 60° water. He logged some 1200 miles in the lakes around Bloomington in the USA before flying to England where he swam another 100 miles around Dover.

Tides, jelly fish, fog, oil slicks, seaweed, sea sickness and shipping in one of the busiest sea lanes in the world were some of the hazards Doc had to face. At dawn on the 14th September he was greased up with five pounds of a ghostly white mixture of vaseline and lanolin. He slipped in to the water at 6.13 from Shakespeare Beach. As the white cliffs of Dover very slowly receded into the mist, Doc maintained steady strokes of 72 per minute, little knowing he needed another 16500 strokes to get him to France. With his wife, Margery, we were on a filthy trawler feeling every movement of the turbulent

EPILOGUE

It was a story on David Lean's film, *Ryan's Daughter* that first brought us to the west coast of Ireland; to one of the most beautiful parts of the world. The pace was slow, the people friendly, often to a degree of embarrassment. We understood with difficulty their dialect and certainly joined in their humour. Fishermen still fished in small boats either rowed or sailed. Farmers still took their milk to the creamery on horse-drawn carts. The Gulf Stream meandered gently across the green lush countryside to the southwest, bringing mild weather, sometimes disturbed by the turbulent Atlantic.

We both fell in love with the country, particularly with a small creek set beneath the beauty of Mount Gabriel. Across the water was one of the oldest farms in the area. It could have stepped right out of a Bronte novel. Often through the early morning mist we watched the farmer drive his cattle along the seashore to new pastures. The lumbering beasts weaved their way in and out of the lobster pots belonging to Jamesy O'Regan. Soon, the sun would burst through the billowing white clouds and do justice to a Turner painting.

On this idyllic site we built a gable-ended cottage in Irish style and the scene was set to sift through three tea chests crammed with the notes made over the years. Many of these notes were scribbled on crumpled pieces of paper written in bumpy Jeeps in the Congo, in vibrating helicopters in Vietnam, or in small canoes tossing about on giant waves far out in the Atlantic whilst chasing mammoth sperm whales; so some of these notes were difficult to decipher. This may account for minor inaccuracies in a tale such as this.

Reflecting back on these hectic years when I covered some 1200 events, I am still surprised at myself that a man who could not bring himself to kill a chicken on our little farm in South Africa, could nonetheless have witnessed the awesome sights described in this book. I probably saw as much action working for LIFE as I did in three years flying for the R.A.F. in World War II. I have seen the pointlessness of bloodshed and have come to detest it in all its forms.

When you were slogging through the hot steamy jungles of Vietnam armed to the teeth with five cameras, or being helicoptered

Left: Ian Anderson, star of Jetho Tull, rides his fast motorcycle at his home in February 1977.
Right: London Heat Wave, June 1976: a very hot Boston terrier.

David Frost with Lord Mountbatten of Burma

Living Dangerously

rain forests to Aguas Calientes. We took the latter. A bus would take us up the ever zig-zagging hairpin bends to the ruins.

In 1911 Hyam Bingham, an American prospector, had been led up to the 'Lost City' by local Indians. About this time it was virtually overgrown, but over the years was disclosed a sight few will ever forget. Apart from the absence of roofs, we looked down on an Inca city, complete with its temples, houses for the elite and houses and workshops for the hoi polloi.

I have always been allergic to heights and from the very top astronomical platform, above the Sun Temple, we had to descend a narrow, tortuous track with a sheer drop of 800 feet to the Urumbamba river below and with nothing to hold on to. Our stay in the beautiful Monaserio hotel in Cusco made up for a lot. Next day we spent ten hours on a 'bucking bronco' train. How our attractive, micro-mini-skirted hostesses managed to serve us with lunch and drinks, while we were quite unable to write up our journals, can only be put down to practice.

We crossed the Andes at 14,200 feet and descended to Puno on the shores of Lake Titicaca at 12,600 feet. We visited the floating islands of the Uro Indians who had built complete villages and schools on bundles of reeds, quite soggy to walk over. Our small smelly fishing boat then crossed the lake for a four hour trip to Taquile Island where another monumental climb up to the summit of the island made me remark, 'I'm glad we've made our wills'. However, the view across the wide azure blue of the lake to Copacabana in Bolivia made it all worthwhile. The almost sheer drop down 500 Inca steps to the little harbour below did not appeal to me one bit. We then had another bitterly cold return trip in our little boat to our hotel and more copious cups of maté de coca.

Arriving in Lima, the capital of Peru, a colourless city rarely seeing the sun, we were met by our guide, Miguel. He told us that maté de coca was from the cocaine leaf! No wonder we had such energy at those altitudes…

turned out to be a sort of 'Outward Bound' course for youngish people. We did venture on a trip to the Grey River and a struggle along a long shingle beach in a howling gale before climbing a treacherous track up to the glacier where the wind made it difficult to stand upright. The glacier itself was breathtaking, with the sun glistening like blue diamonds off the ice. The return into the gale was even more exhausting, a round trip of six kilometres. A six hour journey back to the airport at Puenta Arenas in a rickety old bus through dull country did not improve our tempers.

After that experience we looked forward to Peru. We left Santiago at sea level and three hours later were in Cusco at 11,000 feet. We were advised not to touch alcohol, but the hotel gave us copious cups of maté de coca to help us survive the height. In fact, other than tiredness, as we had been up since 1.30 a.m. that morning, we suffered no ill effects.

Cusco was the capital of the early Inca Empire where we discovered a little about their brilliant civilisation and their engineering ingenuity, for instance in fitting vast granite blocks together so tightly that you could not get a razor blade between the joints in the massive walls. The cathedral built over the Inca ruins contains a lectern weighing a ton and a half of solid silver.

From Cusco we explored the enigmatic ruins of Sacsahuaman which the English called 'Sexy woman' and Pukapukara (the Red Fortress) before travelling up the Sacred Valley of the Incas to Pisaq and its fascinating market where I bought a beautiful alpaca poncho for about £25.

We followed the Urumbamba river down to Ollantaytambo through sensational mountainous country, looking up to the high tiers of Inca terracing and lush green cultivation. It was at Ollantaytambo that we had to climb 450 steps, some 18" high and then on up above this Inca fortress guarding three valleys. Our guide told us we were the oldest couple he had ever had to escort to those heights!

The only way to reach Machu Picchu was by the four day trek along the Inca trail or by a narrow gauge railway down through the

had lent us the money to buy a Piper Cub aircraft and start SkyFotos. We stopped the car, but no way could I make myself go any further. Southern Valley will always look to me the way it was when we were there. Terry walked on down the road but, perhaps fortunately, the trees had grown up and hidden all from view.

Our final destination was Cape Town. The *Time* magazine correspondent in Cape Town, Peter Hawthorne, drove us through Stellenbosch up to Franshoek. En route we passed a massive squatters' camp guarded by police with machine guns. It is estimated there are seven millions squatters in South Africa, a perfect breeding ground for trouble.

Peter Younghusband of the *London Daily Mail* was a colleague of Terry's all over Africa and now runs a successful wine farm. Their old Cape Dutch farm house is aptly named 'Angel's tears'. We wallowed in champagne both at Peter's farm and later at La Petit Ferme where at four o'clock we sat down to lunch.

We were in Cape Town on the momentous occasion of the election of Nelson Mandela as President, resulting in a change of government to black majority rule.

I doubt now if we will ever go back to that country of magnificent wild animals, jacaranda trees, native servants – and insoluble differences.

A few years ago we decided on what was probably to be our last great adventure. We wanted to visit Punta Arenas and Tierra del Fuego in Chile's Patagonia and then fly north into Peru to see the fabulous Inca ruins of Machu Picchu as well as the highest navigable lake in the world, Lake Titicaca.

However, scrambling up to a glacier in Patagonia and climbing 450 Inca steps at around 14000 feet, made us pause to reflect on whether we were a little past sell-by date for such escapades.

We took off on the 12 hour flight to Santiago and another three hours south to Punta Arenas. In fact, we never really saw Punta Arenas or Tierra del Fuego except from the air as our travel agent thought the Explora hotel they had booked us into was nearby when in fact it was 250 miles to the north! Although the hotel was delightful, it

Terry had an unusual experience while travelling on this bus. It was almost full and he had difficulty finding room for his large camera bag, when a rather untidy-looking passenger offered to have it next to him. Rather reluctantly Terry agreed, having noted the nice looking wife who appeared to belong to the passenger. The man turned out to be the American ambassador in Paraguay! He helped Terry lug the gear up thousands of wooden steps to the Canteros Falls. Terry has had his camera bag carried by all and sundry but never before by an ambassador.

Before leaving South America we had to see the famous Iguasso Falls and fortunately chose the superb settler-style hotel Cataratas on the Brazilian side. A one day visit to Paraguay was quite enough for us. We found it run down, neglected and unfriendly, though it is unfair to make this judgement after such a short visit. Next stop was British Airways and England.

What prompted us, I wonder, to pay a visit to South Africa in 1994? After 30 years absence it was an interesting experience – if rather sad in some ways. We arrived at Jan Smuts airport in Johannesburg to be met by an old friend and his chauffeur. There the difference started to be noticed. Jack Rae had built up a massive business and was deservedly successful. Soon we were driving through an avenue of jacaranda trees in full bloom to their beautiful home in the Northern suburbs of the city where the security was intense. Drinks were served in the garden by the swimming pool and after lunch we retired for a siesta to our elegant suite. There was a butler and staff to serve dinner. The difference here is that the Raes look after their servants with pensions. Not always the case in South Africa.

The next day was a trip to nostalgia. After lunch Terry and I drove in Betty Rae's smart golden BMW to Northcliff. The change here was unbelievable. Instead of the many dirt roads we were once used to, a vast motorway system now traverses the country. On earlier drives to Cape Town I had to keep winding up the car windows every time we passed another vehicle, to shut out the dust.

On our way back from Muldersdrift we recognised the dirt road beside Gary Player's wall where the house on the opposite corner once belonged to Dick Mathews, a doctor who so many years ago

thereafter calling it my own! In Klameen I made straight for the kitchen to see if the wooden table was still there where I remembered a dead suckling pig lying, covered in spots and quite unfit to eat. My cousin Nora's house on the finca where we stayed was called 'Stony Broke'. My mother sadly never went to Argentina again though there were many family visits to England.

We regretfully had to leave San Rafael. Nora, though crippled with rheumatoid arthritis but still using her distorted hands, drove us to Mendoza where we boarded a luxurious bus. We had expected rough farm workers with chickens running about inside the bus – but not this one. Instead of the dirt road we thought we would see, we ran on smooth tarred roads over the Andes, the road crossing at 11000 feet with the grandeur of the mountains on either side, some snow-capped, and deep down ravines to the rivers below. Descending into Chile were hundreds of hairpin bends to the Rio Blanco thousands of feet below.

My cousin Kenneth had told us that if you want anything done, wait till you get to Chile. It was true. Everything in Chile seemed to work better than in the Argentine, particularly the Metro, which ran on rubber wheels. The Chilean people are charmers.

We could not get accommodation on Easter Sunday, so after a good dinner at el Novillero washed down with excellent local wine and capped with the all powerful Pisco Sour, we caught the bus at 10 o'clock for Temuco, 425 miles to the south. Once again, the bus was sheer luxury with reclining seats and rising foot rests. As we left behind the lights of Santiago, a steward appeared with a basket tray loaded with delicious tapas such as quail's eggs and smoked salmon. At 6 a.m. we were woken with fresh orange juice, steaming hot coffee and continental breakfast. Total cost for 'dinner', bed and breakfast and 425 miles – $15.60 each!

The next day we caught another bus for the 250 mile journey south to Puerto Varas with its strong German and Red Indian influence. It was bus-boat-bus-boat across the southern Andes to Bariloche in Argentina, starting with the 8700 foot snow-capped Osorno volcano across the deep blue Lake Llanquihwe backed by majestic cumulus clouds.

man, Terence O'Dioghe, who late one night at a friend's apartment summoned the lift to take him down to street level. The door opened and he stepped in – only to find himself falling past eleven floors until he hit the top of the stationary lift on the ground floor. He slowed his fall by gripping the steel cables, dreadfully burning his hands and breaking many bones in his body. Terence told us that his first concern had been ruining his Savile Row dinner jacket!

So began this happy and historic holiday. On the downside Terry was doing a story on what it is like to live with 300% inflation. Not difficult, it seems, if you are a perhaps a middle class farmer. Any australs (now pesos) you possess are changed rapidly into greenback dollars. From then on you deal in greenbacks and barter; but life was much tougher for those in the civil service or on a pension.

We spent a few days exploring Hurlingham where my grandfather had owned several properties. He also owned one in the centre of Buenos Aires, now an expensive area of shops and restaurants. In Buenos Aires too we visited the other Harrods in Florida Street. Hardly comparable to our own in London but I remember the delicious dulce de leche and creamy caramels my grandfather used to bring us in England from that shop before the last war. The family had made their money in shipping and were responsible for the railways. We saw the remains of some of these when we crossed the Andes into Chile.

Visiting the Recoleta cemetery we will always remember the woman we talked to as she stood in front of Eva Peron's tomb. She told us with tears in her eyes that she came here every single day to pay homage.

Sadly, we missed a visit to the grand Opera House where, no doubt, my mother Marjorie saw Pavlova dance and heard Caruso sing. She never complained but life with my father in Kent must have been very different, particularly as their money in Argentinian shares was sadly depleted on the advent of Peron.

I had been to the Argentine with my mother as a child bridesmaid to the various aunts, but remember little. Our next visit all those years later to Finca Klameen near San Rafael did bring back memories of riding Corona, one of my uncle's polo ponies, and alas, the spirits were not on our side that day and refused permission for photography. The materialisation seance went ahead. After snacks and coffee we filed into the study and took our seats. Terry and I sat next to each other. In the dim light I could just make out the gloomy shadow of Alex. After chanting, some strange voices came through, then slowly, very slowly, figures started to build up out of the floor in front of the semi-circle of twelve people. They looked like whiffs of smoke clad in mutton cloth. I whispered to Terry, 'Did you see that?' He nodded. Eventually several figures built up to become life size. One came over to Terry and asked, 'Would you like to shake my hand?' He leaned forward, delved into the ectoplasm and shook a fat, flabby hand. I saw it all. As easily as the figures built up out of the floor so they melted back into it again and Alex woke up out of his apparent trance. Terry checked every corner of the study for possible ruses and he looked around for a fat flabby hand but there were no fat people there. Everyone saw what we had seen. Even Terry will admit there was something there and that it could have been photographed using infra-red film but the spirits would not give him permission.

I did not feel the exerience helped me personally. My visits to a little spiritualist church in Krugersdorp where I would go from Southern Valley on a Sunday evening were more rewarding. Happy times, except when an African tried to stop my car in the dark on my way home!

In March 1991 we were in Buenos Aires and staying at the Hurlingham Club where we settled in to a comfortable room and balcony overlooking the polo ground. My cousin, Kenneth Boadle, was the current President of the club as had been his father and grandfather before him. I must explain that my mother was brought up in the Argentine and met my father after the first World War when he resigned from the Highland Light Infantry and subsequently became social secretary of the Hurlingham Club. Unlike the rest of the family, my parents returned to live in England.

After washing and changing we went down to meet Kenneth and his wife in the lush, green grounds of this very smart club. Every club has its characters and one we met with Kenneth was an Irish-

is to say Beethoven, Bach, Brahms, Chopin, Debussy, Liszt and Rachmaninov. They were guiding her hands on the piano from the spirit world while Rosemary was in a trance.

I have to say she did not *appear* false or insincere to us. She described the characteristics of the various composers. At first, they all looked old so she could recognise them, but now, she said, they all looked in their prime. They spoke to her in English though Liszt came through with a strong German accent. This did not surprise her. She accepted the spirit world totally. 'Why not?' she said.

Chopin had been a good friend ever since he got through to Rosemary to inform her that her daughter had left the tap running and the bath was about to overflow. She found nothing unusual about communicating with people who had passed over. 'I have been able to see and hear since childhood. Members of my family also have this gift. Sadly people outside find it hard to accept'.

Musicians of Rosemary's day were divided, but Richard Rodney Bennett, a leading British composer, was absolutely fascinated and said, 'You couldn t fake music like hers'. Hephzibah Menuhin was also impressed and so, I believe, was Sir Colin Davis. However, a music critic in New York, Alan Rich, was not persuaded, especially by the quality of the music. Rosemary was anything but a talented pianist herself.

This was not however, the first time Terry had been involved in spiritualism from a photographic point of view. Some years ago in South Africa we had very good friends who had lost their son and were naturally devastated. We lost our son, then aged four, under tragic circumstances, and I became interested in spiritualism. Willie Aronsohn had invited a famous Welsh medium, Alex Harris, to fly out from England, and he arranged sittings in his beautiful house in the Northern suburbs of Johannesburg.

Willy and his wife, Gypsy, knew we needed comfort for a similar reason and invited us to join them. I accepted gratefully and Terry contacted LIFE magazine to do a story on the phenomenon. He asked for infra-red film and flash globes, as light would injure the medium. They suspected his sanity. The equipment duly arrived but

beneath. Was the vacuum cleaner reposing in front of the television a gesture? Sellotape held together the broken glass window where they had climbed through.

She was by now slowly collecting herself together, quite cheerfully, sitting on the floor in her old dressing gown, hair in disarray. Yet this girl had style and was seldom, if ever, unattractive. We sat on what some might kindly call a sofa while Marianne brought us mugs of tea. 'Now, with Ben', she said, 'I have finally found the stability that money can't buy. Life is a picnic compared with what I have been through.'

At last the time arrived to go out into the real world, so to speak. The first step for Marianne was a chemist. Here, I watched from outside, Terry as usual hovering with his cameras, alert for the best shots. Marianne was in her element, buying all the cosmetics she could find with PEOPLE Magazine picking up the tab. Next we took her to the Man in the Moon pub in the Kings Road where she was known and greeted by various weird characters.

Years later I saw Marianne on television hosting a travel programme and doing it well. Perhaps the glamour had faded a little but the charm was still there.

Our younger daughter was with us when we visited Trinity College in Dublin housing the longest library in Europe and saw the wonderful Book of Kells, an unusual treat.

The following day was hardly luxurious. We boarded a trawler at Rossaveel for the 75 minute crossing to Kilronan on the Aran Isles. There was no passenger seating, so we sheltered from the spray on the heaving deck, finally docking amid a chorus of bad language when our trawler was nearly rammed by the Galway Bay ferry. We did a mini tour of what seemed more like the 'barren' Isles and managed to get drinks in a small thatched pub before rejoining our trawler for a rough trip back to the mainland.

A strange assignment came for Terry in November 1981 to visit a woman called Rosemary Brown in a rather rundown Victorian house in London's Balham. Rosemary was convinced she was writing music with help from well known musicians of the past, that

Leonora Corbett was with us in the film *Night Alone* and the two of them enjoyed gossiping during their lunch breaks. I was an avid listener! One of Emlyn's stories concerned 'Tam' Williams, as Hugh was always known. He was said to have been found wandering on Hampstead Heath when he discovered the lovely Tallulah Bankhead was a lesbian. That was before the days when they all 'came out'. Emlyn had a son called Brook. He was not named after me but his father told me he liked the sound of the name. When Terry was photographing Emlyn in 1974, I gladly went along.

I met Rex Harrison only once – at the old Playhouse Theatre in London. He held no charm for me but I was young and quite unknown. He was then married to the first of his many wives who was French. Many years later Terry took Cara down to Bognor Regis to photograph Harrison in a George III costume At first Rex refused to dress up as required with the June temperature that day touching 90°F. He sat there sipping ice-cold champagne, never offering Cara or Terry even a glass of water. However he was loath to lose the publicity and finally donned the costume.

From being a star in her own right in the unreal world of the Rolling Stones during its ascendancy, Marianne Faithful lived with Mick Jagger in elegant Cheyne Walk for five years before biting the dust of drugs, poverty and degradation. She had a miscarriage with Mick's baby and at one time contemplated suicide. The daughter of an Austrian Baroness, she was brought up with a cultured background but little money.

On a miserable January day in 1980 we found Marianne living in a sordid and crumbling basement flat in Chelsea. Marianne and Ben E. Fiscal were rudely awakened at noon by our intrusion (previously arranged). A drawn face appeared at the window and let us in. She wasted no time in sending Terry out for a much needed packet of cigarettes. She admitted she and punk rocker Ben broke in and claimed the dwelling for themselves. It is possibly a little more civilised than the squat she shared with Ben in Overdale Road where there were not even basic facilities for washing. In their new residence dampness defaced the walls; light was provided by trailing lamps on wires; lino was lifting from the floors in the bathroom to reveal the filth

said in his best French, 'We don't like crème caramel. She flashed back in very broken English, 'And I don't like your Christmas pudding'.

In 1974 it was the author, Francis King who suggested we join him and two friends on a visit to the Soviet Union, as it was then. Solzhenitsyn was much in the news at that time. When Customs found a copy of the *Sunday Times* in our baggage featuring him, it was immediately confiscated.

The winter was bitterly cold when we landed in Leningrad, now St. Petersburg again. Out Hotel Vadka was undistinguished except for the language problem, but it did have a samovar on every floor. Surely, it was the contrast which struck us most vividly about the country. The people on the streets were shabily dressed; there was a noticeable lack of luxuries of any sort in the shops and only basics in the food markets. And yet the super modern Metro or underground put ours to shame. Everywhere there was wonderful architecture and most surprisingly restoration with an abundance of gold leaf in the Tsarist palaces at Pushkin. This hardly seemed to go with communism. (It was again a surprise to discover how many treasures had been carefully removed and hidden away mostly in Siberia during the war.) The theatre was so much part of Russian life, also the Kirov Ballet and the circus, the latter two being a 'must' for our party.

I, for one, had not expected the Winter Palace, the Hermitage, with its 400 rooms, to be so much a museum. I had pictured the wonderful staircase with beautifully dressed ladies descending it as in *War and Peace!* Nevertheless, there was an exceptional collection of Impressionist paintings among many others. Contrasting again was the Russian museum with its ugly interior and few interesting paintings, though the icons and Russian crafts were better displayed.

I count myself lucky that I worked in films with actors like Hugh Williams and Emlyn Williams. The former was most attractive. Emlyn, in my humble opinion, did not have the respect or should I say the publicity he deserved both as a playwright and as an actor. He told me that as a child he had to walk five miles there and back to school every day, so he had come a long way when we worked together. His sense of humour could be a little unkind, perhaps.

than he appeared on the screen, he was a little overshadowed by his artist wife. She was heavily involved with the New York Museum of Modern Art.

A glorious day followed for our bus trip to Hop to see Edward Grieg's house. It is in a beautiful location and we could not wait to walk the long way down and picture him composing his music there. Would it be unkind to say that some were still sitting in the bus, saying 'Been there, done that'. Well, we had done that now. Next day we were back in England.

When Terry went on a Time Life book assignment to the Pyrenees he asked me to come along as he did not know one wild flower from another! In May one expects to find an abundance of such flowers but we were disappointed, certainly so in France. By comparison, the multitude of different colours alongside the roads in Spain were a great deal more striking.

When I was a child of about nine years old I was posted off under protest to board with the headmaster's children and a handful of others at Hurstpierpoint College in Sussex. I was dreadfully homesick but the walks we took live always in my memory because this is where my fondness for wild flowers began. I would go ahead down 'the Green Lane' or not so happily perhaps, along the Burgess Hill Road, my eyes glued to the banks and to the ditches. I usually managed to find the first primrose, then the first celandine – cowslips always eluded me – and thus enhancing my rather second-rate image. A great treat was to go into Danny Park where violets were a joy and even white ones could sometimes be found in the grounds of this impressive Elizabethan mansion. Penelope Tower, the headmaster's daughter, became my great friend and on her birthday in June we would go for a picnic to Rottingdean after anxiously watching for the clouds which might spoil our idyllic day.

All those years later we were hard at work in the Pyrenees. Miles from anywhere in the Spanish mountains our car packed up, but a small garage at Casteson put it aboard a truck and took us down hill for 50 miles to Barbastro where a mechanic found the trouble and we returned across the Pyrenees into France. At a pleasant little hotel, the Breche de Roland in Gedre, we had dinner, slightly marred by the loud television. Our waitress offered us crême caramel and Terry

CHAPTER XXXIV

Lesley has the last word

In April 1969 I accompanied Terry on a very pleasant story which involved travel all over Europe by train.

The first night of our journey was spent in a luxurious suite at the McDonald hotel in Brussels where Terry was kept busy with endless cables and telephone calls involved in organising our journey. The next morning the train put us in the Gare du Nord, Paris, where we came down to earth having to lug our heavy luggage ourselves due to the absence of porters. We caught the mini TEE (Trans Europe Express) 'Edelweiss' train via Luxembourg to Zurich and checked in to the dreary and cramped Butterfly Hotel. However, swinging Zurich cheered us up and we found an excellent restaurant in the Niederdorfstrasse.

On this extraordinary but most pleasant adventure we seemed to be travelling from one country to another and back again. At one moment we were in Italy, having caught the Cisalpine through the Simplon tunnel to Domodossola where we enjoyed our dinner and Chianti. Of course work was included in our programme. Terry was given permission to ride on the locomotive footplates on all trains.

From Amsterdam we travelled the blue and yellow trains through flat country covered with daffodils and windmills. After dinner in Utrecht we had a night sleeper for a change on the NE Express through Germany. Terry was awake early to shoot our train crossing on the boat ferry into Denmark. We enjoyed our brief visit to Copenhagen where we were able to wander around this beautiful town before dinner. Next day we had a vast, typically Danish smorgasbord at the famous Oscar Davidsons. Later we took the metro to Osterport to see the 'Little Mermaid' and walked round the park with the old windmill and moat and through wide cobbled streets flanked by white shuttered brothels. It seemed like another century – who was the figure behind the frilly curtains?

The next day we were in Norway and had been put on the wrong train, However, this gave us the opportunity to meet Edward G. Robinson and his wife who shared our carriage. Far less sinister

taxis about but a large bribe got me to the airport in the hotel bus. Security men were everywhere, barring any entry to the tarmac. A quick dodge behind excited men engaged in an altercation and I met Arafat coming off his aeroplane. He could not remember my name but said, 'You and your colleague are the only two journalists ever to accompany my fighters into Israel. You are brave men. Come with me on my tour of Tunisia and Algeria'. We covered 500 miles by car with Chairman Arafat, then 53 and a confirmed bachelor, visiting PLO barracks. 'Photograph anything you want,' he said. Quite a break.

In April 1984 I was to spend an afternoon photographing Robert Maxwell for the first time. He was most meticulous with his dress and combed his hair carefully before we started. That evening I returned home and said to Lesley, 'I've met another Ben du Preez!' referring to my erstwhile South African boss!

Richard Branson was and is great fun, the most unassuming and unpretentious man I know. Yes, he does love publicity and will go to almost any length to achieve it. It does not seem to have done any harm to his multi-business empire. I once photographed him in his bath aboard the river long boat in Little Venice, London, which he used as his office and his home. He donned an old flying helmet and goggles of mine and held up a model of his first Virgin Atlantic Jumbo jet in the bath. Despite the fact that he is now probably a billionaire I have never seen him wear a tie. Back in 1984 I went down to his rambling house in Kidlington where he lived with Joan Templeton (they had not yet married) and his lovely little daughter, Holly. The house was a truly lived-in family house with tennis racquets and other sports gear strewn around downstairs. Branson drove a 1940 Humber Super Snipe which he treasured, saying that 'Rolls Royces are not my image'. The Bear at Woodstock was his local pub. He left his public school, Stowe, at an early age and has never looked back. In 1999 he became Sir Richard.

Looking back over those dreadful years of Terry Waite's incarceration in Beirut, I little dreamt that in 1986 we would not see him again for many years. He was with Archbishop Runcie and three American hostages in December 1986 when he mentioned in the interview that he was scared of returning to the Lebanon to try and negotiate the release of other hostages.

In September the police had to break into a house on the Triangle in Brixton, a predominately black suburb of London. They were after drugs. This caused violent riots by the black population. *Time* magazine assigned me to get pictures in this Triangle which was dangerous to enter. The only way was to shoot out of the back window of a car. Lesley volunteered to drive me and we entered the Triangle to be greeted by mobs of unruly blacks strung across the road. Their mood was nastty. I hoped I could get out of the car with a camera and say I wanted to take their picture for an American magazine, as I thought they were sympathetic to America at the time. I was met with a blast of abuse and told, 'Get the f… out of here and with that bloody woman'. Leaping back in the car, Lesley let the clutch in with such a bang that it stalled the engine! A quick restart and we veered off down a side street to escape at high speed. We had our pictures.

Much more pleasant but equally frightening was to be assigned to photograph 'an icon who was once the most beautiful woman in the world'. It was, of course, Ava Gardner, a screen goddess of the 1950s.

The bell to her flat in Ennismore Gardens, overlooking Hyde Park, was marked 'Morgan' who turned out to be her Corgi. Ava opened the door herself. I was almost ready to duck as she had been known to throw things at photographers and hated the media. At 59 then, she was still very good looking but had a broken cheek bone which I had to be careful about. Rarely do we give anyone "kill rights" but with Ava we had to. 'No close-ups.' she said. Lesley came along with me for support but she was hardly needed as Ava could not have been more pleasant or cooperative. She had been out of circulation for eight years, much of the time in Spain with her famous matador, Luis Dominquin. Her earlier life went through three marriages, Micky Rooney, Artie Shaw and the stormiest and last with Frank Sinatra. She then lived alone with her Corgi. Her good friend, actor Charles Gray, lived next door, and after we had finished with pictures, she gave us all glasses of delicious wine and 'tapas' before kissing us 'good-bye'.

I was at the Tunis Hilton in July 1983 when at 6 a.m. a panic call to my room tipped me off that Yasser Arafat was flying in to the airport in half an hour. It was the end of Ramadan and there were no

1981 was the year of the Royal Wedding between the Prince of Wales and Diana Spencer. We started on the build-up to the wedding in February. I was to make several visits to Althorp, pronounced 'Althrop', the country seat of Earl Spencer, and was photographing the Countess selling cheap jewellery to visitors in their local shop. We asked her permission to 'shoot' the Spencer coat of arms. 'Certainly,' she said 'but it will cost you £1,000.'

'Thank you,' I said, 'I will copy it from one of my own plates for nothing.' My father passed down Spencer china to me.

We photographed the infant school where Diana taught; shops she frequented; she and Prince Charles at Ascot and David and Elizabeth Emmanuel who were making the wedding dress. Then there was Harry Secombe, now Sir Harry, who allowed us to copy his wedding invitation and Kiri Te Kanawa, now Dame Kiri, who was to sing at the wedding.

At 5.30 a.m. on the great day, 29th July 1981, I made my way through the crowd, many of whom had been there all night, to the Abbey Life building overlooking St Paul's Cathedral. There was already a hell of a hassle with photographers trying to get window spaces and all I could get was a small ledge only 18" wide on the fourth floor of the building – but with a magnificent view of the cathedral frontage. My worry, balancing precariously on this narrow ledge, was dropping a lens on to the heads of the crowd below, so I limited my cameras and lenses to just three.

What a spectacle of colour. I was able to cover Diana's arrival; the Royal family's arrival; in fact everything apart from interiors of the ceremony; then their departure. From there I ran to Westminster Bridge to get the couple leaving for their honeymoon. I had parked my car conveniently nearby for a quick departure to get my film to the lab for processing, only to find I had locked my keys in the car and there they were on the front seat. I hailed a passing police car. They radioed for a lock expert but he could not open the car door. Taxis were impossible. In desperation, I phoned Lesley who was glued to the television set, hopefully recording the event. She dropped everything and came to my rescue with another key. Phew!

1980 seemed to be a year of covering actors (Derek Jacobi, etc) and writers such as Frederick Forsyth, Phyllis White alias P.D. James, Graham Greene, William Manchester and a lot of other people, but 1981 started with a very rare scoop for a weekly magazine on a big national story.

The Yorkshire Ripper' had been terrorising mostly prostitutes for the last five years of the 1970s and had become a big news story in Britain. A police tip-off sent Fred Hauptfuhrer and myself on a three- hour drive to Sheffield, along with many other media men.

Fred and I immediately headed for the red light district. After speaking to several prostitutes we tracked down Jamaican-born prostitute, Olivia Reivers, within an hour of our arrival. We paid Olivia £50, her night's earnings, to get her off the street for wonderful spooky pictures and interview but also to hide her safely from our colleagues! That January night was bitterly cold and 34-year-old Olivia had put on her scruffy fur coat and stiletto heels. Soon she was in a brown Rover car with a client. The police were watching the area and a radio check informed them that the car was stolen. The bearded Peter Sutcliffe was arrested and named suspect for the many grisly 'Yorkshire Ripper' murders.

Olivia confided in us that she was the luckiest woman alive. Her life had been saved by the presence of the police patrol car and the stolen number plate. She had worked that night with Denise Hall who saw Olivia get into Sutcliffe's car but failed to take the car number which they usually did for mutual safety.

We kept Olivia until the early hours of the morning until it was too late for our colleagues to interview her, then checked in to a local hotel. Still our luck held as the next morning we met up with Denise at the spot where girls were normally picked up by Sutcliffe. So we had the two girls who had been centrally involved.

But that was not the end of the story. A telex from New York told us that the unprocessed film had fallen off a van at J.F. Kennedy airport in New York and been run over by another truck! And after such a scoop it turned out that the lab was only able to rescue one frame that had not been 'fogged'. It ran as a full page in PEOPLE magazine.

sea due to the slow speed we made. Poor Margery was sick, along with several others, for most of the 17 hours we were on the trawler. Half-way across the channel a Russian tanker bore down on us, veering away at the last minute, but the swell nauseated Doc as he swallowed salt water. Taking nourishment was difficult. He used a plastic bottle holding a mixture of milk powder, glucose and canned peaches.

After nine hours in the water and within four miles of Cap Gris Nez in France, the wind blew up to gale-force four and the tide changed, taking Doc slowly out to sea again. His strokes slowed to 62 a minute; his fingers rigidly spread apart, a sure sign of the dread 'channel freeze'. Staring wide-eyed through his goggles and grimacing in pain, Counsilman seemed not to understand instructions to get him close to the boat to minimize the effect of the wind. He was to be in the water another four hours when the tide changed and took him slowly towards France again. Then like a man on some mad mission he realized what was happening and staggered almost unconscious ashore on the beach at Wisant. Victorious! He had been in the water for 13 hours and 17 minutes, covering 26.5 miles. His only comment later, 'It only hurt once – from the beginning to the end'.

Back in London my next job was to cram myself and equipment into a tiny basement office in Mayfair's Berkeley Street. My victim – the very glamorous new editor of *Tatler* magazine – Tina Brown. I have a caption note, 'Regret lack of choice but could only photograph from one position'. Her office was littered with papers on the desk and pictures on every wall. Tina was 26 then, living with the much older Harold Evans, Editor of the *Sunday Times*.

Tina came to the *Tatler* erupting with new ideas to smarten up the layout, replace the fusty traditionalism 'with wicked elegance and make it more provocative intellectually without losing the tittle-tattle'. She soon doubled the sales. Tina was brought up with horses and debs, went to Oxford and wrote plays before editing the *Tatler*. She was to marry Harold Evans and become the toast of New York while editing first *Vanity Fair* and then *The New Yorker* and now TALK Magazine. She has progressed to a larger office!

*Sad farewell at the Gare du Nord in Paris, "Au revoir, cherie."
(March 1969) Chapter XXIV*

*Prince Charles and Diana's wedding in their coach leaving
St Paul's cathedral (June 1981) Chapter XXXIII*

'Doc' Counsilman in his agonising swim across the English Channel to France (September 1979) Chapter XXXIII

Francis Chichester escorted into Plymouth after his non-stop sail around the world (May 1967) Chapter XXV

Girls on the beach — Glorieuse Island

Faery Terns on Bird Island

BEAUTIFUL ISLANDS OFF THE SEYCHELLES
(April/May 1971) Chapter XXXI

Off Mahé at dusk.

Schooner off Praslin Island

NOT ONLY MAN ENJOYS MAKING LOVE

(April 1971)

LEFT: "Hello there."
BELOW: "You're fabulous."

"Wow! That's great."

"She's deadbeat."

Moise Tshombe, President of Katanga (February 1961) Chapter XIII

BELOW: A woman of the Transkei, South Africa

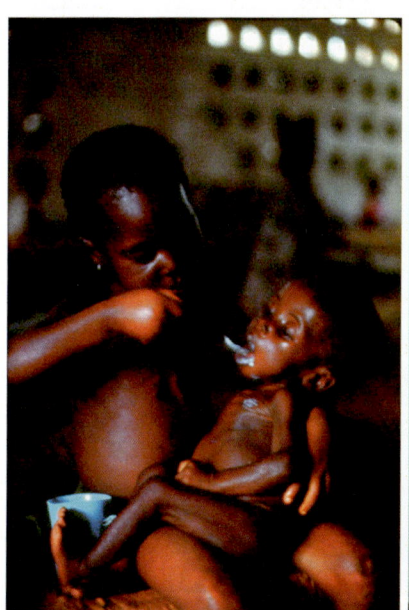

LEFT: The Biafran war, Nigeria. A small child feeds another in a mission station (1968) Chapter XXX

An entire Arab family killed by Israeli jets in a room in Irbid, Jordan (December 1968) Chapter XVIII

Yasser Arafat

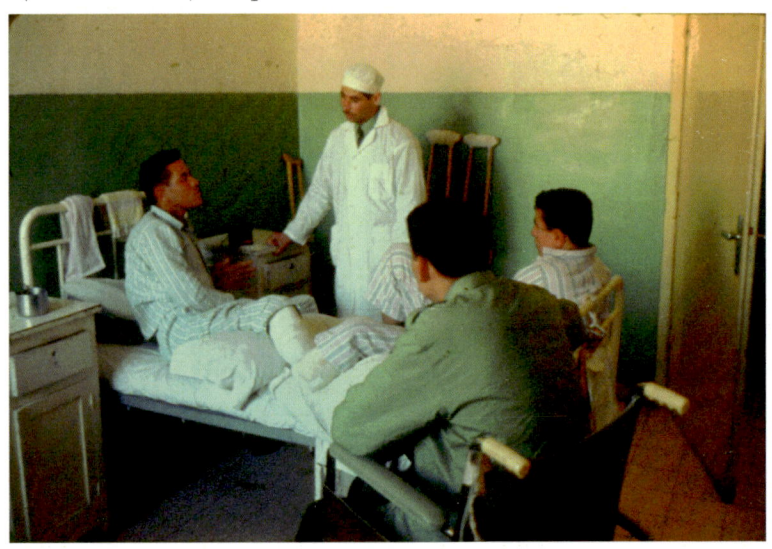

In an Al Fatah hospital in Jordan where many feet were blown off by Israeli 'peanut' mines strewn along the border of the Jordan river (November 1968) Chapter XXVIII

up into the oven baked-mountains of the Yemen, or under the accurate fire of the Viet Cong or the Radfani rebels or being shot at from all sides in the Congo revolution – you develop a sense of personal survival dating back to your early childhood. The bitter lessons learned in a British public school and later as a fighter pilot in the R.A.F. were to contribute to my being alive today. So many young, aspiring foreign correspondents did not appreciate that bullets can hurt, and were killed as a result.

Hopefully, our pictures of wars and violence have helped to bring home to politicians something of these horrors. Even if our photographs lost many of the emotions of the events, they were often able to illustrate dramatically the revolting acts that man perpetrates against man. Nowhere was this more graphically seen than in Vietnam when the war was brought into people's homes as never before. The media coverage was extensive, aided by people who were not worried by cameras and even encouraged us to shoot acts of indescribable beastliness. This accounted for some of the most awesome war pictures ever seen.

I am not intimidated by personalities as I know that Royalty and garbage men are both equally human beings. Usually the famous are more human than those trying to be famous. I could count on one hand the really unpleasant people with whom I have had to deal: three are in showbiz and one is a business tycoon. This says a lot for our race.

Many years on the Black Continent taught me a deep respect for human dignity, something sadly lacking in South Africa and elsewhere. It was no surprise to find that the motto of the University of Nigeria is 'to restore the dignity of man'.

Alas, I have to admit that 'having done it all' has made me blasé, a bit of a cynic and certainly a fatalist. Why a cynic? Because of the times we have been deliberately misled by tycoon business men and by politicians. Some time back the papers were full of reports of a British Chancellor of the Exchequer accusing ten experienced lobby correspondents of misrepresenting him over a briefing he gave them. The ten vehemently denied this and challenged him to produce the taped record of the meeting. 'Regrettably the tape malfunctioned,' they were told. How convenient. One could go on ad infinitum about the belief that diplomacy is a euphemism for legalised lying.

I could not end without commenting on a sad limitation on the freedom of the press, in this case the British press, by the suppression of reporting on certain terrorist activities. If we are confident in our democracy, what do we have to fear? If the political wing of the IRA is allowed to take its seat in the British parliament, how can we out-law its leaders from appearing on television, and who is to be the next to be banned? Surely, the devastating pictures taken of the Inniskillen massacre of the two corporals and many others was the last sort of publicity the IRA would want shown. The media is not an ally of terrorism and nor am I, but if we do not report terrorism there is always the danger of the unknown bringing more fear than the reported facts. We have to face the truth that terrorism is becoming a replacement for war. As we saw in Angola the success of terrorism is never what it achieves but what it *might* achieve which is its potent weapon.

Could this not be better illustrated than by the appalling events which struck New York at 10a.m. on Tuesday 11 September 2001 when desperate men hijacked four airliners crashing two of them into the New York Trade Center, one into the Pentagon and one possibly aimed at the White House? Total death toll of upwards of 3,000 souls. Unbelievable…

Under Section II of the British Prevention of Terrorism Act, which makes it an offence to withhold information of material assistance in bringing terrorists to justice, Mrs. Margaret Thatcher when still Prime Minister said, 'I believe everyone, the media included, have a bounden duty to see that terrorists are brought to justice. Journalists are ordinary people and cannot live above the law. They must impart any information required by security organisations.

Good sentiments, but as this book shows, we could not have infiltrated guerilla groups without 'living above the law' on many occasions, as do M15, M16, the CIA, the police, the Foreign Office and, indeed some politicians themselves. If terrorists believed that journalists and photographers were merely an extension of the security services, we would not live long. It is no good being naive about this. Even Churchill realized it (in a different way) when he said, 'The only people who could order me about are photographers. They are the only people who can ask a girl to lift her skirts without getting their faces slapped.'

In 1963, when LIFE's founder, Henry Luce, wrote the prospectus for the magazine, he must have been looking into a crystal ball. 'To see life; to see the world; to eyewitness great events; to see strange things, machines, armies, multitudes, shadows in the jungle and on the moon; to see man's work, his paintings, towers and discoveries; to see things thousands of miles away; things hidden behind walls and within rooms; things dangerous to come to; the women that men love and their children; to see and to take pleasure in seeing; to see and be instructed. Thus to be seen and be shown is now the will and new expectancy of half mankind'.

It was a tough life domestically. Lesley and I could rarely make plans with any certainty of carrying them out, as against which, we had several glorious honeymoons each year; more than can be said for most other couples who have been married for 55 years!

One thing is sure, if I had to lead my life over again, I would not basically change it.

T. S.

Wat netwerk